TEXTS AND CONTEXTS

By the same author:
Latin Explorations: Critical Studies in Roman Literature
Virgil's 'Aeneid': A Critical Description

TEXTS AND CONTEXTS

The Roman Writers and their Audience

KENNETH QUINN

ROUTLEDGE & KEGAN PAUL
London, Boston and Henley

First published in 1979
by Routledge & Kegan Paul Ltd
39 Store Street,
London WC1E 7DD,
Broadway House,
Newtown Road,
Henley-on-Thames,
Oxon RG9 1EN and
9 Park Street,
Boston, Mass. 02108, USA
Set in Times by Oxprint Ltd
and printed in Great Britain by
Lowe & Brydone Ltd
© Kenneth Quinn 1979

British Library Cataloguing in Publication Data

Quinn, Kenneth

Texts and contexts.
1. Latin literature – History and criticism
I. Title
870'.9'001   PA6003   79-40462

ISBN 0 7100 0279 3

180735

TO GAMBY

v

Contents

Acknowledgments

The author and publishers are grateful to the following for permission to quote from translations: the University of Chicago Press for Smith Palmer Bovie, trans., *Horace's Satires and Epistles*; Indiana University Press for Ovid, *The Art of Love,* translated by Rolfe Humphries; John Murray (Publishers) Ltd and Viking Press Inc. for *Ovid's Amores,* translated by Guy Lee, translation Copyright © 1968 by Guy Lee, all rights reserved, reprinted by permission of Viking Penguin Inc.; Faber & Faber Ltd for T. S. Eliot, 'Seneca in Elizabethan Translation' from *Selected Essays*; the University of California Press for Ovid, *Metamorphoses,* translated by A. E. Watts.

Faber & Faber Ltd and Random House Inc. for W. H. Auden, 'The Epigoni' and 'The Cave of Making' from *Collected Poems*.

Translations printed without attribution are the work of the author.

CHAPTER 1

What? When? Why? and How?

I WHAT DO WE MEAN BY LITERATURE?

Conservatism has always been the mark of the reading public. Throughout the history of western literature, the writer has had to contend with an audience that knows what it likes. Until society reaches a stage where writers can think of themselves as individuals and assert their independence, they are tempted to stick to what will be favourably received, not because it is good, but because people will know what to make of it.

The conservatism of critics in a society which has critics is at least as great. Like the ordinary reader, the critic resents innovation. Change upsets his standards, threatens his definitions: Aristotle talks about history as though Thucydides had never existed because he cannot accommodate Thucydides to his view of the difference between history and poetry. At Rome, the making of literature seems to have been dominated from the outset by the professional critics: the *grammatici.* Impressed by those who claimed to speak as experts on a subject they found too unfamiliar to judge for themselves, the Romans long took it for granted that the only form of writing which mattered was poetry. Poetry meant, not all forms of verse, but verse in what we should call the high style or the grand manner: that kind of poetry which, if it was a representation of life (a *mimesis,* in Aristotle's famous phrase), was an idealized representation of life in myth and legend, or of life at any rate as people liked to think it had been in a heroic past when men had really been men. In short, epic poetry and tragedy. Comedy (which, like tragedy, was always in verse) was considered to run a bad third; Horace in a well-known Satire speculates whether comedy can be regarded as poetry; it is perhaps too close to the way people talk and behave in real life. Poetry in which the poet writes about himself and his contemporaries is a late development. Prose does not emerge as a serious rival of verse until the end of the Republic; prose fiction based on the contemporary world is almost totally lacking—Petronius' *Satyricon* and Apuleius' *Golden Ass*

1

are brilliant, isolated experiments. The modern reader, for whom the short personal poem and fictional narrative in prose set in the world around him are the norms of the literary experience, has to attempt a readjustment of expectations which is not easily achieved.

The Romans, like the Greeks, had no word for literature. They had words, Greek words, which stress what is probably still the essential element in most people's concept of literature, the element of imaginative creation. But these words (*poema, poeta, poesis*), like the Latin word *vates* which the Romans came to use as a substitute for *poeta,* were restricted to creation in verse, and for a long time to verse in the grand manner. These words had first been used in Greece at a time when the act of artistic and imaginative creation occurred only in verse; when there was virtually no prose, no prose at any rate that could cope with the sustained expression of complex thought or emotion. And then, as a result of the conservatism of critics, writers and reading public, people went on assuming that the act of imaginative creation was only possible, or could only appropriately occur, in verse. Aristotle confines himself to poetry, especially to those forms of poetry (epic and tragedy) which enjoyed the greatest prestige in his day. Three centuries later, we find Horace still writing only about verse, because his thinking about what we should today call 'literature' was still tied (by the critical vocabulary at his disposal and the whole Roman tradition of critical discussion) to a concept of imaginative creation from which prose was excluded.

In the last century of the Republic, as intellectual horizons widened, there occurred an expansion of the interests of the reading public which was without precedent. The spate of writing which resulted involved an increasingly large segment of society. The Romans themselves could scarcely have seen where they were heading. Oratory took on more than the practical function of securing acquittal or condemnation, approval or rejection of a policy; it became a kind of entertainment; speeches were revised and published, as being of permanent interest. Didactic poetry came to be practised at a seriously poetical level, transcending its ostensible practical objective. Rome became the scene of intense scholarly activity. We begin to hear more and more of a new concept which the Romans called *litterae.* It became a distinctively Roman concept.

When Cicero speaks of *litterae* he includes everything, both prose and verse, that was worth taking seriously and could be expected to last: *litterae* became for him the symbol of a way of life that offered some consolation for failure in politics; it meant reading books, thinking about books, and the writing which was the natural outcome. More and more it meant books of a particular kind: Cicero had written verse of a sort all his

2

life, but in the end it was to prose that he turned for consolation; taking Plato as his model, he poured out treatise after treatise on the problems of philosophy, especially moral philosophy. Seneca uses the word *litterae* in much the same way a century later of his devotion to bookish studies following his retirement from his impossible relationship with Nero. When he says 'leisure without *litterae* is death' (*otium sine litteris mors est*), Seneca means something that can be regarded as a positive activity, even if a substitute activity; he would not have wanted to leave poetry out, but by *litterae* he has more in mind reading, thinking and writing about the problems of moral conduct. For both Cicero and Seneca, *litterae* included a whole class of books that we today should not think of as belonging to literature at all.

'Literature' means different things today, of course, to the scholar (who may say of a colleague that he is, or is not, acquainted with 'the literature of the subject'), to the businessman (who asks us to send for 'free literature'), and to the poet who dismissed all except the kind of poetry he approved of, saying 'tout le reste est littérature'. A publication such as the *Times Literary Supplement* sees it as its task to cover a wide range of subjects and interests. But mostly when we speak today of literature we have in mind books (not an activity), and books of a particular kind. The Oxford Dictionary definition spells out the implied restriction:

> Literary production as a whole; the body of writings produced in
> a particular country or period, or in the world in general. Now
> also in a more restricted sense, applied to writing which has claim
> to consideration on the ground of beauty of form or emotional
> effect.

When we talk of 'English literature' or 'French literature' it is this 'more restricted sense' we have in mind.

The historian of Roman literature thus finds himself in a quandary. He can hardly follow Aristotle and Horace and leave prose out. But if prose is to be included, what prose? If he attempts to cover all prose, he will find his book cluttered up with much that no one accustomed to the present-day concept of literature can take seriously as literature; is he then to say nothing about Cicero except as a writer of indifferent verse, omit Livy and Tacitus, confine discussion of prose writing to Petronius and Apuleius, arguing that they alone among Roman writers wrote creative prose?

The purpose of this book is to identify those works which possess beyond dispute the status of literature as that term is now generally understood. No more than passing consideration will be accorded to the rest: most didactic prose (textbooks on farming, architecture or public speaking) will be excluded on the grounds that their object is essentially practical, not an extension of the literary experience. Nothing will be said of the speeches of Cicero, however much that might have surprised Cicero. On the other hand, there will be a good deal said about the short poems of Catullus, despite the fact that they had too recently crossed the border between what I shall call 'paraliterature' and what we can regard today as literature for their status to be fully understood by their contemporaries. If it seems strange that the basis of selection should be a concept transferred from modern times to an ancient context, the reader is invited to remember that this is common enough in the history of ideas. One can study ancient economic theory or Roman political thought and do this sensibly and profitably, despite the fact that it involves isolating an area of human activity for which ancient society had no label even loosely corresponding to ours, and employing concepts which would have seemed strange or incomprehensible to those who lived at the time.

Every age responds to the past in the light of its own experience. The major works of the past are inexhaustible, infinitely various in their capacity to stimulate our changing capacity to respond. The critic's task as interpreter is never ended, never definitive. He must guard against sheer failure to respond to the strange and unfamiliar; he must be alert to eliminate misunderstanding. The chapters which follow attempt such an interpretation of the major works of Roman literature. Let the reader keep his Latin text of each author by him as he reads if he can; if he must work from translations, let him take the versions printed here as a starting point, comparing them with others, doing what he can to isolate that which is fundamental and distinctive.

II SURVIVAL OF THE FITTEST

There are a score of Roman poets worth taking seriously, and something like fifteen or sixteen writers of prose: thirty-five writers, or thereabouts, over a period of four hundred years. That is quite a lot; not all of us could name offhand thirty-five English writers of any importance since Shakespeare. Several of the thirty-five will not delay us long, not because what they wrote was no good, but because it falls outside what we today think of as literature. Naturally, by anything you could call a strict standard of quality, even those whose works we can accept as constituting the surviving body of Roman literature are not all in the first class. The best way to put it, perhaps, is to say that there are some thirty-five writers about whom we need to know something (when they lived, what they wrote, what what they wrote was like) before serious discussion of Roman literature can get far.

Before we go any further, however, it is well to be honest and admit at once that what makes Roman literature important and interesting is a mere handful of genuinely outstanding writers. Or rather, not writers so much as individual works. For often we know next to nothing about the men who produced them. Sometimes it is a collection of poems: the poems of Catullus, or the *Odes* of Horace. Sometimes, a major work of startling originality and unmistakable genius: Lucretius' *On the Universe,* or Tacitus' *Annals.* Such masterpieces tower above the relatively unimportant but still familiar-sounding works that are read and remembered for the influence they had at the time, or because they provided the intellectual context from which the really great works stand out, or because the influence they had afterwards is out of proportion to their apparent intrinsic merits.

Take the comedies of Plautus and Terence, or the tragedies of Seneca. As plays they are far from unreadable. Measured against the wholly uninspired dullness of some of the things that have come down to us (the almost unreadable epics of Silius Italicus, Statius and Valerius Flaccus, for instance) they assume a certain stature. But nobody today would really want to put them in the front rank. They had, however, an important influence on the development of Roman literature and thought. A quite special importance accrues to them simply because European dramatists from the Renaissance till the seventeenth century took their inspiration from these vigorous but crude Roman plays. They did so because Plautus, Terence and Seneca were the only models they had. Greek drama, though known to scholars, was little known to the cultivated public, or to the people who wrote plays. We have done better since, so much better that Plautus, Terence and Seneca have lost most of their interest; but the fact that they once had that interest is a hint not to dismiss them out of hand: they would not have lasted so long if they had not been good enough to stimulate others to do better.

All literatures, of course, have their minor writers, and most literatures a host of thoroughly mediocre writers of little importance at the time (except in so far as they helped to create an audience for good literature) and of no interest now except to the specialist. The minor writers of Rome tend, however, to be fussed about beyond their deserts because so much has been lost. Hundreds of writers have been obliterated (we know their names or the names of their works, but nothing, or almost nothing, of what they wrote survives); others have had their works reduced to fragments in the course of the thousand years, almost, which separate the fall of the Roman Empire in the west (AD 476) from the revival of learning in

Italy in the fifteenth century.

The greatest writers have on the whole survived best; because they were the most read, there were more manuscripts to survive. But in case we talk too glibly of survival of the fittest, it is as well to remember that there were some uncomfortably near misses. One is Catullus. With the exception of the second marriage hymn (which survives in an early anthology) all our manuscripts of Catullus go back to a single manuscript, long lost, recovered at the end of the thirteenth century—and then lost again, but fortunately not before copies of it were made. Another near miss is the *Annals* of Tacitus. Our text depends on two incomplete manuscripts; one discovered about 1510 preserves the text of Books 1–6; the other, discovered about 1430, the text of Books 11–16; Books 7–10 and parts of Books 5, 6 and 16 seem gone for ever. One assumes the poems of Catullus and the *Annals* of Tacitus did not figure prominently on the reading-lists of mediaeval monks.

Once we go beyond the first rank survival becomes much more a matter of chance. A really remarkable amount has been preserved that nobody in his right mind could ever want to read today if he were not a specialist: a whole host of learned, obscure didactic poems (a poem attributed to Virgil, but more likely written by Seneca's friend Lucilius, for example, about eruptions of the volcano Etna, which survived no doubt because people believed Virgil had written it); poems written by people who knew the rules for writing poems, but had no gift for poetry, whose poetic imagination was almost wholly deficient; long, dull prose works laden with second-hand, badly reported, inaccurate facts, or supposed facts. It is proper that such works should be studied by scholars. Nothing that has survived so long can be wholly devoid of significance. Such works improve our understanding, ever far from perfect, of the Latin language. Occasionally they provide the only evidence for something the literary historian is glad to know. What is important for our purpose is that those works which are not literature should not be taken to be literature, and that those which are bad literature should be frankly acknowledged to be bad.

More serious are those losses which can only be regretted. The elegies of Cornelius Gallus (a contemporary of Propertius): he was clearly an original and important poet. The poems of Calvus: the poets of the next generation linked his name with that of Catullus; it would be instructive as well as interesting if we were in a position to make the comparison for ourselves. Ovid's one venture at tragedy, his *Medea*: how did it compare with Seneca's *Medea*? The *Annals* of Ennius: one of the earliest and clearly (for we have fragments—500 lines or so) one of the greatest Latin poems; it would be nice to have the lot.

6

What? When? Why? and How?

Almost worse than the known losses is that the literary historian has to set the works which have survived against a background full—not just of holes, but of yawning gaps. Ignorance of the background cannot justify dismissing it from consideration. The background is there none the less, exercising its influence on the major works which have survived; the influence can be sensed, and the literary historian must do what he can to reconstruct its nature, so that the major work can be set in its proper context.

III PRECLASSICAL, CLASSICAL, POSTCLASSICAL

In this book the talk will be chiefly of a mere handful of writers, a dozen or thereabouts, spread over 400 years, from the middle of the third century BC to the middle of the second century AD.

It is usual to divide the period 250 BC–AD 150 into three shorter periods, though there is some question about labels and dates. The terms used here are *the Preclassical period, the Classical period,* and *the Postclassical period.* This avoids such emotionally charged terms as 'the literature of the golden age' and 'the literature of the silver age'. True, the word 'classical' is itself a coloured term, one, indeed, which has generated enormous controversy. 'Classical' and 'postclassical', like 'golden age' and 'silver age', suggest that a high point was reached during the first century BC, from which all that followed is to be regarded as a decline. It is a view of the matter that the Romans themselves of the late Postclassical period were prone to adopt. There is no mistaking a quality which the major writers of the Classical period (Virgil, Ovid, Cicero) have in common, a quality best described perhaps by T. S. Eliot (in his essay, 'What is a classic?') as 'maturity'. But not all writers of the Classical period have that quality. And in so far as the word suggests conservatism, resistance to change, orthodoxy, it is misleading. To their contemporaries, writers like Virgil and Horace, though apt to seem 'classical' in that sense to us, were startling innovators.

It has to be admitted, in short, that the term 'classical' means different things to different people, and some of the meanings are misleading when applied to the major Roman writers. The Latin word *classicus* (a technical term meaning, among other things, 'of the highest class'—for example, the highest class of citizens in the state) begins to be applied to literature in the middle of the second century AD to designate those writers who are considered to belong to the highest class as writers: the passage usually cited is in Aulus Gellius [19. 8. 15]; certain writers are described as 'classical', others are described as 'proletarian' (again of

7

course an assessment of their quality as writers—something like 'run-of-the-mill writers'—not a description of their social status or their origins). When literature began again in the Renaissance, the 'classical authors' were the writers of antiquity who had survived (in the way that we still speak of 'the classics' without meaning any particular ancient writers or any particular period): these authors were held to set the standard for the modern world to aim at in the different areas of literature; they were the models because there were no others. It was a sensible enough idea for the Renaissance; but, because of the natural conservatism of criticism, it easily shaded off into silly ideas, such as the ideas that the classical authors were the permanently valid models of excellence (so that modern works which broke the classical 'rules' were to be condemned), or the idea that all classical authors were first-class, or all pervaded by something that might be called a spirit of classicism. Such ideas, by their persistence long after their silliness has been exposed, have done the study of the classics much harm.

The word 'classical' is really a nuisance. One would like to be able to get away from it. But it has the weight of usage behind it: the terms 'preclassical', 'classical' and 'postclassical' are familiar and convenient. Nor are they wholly meaningless, provided one is careful not to read the wrong meanings into them. I shall take the Preclassical period as running roughly from 250–100 BC, the Classical period as corresponding roughly with the last century BC, and the Postclassical period as corresponding roughly with the first century and a half of the Christian era. A century and a half of experiment and achievement, a century of maturity and consolidation, a century and a half of increasingly unsuccessful attempts to repeat the successes of the past. That corresponds reasonably well to the facts, and the neatness and simplicity of the pattern are a warning against taking it too seriously. Its function is as a framework, upon which to build.

Roman literature doesn't of course come to a stop in the middle of the second century AD. The story of Roman literature and society cannot be said to be complete until the final fall of Rome and the end of the Roman Empire in the west in AD 476, when Constantinople (the ancient Greek city of Byzantium, rebuilt and renamed by the Emperor Constantine, who transferred the seat of government there from Rome in AD 330) became the intellectual and artistic centre of a Greek-speaking Roman Empire (as it had long been the political centre, though, despite the activities of scholars, it never became a centre for literature).

In western Europe, despite the fall of Rome, men continued to go on using Latin as the only language available to them for the organized, precise expression of their thoughts and emotions, or by deliberate choice as the most effective instrument at their disposal, centuries after Latin had ceased to be spoken as a living language anywhere. As a result of the division of the Empire, Greek studies became concentrated in the Eastern Empire, leaving Latin the uncontested literary and administrative language of western Europe to a greater extent than had ever been the case before. For while Rome survived, most educated Romans knew Greek and were acquainted with Greek literature. Greek literature now became almost unknown in western Europe until the dispersal of scholars which followed the capture of Constantinople by the Turks in AD 1453.

In the long history of the Latin language (for a millennium and a half and more European man turned to Latin to record his thoughts and emotions in writing as the only, or the best, or the most congenial language at his disposal) the four centuries from 250 BC to AD 150 seem little more than a flash in the pan. It is roughly the time that separates us today from Shakespeare. But with so long and varied a story to tell, concentration on these four centuries would be an outmoded cultural parochialism, if it were not obvious that during these four centuries, and at no other time, Rome produced writers of the calibre of Catullus, Horace, Virgil, Ovid, Cicero and Tacitus.

I shall give other reasons later in this chapter for regarding the history of Roman literature as interesting and important. What calls for explanation here is why it is sensible to set the end of my narrative, not in AD 476, but three centuries earlier. The explanation is that, though the three hundred years which follow are by no means devoid of interest, they are interesting because a new story is beginning. Old habits of expression and thought continue, and are indeed artificially cultivated; but the cultivation of them is increasingly unproductive, or unproductive at any rate (for a great deal continues to be written) in the sense that the old tradition leads to no new creative expression of the human intellect. Alongside a dying tradition new habits of thought emerge, and with them a new kind of writing in Latin which will eventually supplant the old. On the one hand there is a depressing mediocrity and sterility, on the other the first breath of the Middle Ages. If it cannot be said that the story of Roman literature ceases in AD 150, the story from that point onwards becomes too painful, too devoid of interest, to be worth telling here.

The last true Roman writer to figure in these pages is probably Suetonius. The last writers I shall mention are Aulus Gellius and Apuleius. Gellius is perhaps sixty years younger than Suetonius, Apuleius something over fifty years younger. The writing career of both begins about AD 150. Gellius' eyes are fixed firmly on the past; he writes the Latin of the previous century, if not the Latin of the century before that; his talk and his small talk are all of the great writers of the past and those who still study them. Apuleius is hardly to be regarded as a Roman; he neither lived nor wrote in Rome; the life and values of Roman society find no reflection in his work.

That is even more the case of the major figures of the third and fourth centuries: men like St Augustine (AD 354–430), who was born (like Apuleius) in Roman Africa and spent most of his life there, though he taught for a time in Rome and in Milan before becoming a Christian and returning to Africa; or Ausonius (AD 310–395), who spent most of his writing life on his family estates near Bordeaux. The only true Romans, in spirit or in intention, apart perhaps from the poet Claudian, who struggled hard to preserve the old classical forms, are the scholars and the pedants: men like Macrobius, or Servius (the commentator on Virgil), who reached the height of their careers round the end of the fourth century AD. (See *The Last Poets of Imperial Rome* [2nd to 5th centuries] trans. Harold Isbell, Penguin Books, 1971.) For most of the writers of the third and fourth centuries the influence of Rome as a living social reality, or even as a living literary tradition, is small or non-existent, and it is better to call these writers Latin writers, rather than Roman writers, and their work Latin literature (meaning by that literature in the Latin language) rather than Roman literature, in order to keep the term 'Roman literature' for literature produced in and somehow bearing the stamp of the city of Rome.

Latin literature is obviously a convenient term also for the vast literature of the Middle Ages, much of it mediocre, but much too breathing a new spirit and using the Latin language in new and unexpected ways. Take, for example, this anonymous twelfth-century lyric:

> Redit aestas cunctis grata,
> viret herba jam per prata;
> nemus frondibus ornatur,
> sic per frondes renovatur.
> Bruma vilis, nebulosa,
> erat nobis taediosa.
> Cum Aprilis redit gratus
> floribus circumstipatus,
> Philomela cantilena
> replet nemoris amoena,
> et puellae per plateas
> intricatas dant choreas.

Summer is coming back, welcomed by all. The grass is green now in the meadows, the wood is decked with foliage, made fresh

again thus by its foliage. The wretched, foggy winter was weari-
some to us. Now that welcome April is back, crowded around
with flowers, the nightingale fills the pleasant woodland scene
with her song, and along the paths the maidens dance their inter-
twining dances.

There is little opportunity for originality in description of the spring
scene. Much the same imagery as in this simple lyric can be found in
Lucretius, or in Chaucer. But take the first spring ode of Horace (*Odes* 1.
4. 1–8):

Solvitur acris hiems grata vice veris et Favoni,
    trahuntque siccas machinae carinas,
ac neque iam stabulis gaudet pecus aut arator igni,
    nec prata canis albicant pruinis.

iam Cytherea choros ducit Venus imminente Luna,
    iunctaeque Nymphis Gratiae decentes
alterno terram quatiunt pede, dum gravis Cyclopum
    Volcanus ardens visit officinas.

Winter's grip relaxed, spring's quickening winds are welcome back.
The winches drag the dry hulls.
Beasts now are not happy in their stalls, ploughman at his fire,
fields not white with hoary frost.

Cytherean Venus leads her dance now beneath a hanging moon;
together nymphs and graces neat
tap the ground, first one foot then the next; Vulcan ruddy-faced
inspects his busy Cyclops factory.

The twelfth-century poem is simple, uncomplicated, joyful, direct, the
Latin little more than a jingle by comparison with the intricate rhythms,
the complex syntax, the imaginative density of Horace's observant,
reflective, unspontaneous lines. It is not a matter of linguistic evolution,
for in the main the literary writers of mediaeval Latin (as distinct, for
example, from the writers of feudal documents) are men of some learning
who write a Latin as pedantically correct (according to the rules of
Roman Latin) as they can. It is a matter of men whose minds work
differently in a social ambience that is no longer recognizably Roman.
Their instinct is to keep the grammatical forms of Classical Latin, but to
abandon a style which they cannot make the expression of their own more
straightforward, less carefully controlled feelings. To the ear of the
modern reader attuned to Roman Latin (any Roman Latin from Plautus

11

to Juvenal), their Latin sounds oddly foreign. Take, as another example, these lines, which also belong to the twelfth century. They are put in the mouth of a bishop attached to the court of the Emperor Barbarossa and later became familiar as a German students' drinking song:

> Meum est propositum in taberna mori:
> vinum sit appositum morientis ori,
> ut dicant cum venerint angelorum chori,
> 'Deus sit propitius huic potatori.'

> I am resolved to die in a tavern,
> Let wine be close to my lips as I die.
> Then the choirs of angels when they come will sing,
> 'May God be merciful to this drunkard.'

It is not merely the metre or the sentiment which is not Roman: it is the unmistakable style of a man composing in a language not his own, a language, indeed, which for him is dead, so that the life he infuses into it is that of an alien spirit.

This is even more clearly the case with the writers of what it is becoming usual to call 'neo-Latin', by which is meant the Latin used by educated men from the beginning of the Renaissance, throughout the fifteenth, sixteenth and seventeenth centuries down to the late eighteenth century, and, indeed, though increasingly as an affectation, to the present day, chiefly for scholarly purposes (for example, Newton's *Principles*), but also for the expression of their thoughts and emotions, in both prose (for example, Erasmus' *The Praise of Folly*, 1509, Sir Thomas More's *Utopia*, 1516) and verse (for example, the Latin poems of Milton). Neo-Latin differs from mediaeval Latin in being more elaborately classical (it is the work of men who don't just know Latin, but know their classical authors intimately), and usually in being even deader. There is little that can be compared with the Latin poetry of Dante (late thirteenth, early four-teenth century) and Petrarch (fourteenth century), those two giants of pre-Renaissance Italy. Indeed, where poetry is concerned, the usual level is that of elegant pastiche. Here, as an example of something more ambitious, is a lyric written in the first half of the sixteenth century by the great scholar Julius Caesar Scaliger:

> Dulci turdule docte gutturillo
> asperas animi levare curas,
> cantillans modulos minutiores,
> condito mihi pectoris medullas,
> cantiuncula ut inquietiore
> oblitus veterum miser malorum

mentis improbus acquiescat aestus.
Da mi blandula murmurilla mille,
mille anfractibus implicata, quod sit
pote eludere vortices Charybdis.
O princeps avium beatiorum,
quot grato dominum excitant susurro,
rex nostrae volucelle vocis almae,
dulci turdule docte gutturillo.

Little thrush, skilled with your tiny throat to lighten the sharp cares of my mind as you sing your slender melodies, soothe the inner recesses of my heart, so that, through your tiny, never-ceasing song, the evil, wretched seething of my thoughts may find peace, forgetful of past wrongs. Give me a thousand charming gentle songs, wrapped in a thousand trills, something to mock the whirlpools of Charybdis. O first among happier birds, of all those that awaken their master with their sweet murmuring, little bird-king among our charming singers, little thrush, skilled with your tiny throat.

The spontaneity of twelfth-century lyric has gone, and with it most of the poetry. This is a learned poem by a learned man, skilfully exploiting two of the best known poems of Catullus. But set against this ponderously whimisical trifle the lines Catullus wrote. Here is the first sparrow poem:

Passer, deliciae meae puellae,
quicum ludere, quem in sinu tenere,
cui primum digitum dare appetenti
et acris solet incitare morsus,
cum desiderio meo nitenti
carum nescio quid lubet iocari,
et solaciolum sui doloris,
credo, ut tum gravis acquiescat ardor:
tecum ludere sicut ipsa possem
et tristis animi levare curas.

Sparrow, my mistress' object of delight—
with you she often plays, holds you in her lap,
offering finger-tip to eager beak,
soliciting your darting nip
(for there are moments when my radiant love
finds a kind of comfort in this idle play.
You are a consolation in her pain. She hopes

to soothe, I feel, her brooding love thereby):
if only I could play like her and sport with you,
and lighten passion's burden in my heart!

And here are two lines from the first kisses poem of Catullus:

da mi basia mille, deinde centum.
dein mille altera, dein secunda centum.

Give me a thousand kisses, then a hundred,
another thousand then. Then a second hundred.

It was presumably no accident that Scaliger's son, the even more prodigiously learned Joseph Scaliger, edited Catullus. But for all the learning, this is the Latin of a man who, though saturated in Latin, cannot write a Roman poem. Though Catullus' Latin is syntactically complicated, it is a complexity that heightens the vitality of the thought; in Scaliger's poem the effect is almost exactly the opposite.

The difference is not after all anything to be surprised at. Roman poems need Romans to write them; they are the expression of a society's ways of thought and feeling, not a linguistic exercise. Between a given society and the use it makes of its language for the expression of its thoughts and feelings in literature there exists a relationship that cannot be creatively imitated by someone who is attempting to manipulate the same linguistic instrument in another culture. With all the learning in the world, a Roman poem (unless it is straight pastiche) cannot be written by a Frenchman a millennium and more after Rome had ceased to exist.

IV   THE CONTEXT IN TIME AND PLACE

The importance of context is put thus by a recent writer on Horace (J. Petter, *Horace,* trans. B. Humez, 1964, 34):

Around the writer, and at the very center of the inspiration that makes him a writer, we must re-establish the presence of a literary universe. To conceive of writing tragedies, one must live in a sphere where tragedies are written; to have the idea of expressing oneself in writing, one must know that this is possible and be concerned with what others have written. It is not the obligation of each poet to invent poetry, or the satire, or the ode; he receives them, as he received words themselves in his childhood. In a non-literary civilization, he would not have written; living in another literary atmosphere, the same man

would have written something else; brought up among the mute
he would never have spoken.

The intriguing thing about Roman literature is that it seems to start
from nothing, or next to nothing; to spring into existence fully grown, as
the goddess Athena in Greek myth sprang from the head of Zeus. The
earliest things in Roman literature are said to have been two plays, a
comedy and a tragedy (though some say only a tragedy), produced in 240
BC by a Greek from Tarentum called Andronicus who became the
slave of a member of the family of the Livii (he had probably been a
prisoner of war) and was known as Livius Andronicus, having in the usual
fashion added to his own name that of his Roman master and *patronus*.
Before that there was virtually nothing, apparently: some crude forms of
native Roman farce, some simple songs of famous men of the past to be
sung at drinking parties, some hymns; nothing that you could call
literature. Yet within little more than a generation, Roman drama sprang
into full adult existence and Rome possessed at least one major epic
poem, the *Punic War* of Naevius. Obviously, it cannot have happened
quite like that.

Where literature is concerned, the three centres of the classical world
are, in chronological order, Athens, Alexandria and Rome. The
language of the first two is Greek; of the third, Latin. Literature did not
begin in Athens; it began with Homer on the Mediterranean seaboard of
what we now call Turkey, perhaps in the eighth century BC; but it was
Athens which became in the fifth and fourth centuries the centre of the
classical age of Greek literature, the home of the drama, the home of
philosophy and intellectual inquiry, the centre to which others journeyed
to listen and to learn, or to make their reputations as teachers. Towards
the end of the fourth century, where poetry proper is concerned (not, that
is to say, the drama—and not philosophy) the centre shifts to Alexandria,
the great new harbour city in Egypt founded by Alexander the Great in
331 BC which quickly became the home of an artificially stimulated court
culture, famous for its great library and as the birthplace of literary
scholarship; the richest period of Alexandrian poetry falls in the half-
century from 290 to 240 BC (the fifty years before the Second Punic War
between Carthage and Rome), a period which overlaps with the flourishing of the brilliant new comedy of manners (the so-called New Comedy)
at Athens, the heyday of which falls in the sixty years from 320 to 260 BC.

Rome is thus, when literature begins there around 250 BC, the direct
beneficiary of these two centres of intellectual and social life in the
Hellenistic world (a term used to designate the Greek-speaking culture of
the eastern Mediterranean from the death of Alexander the Great until

well into the Christian era). From Athens came the drama (the comedies of Menander and others, on which Plautus and Terence based their plays) and the ideal of a new kind of social life (greater freedom for women than the social organization of classical Greece had permitted, romantic love, and comfortable, sophisticated living). The contribution of Alexandria was that of a city where intellectual life had no cultural roots outside the court and the administrative élite: the notion of literature (or at any rate poetry) as something to be studied and practised in small groups, the notion of the literary scholar as a man of standing, comparable to his Athenian counterparts, the philosopher and the rhetorician. Both Athens and Alexandria remain centres of learning long after the middle of the second century BC. But the creatively productive period of comedy at Athens and the creative period for poetry at Alexandria are past before Roman literature begins.

Rome in 250 BC was already a city of some importance, though two centuries more were to pass before Rome could claim to rank in its turn as the centre of literary and intellectual creativity in the Mediterranean world. The time perspectives of classical antiquity are very long; they extend almost as far back into the past from the starting point of my narrative in 250 BC as they extend forward into the Middle Ages from my chosen cut-off point in AD 150. And yet the classical world can seem curiously timeless. Take the way Greek literature remains dominated by Homer's *Iliad* and *Odyssey*; Athenian drama in the fifth and fourth centuries continues to draw on the same body of myth; so does Apollonius a century later; so does Valerius Flaccus at the end of the first century AD.

Athens looks east and south, Alexandria east and north. Rome looks west. Until the third century BC the Romans stood on the edge of the Mediterranean world. Perhaps that is why Alexander did not think conquest of Rome worth while; the east was what mattered; the west was a backwater. But it was a backwater which contained a tough, pragmatic, small nation of soldier-farmers with a genius for organization and a moral impulse to put things right which made it impossible for them to stay long out of anyone else's business. As their political horizons expanded, it was natural that their first concern should be with what went on in the western Mediterranean: in Carthage, in Spain and later in Gaul and the rest of what we now call western Europe. Their involvement with what went on behind their backs in the eastern Mediterranean was slow and reluctant. Yet, inevitably, the Greek world fell in its turn, first under the influence, then under the direct rule of Rome: Greece became a Roman protectorate in 146 BC and a Roman province in 27 BC. Alexandria fell to Caesar's adopted heir, the future Emperor Augustus, in 30 BC.

16

For the first five hundred years of its existence—until, that is, the middle of the third century BC—Rome seems to have got on very well without literature. The Romans of the early Republic, when Rome was a small town struggling for its existence against hostile neighbours, had little use for poetry, and this was an attitude that hardened, when Rome began to be subjected to foreign influence, into the forthright conservatism of those who liked to think of themselves as Romans of the old school. Cato the Censor, writing in the middle of the second century BC, gives this picture of the old Roman:

> The custom was to dress respectably in the forum, at home to limit oneself to what was adequate. They spent more money on horses than on cooks. They had no respect for poetry. Anybody who spent his time on poetry or devoted himself to dinner parties was called a 'crassator' ('good-for-nothing', or 'loafer').

Cicero tells us that Cato denounced the Roman governor Marcus Nobilior for including poets on his personal staff (he had taken Ennius with him to Aetolia). One almost wonders whether the story (discounted by modern scholars) that the great library at Alexandria had been destroyed by fire while Caesar was besieged in the city was not wishful thinking on the part of latter-day Catos.

There must always have been Romans who knew Greek. It is hard to imagine that in the early years such Romans were numerous, or that many Greeks found their way to Rome. None the less there is abundant evidence that the influence of Greek culture upon Roman life and institutions is ancient (at least as old as the sixth century BC) and pervasive, and from this influence literature can hardly be excluded. Why should a Roman who had the leisure and the wealth to permit himself such refinements not have read the occasional book in Greek; or, if he could not read, have had a Greek book read to him by a Greek-speaking (and Greek-reading) slave? Homer was at least as old as Rome itself—Cicero thought older—though it was not till the text of Homer was put in order and written down that one can imagine copies of the *Iliad* or the *Odyssey* circulating even among the rich and relatively enlightened in Rome. According to tradition, that happened about thirty years before the expulsion of the kings from Rome and the foundation of the Republic.

Any Roman during the first two and a half centuries of the Republic who had the money and the leisure and the opportunity to travel was able to come into living contact with Greek literature. There is a story, for example, of an embassy to Greece in 453 BC out of which emerged the Twelve Tables of the Roman Law. The members of that embassy might easily have witnessed the performance of a trilogy by one of the great

Athenian tragedians; they might even have been introduced, as distinguished visitors to Athens, to Sophocles or to Euripides (Aeschylus had
died a few years before). A century and a half or so later a member of
another embassy, to Alexandria in 273 BC at the end of the war with
Pyrrhus, might have spent a free day, if he was so minded (and was
regarded by his hosts as important enough), in the great library (built by
Ptolemy I, who died in 283–282 BC). A Roman coming a little later
(during the First Punic War, say) might have met Apollonius (died after
247 BC) or Callimachus (died about 240 BC) working in the library. One
imagines there were not many to whom these things happened. Rome of
the fifth and fourth centuries, even Rome of the first half of the third
century, must have seemed a long way from Greece and Greek Egypt.

It was not necessary, however, to go as far as Athens or Alexandria to
come in contact with Greeks and Greek civilization: one had only to
make one's way south into the boot of Italy, or over the strait of Messina
to Sicily, where Greeks had lived in Greek-speaking cities with all the
appurtenances of Greek cultural life since the eighth century BC. A
Roman who found himself in Croton around 520 BC might have met
Pythagoras there; a Roman who found his way to Syracuse around 475
BC might have been present at the première of the 'Prometheus Bound'
of Aeschylus; he might have met Aeschylus himself during one of
Aeschylus' visits to Sicily (Aeschylus died in Sicily, at Gela, in 456 BC);
or, to advance into the fourth century, our imaginary Roman might have
conversed with Plato during one of Plato's three visits to Syracuse (389,
367, 361 BC). One imagines few did. Until the end of the third century the
hostile war-like hillsmen pretty well barred the way between Rome and
the south of Italy, unless one made the journey from Rome to Tarentum
or to Syracuse by ship.

During the first 250 years of its existence the Roman Republic seems to
have produced few travellers, and few men appreciative of things Greek.
Most Romans of the fifth and fourth centuries (the period which saw the
great flowering of Athenian culture) would have been content, we can
imagine, to agree with Virgil's Anchises, though they would probably
have preferred to put the matter more plainly (Virgil, *Aeneid* 6. 847–53):

> 'Others will force on breathing bronze a softer line,
> I well believe, tease from marble the living face,
> plead cases better, plot with rod orbits
> in the sky, predict the planets' rise.
> You, Roman, remember that to govern nations
> will be your culture, and to add to peace a way of life:
> mercy for the conquered; with the proud, unending war.'

18

They might perhaps have allowed there was some use in pleading causes, though one suspects they would have been suspicious of Greek oratorical polish and disposed to agree with Cato, who said (as late as the middle of the second century BC), 'Master the facts; the words will follow' (*rem tene, verba sequentur*).

Some Greeks came to Rome. Greek sailors and traders: the Romans were still a land people; it is likely they allowed others to sail such ships as found their way to the Tiber. Ambassadors from various Greek-speaking communities in the eastern Mediterranean: we hear of an embassy from Rhodes in 306 BC; one imagines diplomatic contacts were not infrequent. The Romans of course were busy with other things than trade or the arts. They were occupied before all else with carving out that reputation for tough, unimaginative brutality which has dogged them in modern times, perhaps because the nineteenth century spent more time on Roman history than on Roman literature.

But before the end of the third century the picture starts to look different. Part of the credit must go go Pyrrhus of Epirus, a second cousin of Alexander the Great with visions of grandeur. Pyrrhus claimed descent from that Pyrrhus (also called Neoptolemus) who was the son of Achilles, and more remotely from Aeacus (a son of Zeus and the nymph Aegina, and one of the judges of the dead in Hades). He comes into the picture because the Greeks of Tarentum invited him to Italy (southern Italy) to put up a show of strength in the face of Roman interest in extending their influence south after gaining control of the hill country. Pyrrhus perhaps regarded Italy and Sicily as a fresh world to conquer (the only one his distinguished cousin had left untouched); he can have had little thought of civilizing the Romans, but he was more effective in that (if indirectly) than in conquering them.

He landed in Italy with his Macedonians and his elephants in 280 BC, the first great invader of Roman Italy. It took the Romans five years to drive him out of Italy and five years more to capture Tarentum (270 BC). During that time a lot of Romans travelled south. Many of them learnt some Greek (or took Greek-speaking prisoners of war home with them as household slaves, and thus improved their Greek at leisure), and not a few must have returned home impressed by what they had seen. It was not the only case in history of the civilizing influence of war: as with the Normans in France (if not in England), it was the conquerors who were civilized, not the vanquished. The process had begun which Horace summed up in his memorable phrase:

Graecia capta ferum victorem cepit.

Greece imprisoned took its rude conqueror prisoner.

19

What? When? Why? and How?

A further exposure to the civilizing influence of the Greek-speaking south was soon to occur. History books call it the First Punic War. As well as to Africa it took the Romans to Sicily. The fighting lasted nearly a quarter of a century (264–241 BC), and when it was over Sicily (apart from the Kingdom of Syracuse, which was allowed to remain independent in return for its loyalty to Rome) became the first Roman territory overseas (what the Romans called a *provincia,* the seat of a permanent administration and a supporting garrison of troops). In later centuries when their minds had been exposed to the Greek philosophy of Stoicism and they had made of it a working, pragmatic philosophy compatible with Anchises' injunction 'to add to peace a way of life', the First Punic War provided the Romans with the edifying legend of Regulus, the general strong in defeat. Regulus was defeated by a Carthaginian army in Africa in 255 BC; according to the legend, he was sent back to Rome as a prisoner on parole to convey the Carthaginian terms of peace. Whether he would have recognized himself as the Regulus of Horace's ode is doubtful (3. 5. 41–56):

> His chaste wife's lips, the story goes,
> his little children, like a man who has lost
> his civil rights, he thrust aside,
> gaze bent grimly on the ground
>
> till he had won firm acceptance from the Senate
> of a proposal never made till then,
> and, surrounded by his grieving friends,
> had hastened on his way, an unprecedented exile.
>
> And yet he knew what the barbarian torturer
> had ready for him. All the same,
> he forced his way through the kinsmen who
> barred his path, the people blocking his return,
>
> for all the world as if he had come to the end
> of some protracted court case entered into for
> the sake of others, and were on his way to Venafrum's
> fields, or Spartan Tarentum.

Horace, like Livy, mythologizes the heroes of the old Republic. Regulus can hardly have been the civilized Stoic, the enlightened *patronus* Horace's portrait implies. And yet the elements of continuity in the Roman character and way of life are there. They are present too in Horace's expression of the character of Regulus. If the formal indebtedness of Roman literature to Greek literature is evident at every turn

(Horace's ode is a meticulous adaptation of Greek sixth-century lyric structure), that indebtedness does not suppress or strangle what is Roman in Horace's poem, or transform it into something derivative and alien, a kind of high-grade parody. Rather it is the alien structure which liberates the Roman content from inarticulateness and incoherence. From the Greeks the Romans learnt the forms of literature, not the spirit. The result was a new self-awareness that in its turn infused life into a consciously acquired capacity for accurate, elegant expression. The spirit remains all the more unmistakably Roman because the alien form has endowed the Roman thought with a new eloquence of expression.

V THE USE OF LITERATURE

Rome in 241 BC, the year the first war with Carthage ended, was not a liberal society. We must take with a grain of salt the glamorized version of third-century life which we find in the pages of Livy. The restraints of class were rigid, the claims the state made upon its citizens onerous. The need to win a livelihood from the land or from the labour of one's hands at a craft left the vast majority of the population little time for the things of the mind except in the most casual, desultory fashion. Throughout antiquity the struggle for survival against a hostile environment weighed heavily upon the ordinary inhabitant of Italy; the poverty of small-time farmer and urban plebeian alike was real and oppressive.

There was of course a wealthier, more leisured class, even in the third century BC, among whom the ability to read and write and the leisure to make use of that ability cannot have been uncommon. Among these there must have been a good number experienced in organized verbal communication in writing. The formulae of religious ritual had to be known, employed and transmitted to others. Even a rudimentary legal code requires men versed in putting words together clearly, able to frame a law, experienced in the application of precedents. It seems the typical pattern that organized, disciplined, recorded, preserved expression in words begins with a society's prayers to and worship of its gods, and with the business of telling its citizens what they may and must not do and the prescription of precise penalties for those who disobey or fail to heed society's injunctions. In time the practitioners of these crafts become skilful in the manipulation of words and extend the area of daily life which they make their concern. The business of government calls for recording who was elected to what office and what occurred during the year the office was held, and with the passage of time the record naturally becomes less bare. Religious ritual, law and the public record are the obvious, useful functions of organized verbal communication. So it was at Rome.

The outcome was a set of texts which were transmitted and added to from generation to generation. Most of these early texts have been lost, but not all. Livy tells us (6. 1. 10) that after the sack of Rome by the Gauls in 390 BC, the Romans were able to recover the written texts of certain treaties and laws, among them the Laws of the Twelve Tables and even some legal texts dating from the time of the kings. Documents dating from the fifth century still existed in the Classical period; the text of the Laws of the Twelve Tables seems to have been commonly consulted by those who made the law their concern. From early times some texts seem to have been cast in metrical form. Such are the Arval and Salic hymns, the epitaphs of famous men, for example those of the family of the Scipiones. The word which was to become the ordinary Latin word for a poem (*carmen*) originally denoted any organized verbal structure: a hymn, for instance, or the formula of a religious ritual, what the Romans called *condita verba,* as opposed to the *incondita verba* that Virgil represents the lovesick shepherd Corydon singing to the hills and woods.

The everyday uses of organized, recorded expression of thought fall outside what we mean by literature. Recognition of a text as belonging to literature is accompanied by a reversal of the relationship that existed between that text and the circumstances which produced it. The use the text served has passed, and the text survives on its own merits, because it gives pleasure to people other than those for whom it was originally written, or because it is inherently memorable or moving. It is in the nature of literature to be, for everyday purposes, useless.

In all societies individual texts can cross the border that separates everyday usefulness from literature, though it is uncommon for a national literature to begin exclusively in that way—societies tend to learn from one another about literature, as the Romans learnt from the Greeks—and still more uncommon for this transfer from everyday use to literary status to continue as a significant factor. Pretty soon, and more and more, we have texts for which there never was a use: they started life as literature, were written as literature.

This is not to make uselessness for everyday purposes the criterion of literary texts, or to deny usefulness to literary texts altogether. My argument is that in the case of a legal text, or a text which was composed as part of a religious ritual, usefulness is fundamental: the social need existed, the text was written to meet it; it does not have to possess other merits. In the case of a literary text, usefulness is a secondary concern, or no concern at all; what determines the literary text's survival, what makes it good or bad, is its merit as literature.

As a society becomes more complex, the range of usefulness of organized forms of expression becomes more diverse, to include things that make life more agreeable or more civilized, or a society more capable of realizing its aspirations, or more completely aware of the nature of its human destiny. Plainly, literature can discharge a useful role in this process of expansion of the cultural and moral self, but that is not normally why writers start writing, or go on writing, nor is it a valid basis for judging the literary quality of a text. Writers start writing because they have seen the thing done in other societies, or languages, and go on writing because they want to write; the consciousness that they are fulfilling a social function is secondary, or comes afterwards. They are perhaps apt to write better if they are conscious of fulfilling a social function as well, of being understood and wanted. But that is not why they write. Nor do writers stop writing because they fulfil no discernible social function, though they may write less well. Indeed, the history of Roman literature is in large measure the history of the discovery and then the loss of a social function.

The uselessness of literature is not something that disturbs us today, but it disturbed the Romans. Throughout their history they were distrustful of talk if it seemed to lead nowhere, or was not called for by an occasion that could be pointed to. Often they felt they had to give a literary text a façade of utility, a pretence of usefulness where no useful object was in reality aimed at. That attitude is clearly one reason for the popularity of didactic poetry; it helps to explain why Cicero regularly cast his popular treatises on philosophy and oratory in the form of long letters written to help personal friends; or why he published speeches against such notable figures as Verres and Catiline, some speeches never delivered, instead of issuing a justification of his actions that made no claim to be called for by the requirements of an actual occasion. Everybody knew that that long string of speeches against Verres which we call the *Actio secunda* had never been delivered; everybody understood that the *De Finibus* was not really written to help Cicero's friend Brutus grasp the problems of moral philosophy; everybody understood that Virgil's *Georgics* was not written to help farmers. Nobody was deceived; but everybody felt more at his ease in reading a work that had a built-in explanation of how it came to be written. The force of tradition is not to be discounted in all these cases, but tradition alone is seldom the determining factor in a writer's decision to do what he does in the way he decides to do it.

The question whether *poetry* was useful or not seems to have preoccupied Horace all his life. It was, fairly plainly, one of the factors that drove him back to the explicitly moral statement of the *Epistles* in retreat from the only implicitly moral statement of the *Odes*. His final verdict was a compromise, and an evasion (*Ars Poetica* 343):

23

What? When? Why? and How?

Omne tulit punctum qui miscuit utile dulci.

He comes out on top who combines usefulness with pleasure.

The Romans were a moral people. Greeks might talk a lot about morality, but to Roman eyes the Greeks were morally frivolous, if not downright immoral in their conduct. The Romans were thus impelled to create a use, or an apparent use, for literature: literature becomes at Rome the expression of moral concern. Actually, it was an old use, one that had been lost in Hellenistic Athens and Alexandria. It is in the nature of the comedy of manners to assume a permissive attitude to morality. In a court literature where poets write for one another, there is nobody left to instruct; all that matters is technique. The Romans restored to literature its moral function, and gave it a new emphasis which literature has never since quite lost.

One explanation for that new emphasis is to be found in the intensely personal nature of the major writers of Rome from Catullus onwards. It is the difference between poetry which merely expresses the awareness of a society (more eloquently, more pathetically than the poet's contemporaries, but drawing still on the common heritage of sensibility and moral feeling) and poetry which actively seeks to manipulate the awarenesses of the poet's contemporaries, in order to convey—not what everybody feels, but what the poet himself feels and wants his contemporaries to feel. The *Iliad* and the *Odyssey* are examples of the former; Virgil's *Aeneid,* of the latter. It hardly matters who wrote the *Iliad* and the *Odyssey,* or when: no more than a small effort of the historical imagination is called for from the modern reader. Virgil's *Aeneid* challenges Virgil's readers to see some of the central problems of the poet's time through the poet's eyes. Even the elegiac poets, who may be thought to flaunt the uselessness of poetry, are seeking to manipulate the feelings of their contemporaries in favour of a lifestyle that challenged all traditional concepts of the individual's duty to the state. It is this close relationship between Roman society and the individual writer in that society which makes it important to see the masterpieces of Roman literature as the works of individuals living in, and reacting to, an evolving and constantly changing social environment.

VI   A FIRST LOOK

Roman literature begins with a period of provincialism or cultural colonialism lasting from the close of the First Punic War (241 BC) until the emergence of the feeling, which followed the Social War, as it is

24

called, of 91–87 BC (a struggle between Rome and her allies within Italy) and the resultant extension of Roman citizenship to Italians generally, that Rome was really one country, united by common aspirations. For simplicity's sake, we may speak of the century and a half from 250 to 100 BC. This is what I have called the Preclassical period; it is the period of Plautus, Terence and Ennius, the period which sees the creation of a Roman tradition of dramatic and narrative poetry.

The essence of cultural colonialism is a feeling that one is on the periphery, that what one does can only be derivative. A Roman writer of the Preclassical period could hardly escape the thought that the centres of civilized life were Athens and Alexandria; the only models from which he could learn were Greek models. To possess such an awareness is the first step towards cultural sophistication. Naturally, a polarization easily occurs. The enthusiasm for everything Greek which characterized Roman society at the turn of the third and second centuries BC was vigorously resisted by those who proclaimed the superiority of the old Roman way of life; their leader was Cato. A similar sense of being located on a cultural periphery is easily seen in those who lived and wrote in the English-speaking countries of the British Empire in the nineteenth century: they cannot escape the feeling that the centre of things is London; that the place to write a novel about is London, or at any rate England—not Australia, or Canada, even if the writer has never been to London and knows about it only from books. At Rome, the sense of cultural isolation was intensified by language; the only available models were those of a foreign tongue. One can compare the situation that faced those who set out to create a national literature in the countries which emerged out of the old Austro-Hungarian empire after the First World War. The need was felt to create a national literature in Hungarian or Czech comparable to that which existed in German; for the established forms (the novel, the complex short poem) the only available models were German models (or the less familiar models of French and English); the new national literature could not escape, to begin with, the status of a derivative literature. At Rome, this was not a period of colonialism, of course, in the political sense: Rome was never anybody's colony. On the contrary, this was politically a century and a half of conquest. Rome enters the period mistress of Italy south of the Po valley down to the toe, possessed of her first province (Sicily); before it is over she will have conquered Carthage twice more and established her influence as the leading Mediterranean power in Greece itself. The idea of Italy as a country will have started to gain ground.

This period of colonialism is followed by a period which extends from the end of the Social War until the death of the Emperor Augustus in AD

25

14. It is the period of the anguish of the Republic and the Augustan Age. For simplicity's sake we may speak of the last century BC, and call it the period of Classicism. To this period belong two of Rome's greatest prose writers, Cicero and Livy. But it is above all a period of achievement in verse: practically everything that is first-rate in Roman poetry outside the drama was written during the three-quarters of a century from 60 BC to the death of Ovid in AD 17; the only possible addition is Juvenal, who lived a hundred years after Ovid.

The Classical period is followed by a period of prosperity and totalitarianism, the first century and a half of the Empire; or to be more precise, the period AD 14–150. In this period there are two high points: the age of Nero (the main writers are Lucan, Petronius and Seneca) in the middle of the first century AD (AD 54–68) and the age of Hadrian and Trajan (the main writers are Juvenal and Tacitus) half a century later (AD 98–138). The two high points are separated by the productive mediocrity of the reigns of the Flavian emperors Vespasian, Titus and Domitian. The Postclassical period is a period of decline, not in output (it produced a host of minor writers), but in quality, by almost any standard; above all, it is characterized by a failure of that capacity to express the awarenesses and aspirations (and often the despairs) of a whole society which is characteristic of the Classical period. Writing becomes a pastime for gentlemen. The typical figure is the younger Pliny; Martial is perhaps the only professional writer of the period. Verse in particular in the Postclassical period is marked from the outset by something like that 'dissociation of sensibility' (to use Eliot's famous phrase) which separates the English Metaphysicals of the seventeenth century from the poets of the English Augustan Age. The most significant development of the period in literature is the reversal in importance of verse and prose (see Chapter 5).

The chief writers arranged in their three periods are as shown in Tables 1 and 2.

Naturally, the facts are not as simple as a chart makes them appear. Prose writers write verse and poets sometimes write prose. Actually, there is only one writer for whom a place can seriously be claimed in both lists. This is Seneca, the tragedian and philosopher (not to be confused with his less famous father, 'Seneca the Elder', often called 'Seneca the Rhetorician', the writer of model exercises for young lawyers). Oddly enough (though we have some of Cicero's verse, and some verse by Petronius), only one prose work (the *Euhemerus* of Ennius) has come down to us from the sixteen poets. Several writers in both lists wrote in more than one tradition. Cicero in prose and Ovid in verse possessed the most diverse talents: Ovid even wrote a tragedy, *Medea* (two lines

26

Table 1   The major Roman poets

(In order of date of death, if known; writers in square brackets are mentioned only in passing)

THE POET AS STORYTELLER	THE POET AS TEACHER	THE POET AS HIMSELF
	The Preclassical period (250–100 BC)	
[Livius Andronicus, c.284–204 BC]		[Lucilius, 180–102 BC]
[Naevius, c.270–200 BC]		
Plautus, 254–184 BC		
[Ennius, 239–169 BC]		
Terence, 185–159 BC		
	The Classical period (87 BC–AD 14)	
	(i.e., from the end of the Social War to the death of Augustus)	
Virgil, 70–19 BC	Lucretius, c.100–c.55 BC	Catullus, c.84–54 BC
Ovid, 43 BC–AD 17	(Virgil)	Tibullus, c.60–19 BC
	(Ovid)	Propertius, c.60–c.15 BC
		Horace, 65–8 BC
		(Ovid)
	The Postclassical period (AD 14–150)	
Lucan, AD 39–65	[Manilius (reign of Tiberius)]	[Persius, AD 34–62]
(Seneca, counted among prose-writers)		(Statius)
[Valerius Flaccus, died AD 92/93]		Martial, AD 60–114
[Statius, AD c.45–96]		Juvenal, AD 60/70–c.128
[Silius Italicus, AD 26–101]		

Table 2 The major Roman prose-writers

HISTORY	OTHER DIDACTIC PROSE	PERSONAL (i.e., letters)	ORATORY	IMAGINATIVE PROSE
		The Preclassical period (250–100 BC)		
	[Cato, 234–149 BC]		(Cato)	
		The Classical period (87 BC–AD 14)		
[Caesar, 100–44 BC] Sallust, 86–35 BC Livy, 59 BC–AD 17	(Cicero)	(Cicero)	Cicero, 106–43 BC	
		The Postclassical period (AD 14–150)		
Tacitus, AD c.55–117 [Suetonius, AD c. 70–c.160]	Seneca, AD c.4–65 (also wrote verse tragedies) Quintilian, AD c.35–c.95	(Seneca) Younger Pliny, AD 61/62–c. 113		Petronius, ?–AD 65 [Apuleius. fl. c. AD 155]

survive). History seems to have produced the most single-minded writers.

A more serious objection to a chart of this kind is that it obscures the continuity and coherence of a tradition. A literary tradition is more than a string of names spread out in the columns of a time chart. Literary events, like ordinary historical events, are linked in a cause-and-effect relationship; they are linked as well by a process of development similar to the process by which Henry Ford's Model T becomes, by diversification and elaboration through a long series, the range of new models placed on the market each year. Moreover, while ordinary historical events fade into the past and are forgotten except by the historian, and old Ford cars not merely wear out but are superseded because nobody except the crank or enthusiast wants them any more, the events in a literary tradition (as in music and the plastic arts) enjoy an odd kind of timelessness. True, some works die or fade away, and are known only to the scholar or research worker. But the really great works, the classics, live on, not merely as something still remembered, but as present and immediate for all interested in literature, or that particular literary tradition. Shakespeare is as present in the sensibility of the twentieth-century reader or writer as is Ibsen or Eliot; perhaps more present despite his relative remoteness in time, more easily turned to, more easily alluded to, more easily read for enjoyment. Though the culture Homer expressed receded into the past, though the form he used (Homeric epic) became superseded as social circumstances changed, the *Iliad* and the *Odyssey* remain, timelessly present as a source of inspiration and allusion throughout classical antiquity, as perhaps only the Bible is for those of us for whom the Bible remains a timeless source of inspiration or guidance. For a Roman knowledgeable about literature in the time of Cicero—for Cicero himself—Ennius and the so-called early Roman writers are not figures of the past in the way that the great Romans of ordinary history had become figures of the past. They are present and familiar; the more present and familiar the greater they are, not the closer in time.

The principal works of the Roman literary tradition can be classified as follows:

1. *The poet as storyteller* (narrative and dramatic poetry): The terms 'Poet as Storyteller', 'Poet as Teacher' and 'Poet as Himself' correspond to the titles of Chapters 2–4; for details of the individual works mentioned, see the relevant chapters.

(a) Narrative poetry: Two major works, both belonging to the Classical period, the *Aeneid* of Virgil and the *Metamorphoses* of Ovid; the reputation of each has varied from century to century, but both have exercised a powerful influence upon western literature and upon western thought and imagination. To this group belong also a number of works, all written in the Postclassical period, which are major in intention, but of little appeal to modern taste (Lucan's *On the Civil War*), or frankly dull (Silius Italicus' *The Punic Wars*, Statius' *Theban War* and *Achilles*, Valerius Flaccus' *Voyage of the Argonauts*).

(b) Dramatic poetry: The Preclassical period has bequeathed to us a large body of plays by one comic writer (Plautus, twenty-one plays survive) whose influence on the beginnings of modern drama in the Renaissance down to the seventeenth century was. enormous. Both Shakespeare and Molière drew upon his plots and followed him in writing a kind of comedy of situation that bordered on farce in its pursuit of brilliant stage effects and intricacy of plot. A smaller group of technically better-written plays by a second writer (Terence, six plays survive) has had less influence. Of the many other comedies and the many tragedies that were written in the Preclassical period only fragments survive. The only Roman tragedies we possess are nine plays, all on traditional Greek themes, by Seneca. These bookish, spectacular, rhetorical plays also exercised an enormous influence upon Elizabethan and seventeenth-century French drama. A tenth tragedy (the *Octavia*), doubtfully ascribed to Seneca, is the only surviving example of a tragedy on a Roman theme (*fabula praetexta,* a type common in the Preclassical period); this play, about the fate of the princess whom Nero divorced in order to marry his mistress Poppaea, is important for its influence on later drama (the Roman plays of Racine; less directly, the historical plays of Shakespeare).

2. *The poet as teacher* (didactic poetry): Represented by one major work belonging to the Classical period, Lucretius' *On the Universe* (*De Rerum Natura*). Though long denounced as an enemy of religion and dismissed as a weaver of fantastic theories, Lucretius has in the last hundred years come into his own. Now that his ideas are less subject to bigoted attack, his genuine moral purpose has been sensed. The remarkable agreement between his theories and the findings of modern physics has naturally been much to his advantage. At the same time his real stature as a poet has been recognized. To be grouped along with *On the Universe* are two more works, both of the Classical period, hardly major works in size or in intention, but works which express a highly civilized sensibility and are the product of a highly cultured sophistication: these are Virgil's *Georgics* and Ovid's *Art of Love*. For centuries after literary refinement began to return to western Europe (from the fifteenth century, say, till the eighteenth), literature would have been the poorer and cruder, and certainly the duller, without them. Also under the heading of 'The Poet as Teacher' must come Ovid's uncompleted poem

on the Roman Calendar, the *Fasti,* and perhaps also Manilius' *On the Stars* (early Postclassical period); the former is still occasionally sampled, less for its information about the Roman calendar than because it is, like Ovid's *Metamorphoses,* a repertoire of stories from legend (though more briefly told); the latter is a work of monumental difficulty intelligible only to the scholar.

3. *The poet as himself* (personal poetry, including satire):

(a)   First and foremost under this heading come three collections of short, or at any rate much shorter, poems, all of the Classical period. These are the Catullan collection, the *Eclogues* of Virgil and the *Odes* and *Epodes* of Horace. Some of the poems of Catullus and many of the odes of Horace are among the best-known things in western literature.

(b)   Almost as well known as these, but hardly to be put in the same class, are the elegies (i.e., poems written in 'elegiac couplets', combinations of hexameters and pentameters) of Propertius and Tibullus and the *Amores* of Ovid (along with which have to be grouped a number of Ovid's less well-known collections of elegiac poems, such as the *Tristia*). Apart from a modern revival of interest in Propertius (due to Goethe in the nineteenth century and to Ezra Pound in the twentieth), the reputation of the elegists has waned greatly since the seventeenth century. In the same formal category belong the *Epigrams* of Martial and the *Silvae* ('Undressed Timber') of Statius.

(c)   Under the same general heading belong three collections of verse in a more relaxed, conversational style (and, on average, rather longer), the *Satires* and the *Epistles* of Horace and the *Satires* of Juvenal. All three collections were much admired and imitated in the seventeenth and eighteenth centuries in France and in England, but few would now put them in the front rank. In this same group, but a long way behind in general estimate, come the *Satires* of Persius.

4. *The uses of prose*: The bulk of surviving Roman prose greatly exceeds that of verse. Much of what survives, however, has little claim to be regarded as literature in the sense that the term literature is used in this book. The voluminous *Natural History* of the elder Pliny both falls outside literature and, unlike the didactic writings of the elder Cato or Cicero or the prose of the younger Seneca, is of little importance for the development of literature.

Perhaps only one work can claim an undisputed place in the front rank of literature. This is Tacitus' *Annals,* the history of the imperial court from Augustus to Nero. The rest of Tacitus (his *Histories,* his biography of his father-in-law Agricola, and his monographs on Germany and the history of oratory) and the remainder of Roman historical writing— Livy's huge *History of Rome from its Foundation,* Sallust's monographs

31

on *The War with Jugurtha* and the *Conspiracy of Catiline,* Caesar's *Gallic War* and *Civil War,* Suetonius' *Twelve Emperors* (from Julius Caesar to Domitian), despite their individuality, their high level of general competence and the moments of brilliance to be found in nearly all, cannot stand comparison with the *Annals.*

The enormous oeuvre of Cicero is, like Roman drama, important for its influence on the development of western literature rather than for itself: Cicero was much more than an orator and politician. He created not only the highly flamboyant, rhetorical style which most people think of in connexion with his name, but also at least two other styles. One is the faster moving, less showy style which he used in his semi-popular treatises on philosophy and oratory. The other is the compact, subtle style of conversation improved upon, which we find in Cicero's letters. Hardly less important for the development of European prose are the letters and the philosophical monographs of the younger Seneca ('Seneca the Philosopher'). If Cicero's treatises hardly count as literature, Seneca's *Letters to Lucilius* provide one more instance of a work that crosses the border from paraliterature to undeniable literary status: they are an eloquent, elegant and candid expression of an unusually cultivated mind, the honest, sombre (but not cynical) thoughts of a man who had led an unusually interesting life, and who had cultivated and mastered the art of expressing his thoughts in a sinewy, incisive and yet simple and highly readable prose which perhaps reminds the modern reader more of Voltaire than of any English writer. Comparison with the *Letters* of the younger Pliny, that shallow, precious commentator on the Roman cultural scene in the second half of the first century AD for whom little more than the veneer of culture matters, is instructive.

Finally, two prose works whose status as literature is unquestionable. One is Petronius' strange satiric narrative fantasy traditionally called the *Satyricon*; the other is Apuleius' even stranger and more fantastical tale, the *Golden Ass.* Petronius belonged to the court of Nero; his tale, though the first sustained piece of Roman imaginative prose, is truly Italian in spirit: it is racy, ironic, derisive of convention and sham, ribald, the sort of prose tale Plautus might have told. But despite its return to fashion in recent years, the *Satyricon* must forfeit any claim it might have upon a place in the front rank, by reason of its originality and verve, as a result of its wilful, slapdash eccentricity. The *Golden Ass* is the work of a Romanized African who wrote more in the spirit of Greek romance than in the tradition of Roman satire.

If to begin with the styles of the Roman poets are oddly hard to tell apart, this is not so of the writers of prose. All the major writers have their own easily recognized individual style. Yet, despite this interest in style, the Romans seem to have been curiously negligent of the literary uses of prose. Why imaginative prose came so late and indeed never established itself at Rome (both the *Satyricon* and the *Golden Ass* are highly eccentric works) is a question that will be discussed in Chapter 5.

VII A PRELIMINARY ASSESSMENT

This is the point to pause and take stock. Some preliminary assessment is desirable of a literature so ragged and fragmentary in the form in which it has come down to us, if only as a justification for asking the reader to proceed.

Three literatures of western Europe offer an unparalleled continuity and richness: Greek, English and French. To those of us who live in the English tradition it has for centuries seemed almost inconceivable that a nation could exist which had no literature, as was the case at Rome for something like 500 years, or that there should come a time when our own literature might wither away and die, as happened to Roman literature in the second half of the second century AD.

Or rather, it would have seemed so until recently. There are signs that our generation (I speak of myself and some of those who will read this book) is the last in which literature occupied a natural and central place in cultural life. I use the past tense because it seems to me that the generation after mine already does not accord literature that central place, and that the likelihood that literature will in the foreseeable future recover the importance it possessed for us is not great.

Already in the eyes of the generation before mine, to be a writer seems to have been something less honourable than it had been in the days of Queen Victoria; certainly literature was a less natural activity for a cultivated man than in the days of Queen Anne. It was still not uncommon, however, for ordinary, non-literary people to write verse. Universal literacy, the ability to read and write, that great triumph of modern education had still not reached its inevitable goal, the flow of popular journalism which now overwhelms us. Nor was there the same mass of paraliterature and non-literature: advertising matter, commentaries on the news, reports of committees. All these things existed, but we had not reached the point where the ability to read meant the imposition upon us of an unending stream of print that had to be read if we were to survive as citizens of an increasingly complex society. Nor was much alarm felt at the increasing role of literature as an activity for people who were content to let their minds idle, as the motor of a car idles when it turns over while the car is standing still. Despite occasional warnings such as Mrs Q. D. Leavis's *Fiction and the Reading Public* (published in 1932), it was not generally foreseen that catering for this market might in the end supplant the production of serious books by making them economically unviable.

Since that time books have multiplied beyond belief. But increasingly they are different books catering for a different public. My generation could expect to find in any large town two or three bookshops that carried a pretty fair selection of the English classics. Today I doubt that you would easily find the works of Pope or Shelley anywhere except in a university textbook store—and not even there, if the author you wanted didn't happen to be prescribed for some course. You might not be able to lay your hands on a copy of a particular novel of Dickens, say, except in a university library. Most of the English classics are still available in cheap modern editions, but even 'serious' bookshops now carry only very ragged stocks of such books. Literature is becoming increasingly an academic subject; more and more the classics of western literature are read only by those who have to read them.

The time and attention devoted to reading by individuals has clearly shrunk; the growth to maturity of film, radio and television has meant that all three impose a claim upon the attention of cultivated people. It no longer seems out of the question that the time may come when serious literature will disappear altogether simply because there will be too few people interested to justify the huge capital outlay involved in marketing a book. Poetry is obviously the most vulnerable. The uselessness of poetry, which was once its glory, is still vaunted, if on an increasingly petulant note, by old practitioners, as in these lines by W. H. Auden (from 'The Cave of Making'):

> After all, it's rather a privilege
> amid the affluent traffic
> to serve this unpopular art which cannot be turned into
> background noise for study
> or hung as a status trophy by rising executives,
> cannot be 'done' like Venice
> or abridged like Tolstoy, but stubbornly still insists upon
> being read or ignored.

There is an element of pettiness in a defence of poetry reduced to such terms. If poetry survives at all, its survival is likely to depend on 'little magazines' and other technologically cheap forms of circulation. But that will only increase the tendency for reading and writing poetry to become an occupation for eccentrics.

There is little point in deploring what cannot be resisted, and what may not in fact occur. The pendulum may swing the other way. But the possibility of an affluent and reasonably well governed society with no place in it for literature (either the writing of new books and poems, or the reading of what the past produced) exists. We begin to see that a society can get on without literature.

Part of the interest, therefore, that Roman literature has for us lies in the fact that it lacks that continuity of assured development which till recently those of us whose mother tongue was English or French were apt to take for granted, as a normal, inevitable development, as one aspect of social continuity, or even progress. Over a period of four centuries we can see Roman literature begin in a sudden blaze of activity, reach within a couple of centuries an astonishing maturity, and then subside into apparently irredeemable triviality and mediocrity. We are interested in how it happened. It might happen to us.

Involved in this process of rise and decay is a fundamental conflict in Roman society between the state and the individual. It is to be found of course in all societies. But in Roman society its effects are unusually apparent and ultimately destructive. In literature, it becomes the conflict between the public and the personal modes, the conflict between literature as entertainment and literature as the expression by the individual of his own personality. On the one hand, there is the possibility of a large audience, the possiblity of viable social function; if the writer is appreciated, he can feel he is worth his salt. On the other hand, there is the likelihood of no more than a small hypercritical élite more interested in technique than in what the writer has to say and the frustrating feeling of fulfilling no social function. These are the Scylla and Charybdis which confront the writer at Rome.

The conflict is occasioned in large measure by the shift from an oral literature to a written literature: Plautus had a wide audience, for whom he had an immediate appeal; Horace wrote for a small audience of those seriously interested in difficult poetry. The shift is largely the consequence of that characteristically Roman institution, patronage: the special relationship between the man of influence and those whom he protects, partly as a social obligation, partly because those who claim his protection can in their turn help him by their support—in elections, for example. In the Preclassical period the typical Roman writer is a non-Roman, to begin with little more than a kind of tradesman (Plautus is said to have been a stage carpenter who took to writing plays), later a provincial, or a refugee intellectual. He finds the support he needs from a patron interested in literature. A group grows up in which literature is discussed; concentration on the kind of writing which lends itself to close discussion, and an obsession with style are natural consequences. The relationship between the writer and his audience exerts a powerful influence on the form literature took in the latter part of the Preclassical and in the Classical period. It is an early instance in western literature of the interaction of criticism and creative writing. In the Postclassical period Roman literature becomes a court literature. There is a return to a form of public performance, the recital given by the writer of his works. But it is an artificial kind of public performance corrupted by preciosity and rhetoric.

The metaphors of physical decay ('wither', 'die', etc.) obviously provide too facile an explanation, as do metaphors which invite us to imagine a national literature as something that moves through time, so that we can say, for example, that a movement 'loses its sense of direction'. A more sensible approach, I think, lies in seeking the social function, not so much of literature in general, but of the individual work in the context in which it comes into existence. But some general statements also are possible. One can say that Roman literature begins as an oral literature (in the drama, which comes to life on the stage), and then never quite succeeds in managing the transition from an oral literature to an essentially written literature. The quality of what is written improves, but at the same time the writer is deprived of a valid social function. The writers of the Augustan Age were able to persuade themselves they had recovered a social function. It became increasingly evident that, with rare exceptions, the writers of Imperial Rome could have none except the cultivation of their own ego. None at any rate within the framework of society as it existed. Equipped with modern technology they might have been able to revert to an oral literature and free themselves from an outmoded preoccupation with the written word. Perhaps that is what we should do.

VIII   SOME QUESTIONS OF METHOD

Ideally, there are three requirements the literary historian can be expected to satisfy. The reader who wants facts feels entitled to be told such things as are known or reasonably supposed about who wrote what and when. The author's responsibility in discharging this function is to be clear, concise and scrupulous. A second requirement, less easily met, is descriptive evaluation of the surviving works of the major writers. Here something more is expected of the literary historian than clarity, conciseness and scrupulousness; it is not as widely supposed today as it was a generation ago that a work of literature is so easily described, or the reputation of a writer so commonly acknowledged and immutable, that the literary historian need only perfunctorily discharge his critical obligation; he has, moreover, an increasing duty, where Roman literature is concerned, to readers whose literary taste is discriminating but who know little about Roman literature or Roman society. A third requirement is a readable, continuous narrative for the benefit of those who will turn to the book, not merely for facts and critical assessments, but for guidance in understanding the influences and trends which constitute the literary and cultural environment of a writer and the evolving literary tradition in which the writer works. Books which attempt to discharge all or some of these requirements are listed in the Bibliography. The facts about Roman literature (dates, names of works, summaries of what the works contain and the like) are not hard to come by, and I have devoted little space to them here, in order to concentrate on more interesting and less straightforward matters where it seemed to me the general reader was less well served by the books available to him.

To meet the requirement of a continuous narrative, most literary historians arrange their material in chronological order. It is the obvious method, but it has certain disadvantages. One is that, if you begin at the beginning, it is some time, where Roman literature is concerned at any rate, before you get to anything really worth talking about. For it is the convention of chronological narrative that what is still to come cannot be discussed: you can only discuss what has already been dealt with or is now being dealt with at the point you have just reached; serious comparison of works belonging to different periods is almost impossible. Another disadvantage is that in a chronological survey space has to be found for good and bad alike, and this is apt to leave insufficient room for proper discussion of those works which the average reader wants most to know about.

This book attempts a radical reversal of emphasis, in order to restore the major work to the front rank of importance. That will be the subject of the following chapters. But before we begin, a word has to be said about the problems raised by the fragmentary nature of our knowledge and the sheer remoteness in time of Roman society.

We know a good deal about the political history of Rome, but we know much less about its cultural and intellectual life. So much of what the Romans wrote simply did not survive the Dark Ages: of the 750 or so Latin writers we hear tell of, only one in five is represented today by anything you could call a complete work, or a substantial portion of a complete work; if we confine our attention to the four centuries 250 BC–AD 150, those who are left more or less intact amount to a few dozen out of several hundred. Our knowledge of the men who made what has survived is hardly less woefully incomplete: we know a good deal about

Cicero, and more about Virgil and Horace than we know about Shake-speare; but we know precious little about Catullus, practically nothing about Lucretius or Propertius or Petronius. About the impact these men and their writings had on their contemporaries we know, usually, nothing at all: a chance remark by Cicero about Lucretius (what impressed him most was Lucretius' technical skill as a poet); a peevish *obiter dictum* about Virgil's *Aeneid* by Augustus' admiral Agrippa (Virgil's trick of packing fresh, complex meaning into phrases woven out of ordinary, everyday words of Latin exasperated him); a largish handful of compli-mentary remarks by poets on their contemporaries or their immediate predecessors (all comments the occasion of which precluded serious criticism); Cicero on his predecessors in oratory, or on the old Roman poets; Quintilian's brief survey of Roman literature; Macrobius on Virgil. From all these it is possible to glean something about what the Romans made of their leading writers, but not much.

Fortunately, a good deal remains which it would be almost patronizing to describe as first-class, since it includes several of the greatest master-pieces of western literature. And, according to a common view of literary studies, the intrusion of biography into literary history can be dismissed as an unfortunate heresy: what matters, we are told, is poems, not poets. Those who accept this argument easily reconcile themselves to ignorance about the poet's contemporary audience. It makes judgment of a work hard when that work was written two thousand years ago. But then judgment is never easy.

The real trouble with judgment where Roman literature is concerned is that, if you admit the relevance of judgment to criticism, you have to answer the awkward question: Whose? Are we to attempt to reconstruct the reactions of Virgil's contemporaries? Or is the standard to be the reaction of the intelligent modern reader on first looking into Virgil's *Aeneid*? Or do we appeal to some more absolute judgment—the 'verdict of the ages'? None of the three, when we look into the matter, proves to be anything you could call a reliable criterion.

One difficulty in appealing to the judgment of Virgil's contemporaries is that we have very little idea what they made of the *Aeneid*. Agrippa's comment hardly constitutes representative contemporary reaction. Another difficulty is that there is reason to suppose that the way literature went in the second half of the Augustan Age virtually deprived the Augustan poets of an audience competent to contribute from their repertoire of awarenesses (what they expected of literature and could respond to) anything like an adequate understanding of Virgil's poem. Somehow, about that time the expectations of the reading public seem to have shifted and shrunk. I spoke before of a 'dissociation of sensibility'. It is a phenomenon as important as it is elusive, but it seems to help to explain Ovid; it perhaps helps to explain what went wrong with Propertius' fourth book. A third, less straightforward difficulty about accepting the view of the writer's own contemporaries is that formulated in Eliot's famous essay on 'Tradition and the individual talent': our understanding of the great works of the past keeps changing because each new work which appears modifies our understanding of all its predecessors.

It isn't obvious that appealing to the judgment of our own contemporaries is much better. Our ideal modern reader is apt to misunderstand and to fail to understand so much. He is exposed to the typical mistakes of the good student essay which substitutes empathy and enthusiasm for understanding. He misses things that are there, and sees things that aren't there.

Where the verdict of the ages is concerned, the trouble is that valid, absolute, timeless judgments are hard to come by. As has already been hinted, the reputation of those Roman writers who have been commonly thought great (in the sense that they have been thought great more often than not) has fluctuated alarmingly, seldom more alarmingly, indeed, than in the case of Virgil's *Aeneid.* Many have considered the *Aeneid* the greatest work of Roman literature, others have dismissed it as derivative and insincere. The 'verdict of the ages' permits at best the loose, vague front-rank placings advanced in our preliminary assessment in Section VI. They are a starting point. They do not constitute criticism.

The concept of a verdict of the ages is an attempt to substitute some more absolute standard than fluctuating opinion. But it is hard to see what greatness can mean unless we relate it to a writer's contemporaries. For great works do not grow in a vacuum. They are the writer's attempt to cope with his environment. The same work may sometimes be both a success and a failure; a success, because it works as a work, so to speak—it is well put together; a failure, because it did not work for its contemporaries. Horace's *Odes* seem to have been something of a failure in that second sense. Virgil was perhaps afraid when he saw the misunderstanding, or failure to understand, which greeted the *Odes,* that his *Aeneid* would be similarly misunderstood; it may be one reason why, when he was dying (four years after the publication of Horace's first collection of *Odes*), he asked for the poem to be destroyed.

It is not hard to distinguish the work which is startlingly and creatively fresh and innovatory from a work which is intrinsically incompetent or shoddy. Where content is concerned (in so far as it is sensible to talk about content, as distinct from form), it is not hard either to distinguish the work which expresses a startlingly fresh insight from a work whose thought is facile or meretricious. But in neither case is this a matter of judgment which is self-evident and independent of the work's historical context: a work which is so new in its day that its contemporaries fail to appreciate it or even to comprehend it (so that proper comprehension and appreciation come a generation or a century later) may seem to us trite or commonplace, simply because so many writers have done the same thing since. A work which dominated the minds of its imitators thus becomes hard to see in its original freshness; or a work which expresses the feelings of a moment in history of unusual sensitivity of insight in a particular area of human experience (about the horror of war, for example) may seem to an age that lacks that insight dull or pointless. The only valid conclusion, apparently, is that separation of the work from the environment which produced it, from the problem to which the work represents the writer's solution, or attempted solution, is artificial and misleading.

IX   EXPLAINING LITERATURE

F. W. Bateson has maintained in his *English Poetry: a Critical Introduction* (published in 1950) that a given society (by which he means, roughly, a given culture in a given time) either finds, or fails to find, its own characteristic literary expression; in that society, to put the matter another way, only one form of expression will really work. The kind of relationship he has in mind between social context and literary work is readily understood from some of the chapter headings in the second half of the book: among the more immediately convincing examples are 'The Yeoman Democracy and Chaucer's "Miller's Tale"', 'The quickest Way out of Manchester: four Romantic Odes' (Wordsworth's 'Intimations of Immortality', Coleridge's 'Dejection', Shelley's 'West Wind' and Keats's 'Grecian Urn') and 'From Escapism to Social Realism: two poems about Oxford' (Lionel Johnson's 'Oxford' and Auden's 'Oxford').

There is a strong element of paradox and challenge in Bateson's argument, which amounts to a sophisticated revision, with a sprinkling of Marxist literary theory, of the would-be scientific objectivism of Taine's *Littérature anglaise* and its three determining factors of race, social milieu and moment in history. It is important not to take such theories too seriously. The most we can expect from them is that they will explain the past; they are not to be used, that is to say, to predict the future. True, explanations in the social sciences can be so glib they hardly explain anything because they seek to explain everything. They can lay themselves open to the natural scientist's complaint that they are not falsifiable and draw us into a game in which there is no such thing as being right or wrong. But if we do not take them too seriously, they can be useful, if only in provoking thought.

It seems sensible to suggest that there exists an ideal expression in literature for a given society, much as you might say there is an ideal form or structure for a university in a given society—one that works better than any other in that society. It seems no less sensible to say of a university or society at a particular stage of its development that it found, or failed to find, that form or structure which was alone fruitful at the time in question. The prescription for this ideal form cannot be drawn in advance: one can only attempt to assess the success or failure of what has happened, or is happening, and offer an explanation of that success or failure. One can point, however, to a two-way process. The best university isn't that which gives the student public (or the public in general) exactly what it thinks it wants, any more than it is one that ignores completely the needs of its students and the public it serves. It is one that reacts fruitfully to those needs. So with literature. The writer whose work will last is the writer who reacts fruitfully to the intellectual pressures of his environment and brings to the level of conscious understanding those latent intuitions which contemporary society (or a significant section of it) has developed as a result of its own, unique experience of the delights and anguishes of the human condition. To do that he must often draw out his contemporaries, instead of giving them what they would most readily admire.

There is thus a sense in which we can 'explain', if not Homer (for the appearance of the individual of genius ultimately defies explanation), at any rate the Homeric poems. First, we postulate a society that looked backwards. The society for which Homer wrote (for the society of the poems had vanished from the earth by the time Homer wrote) found it comforting, we can suppose, to look back to the glories, or supposed glories, of the Bronze Age, when men were not just men, but more like supermen, sprung from gods and still mixing with gods on earth; it was an escape from a sordid, decadent present (the present, more or less, of the *Works and Days* of Hesiod). Catullus, centuries later, was to feel much the same when he wrote his epyllion of the Heroic age, the *Marriage of Peleus and Thetis,* and added a tailpiece denouncing the moral decadence of his own day. The society we postulate for Homer was aristocratic in its sympathies, committed to heroic ideals of individual valour on the battle-field, disposed to look upon war as a gentlemanly affair; not wholly insensitive to the suffering of war, but accustomed to the idea that life was cheap. It was a society which was illiterate. Reading and writing were, if not unknown in the strictest sense, at any rate not things which were

41

available to the poet and his audience. The poet carried his poem in his head; his audience knew the poem only through oral performance by a professional performer. It was a society which had no theatres, no notion of anything we could call dramatic performance. As the story unfolds, the characters in the narrative speak, often at length, and we must suppose that a practised performer might be able to make his listeners feel it was Achilles or Ulysses himself speaking. But they had no knowledge of a poetic form in which narrative was wholly absorbed into dialogue. Nor, we may imagine, would they have much liked it that way. Drama is a relatively sophisticated taste; Homer's audience was content with a good story.

The Homeric poems are commonly grouped along with other epic poems which were known to their contemporary audience through oral performance and the label 'oral epic' is used to distinguish them from what are called 'literary epics', poems such as Virgil's *Aeneid* or Milton's *Paradise Lost*. But this convenient distinction is misleading. For one thing, the *chansons de geste,* though written for oral performance, were written down and organized in writing by the poets who composed them. Virgil's *Aeneid,* on the other hand, though its dense sophistication can only have been fully appreciated by those who had studied the written text, was known to its contemporary audience, and probably throughout the Postclassical period, primarily through oral performance; the same is true of Lucan's *On the Civil War*; both poems, in other words, have this quality of oral performance in common with Homeric epic and differ in this respect from poems like *Paradise Lost* which were composed for private reading by individuals. Moreover, French society in the Middle Ages included an educated class aware that earlier, superior literatures existed: the Homeric poems develop out of the society in which Homer lived. They are in fact the only possible sustained literary expression of that society.

By the same token, Homeric epic was doomed to decay when the society which produced it decayed. The *Iliad* and the *Odyssey* did not lose their appeal; throughout antiquity men continued to regard them as the greatest poems ever written. They remain masterpieces today. But the *Iliad* and the *Odyssey* ceased to represent a way of doing things that was artistically valid. The loosely structured form of oral poetry ceased to interest poets: they could now do better. The introduction of writing had helped; they had also learnt more about their business. Their audiences might have been content with fresh versions of the same old thing; but quickly they were accustomed by the poets themselves to expect—of a living poet—if not better poetry, at any rate different poetry. At the same time the ideals and assumptions the *Iliad* and the *Odyssey* express ceased to be ideals and assumptions which later poets found it natural, or exciting, to put into words over which they had taken artistic pains.

It is one of the extraordinary properties of works of art that they both die and continue to live. Or rather, all die, in the sense that no artist wants to do things that way any more; and some live on, because they are too good to be forgotten. Shakespeare and Mozart are as popular with audiences today in Moscow and Tokyo as they are in London or Toronto. The fact that Shakespeare and Mozart are artistic and social anachronisms in each of these places has little effect on their popularity. But nowhere in the world today does any serious composer think of writing music like the music of Mozart, or any serious dramatist of writing plays like the plays of Shakespeare. The writer who is worth his salt loses interest in doing things in a way that no longer corresponds to his capacities as a writer, or to his audience's capacity for appreciation and understanding. His instinct tells him that, though repetition of the great works of the past remains possible, the two-way relationship between him and his audience can no longer continue on the old basis. The temptation to go on giving the public what it wants has to be resisted, or it will prove fatal. One of the obsessions of the creative writer is the danger of losing touch with that section of contemporary society which for him really matters. The image of the dinosaur dominates the creative mind. Keeping in touch doesn't mean becoming like your audience; it is rather a matter of intelligent resistance, of building up between yourself as a thinking person and the society around you a fruitful tension.

We see that tension in the next great age of Greek literature, in Athenian drama of the fifth century BC, especially tragedy. The theatre is an artistic innovation, offering possibilities to the dramatic poet that are not available to the writer of narrative poetry. The organization of dramatic performances virtually depends on the use of written scripts, though the written work remains available for the great majority of its audience only in its spoken form. The theatre depends too on the existence of a community with the resources to build a theatre, and the leisure and the social structures needed to organize performances. In the form tragedy assumed in Athens in the fifth century, performance depends on an audience which possesses an interest in moral reflection, and even in intellectual subtleties; it is no accident that Athenian tragedy is contemporaneous with the active beginnings in Athens of moral philosophy: the Sophists, Socrates, Plato. The Athenian dramatist has at his disposal a society which is interested in dramatic situations and in ideas and is content to see stories it knows already retold for their dramatic possibilities; a society which is mature enough to have got away from the simple, sentimental backward-looking of Homer's contemporaries, possesses a sense of the duration and continuity of human experience, and has developed a tragic view of the world. Such a society has much more demanding expectations in the matter of literary structure; it expects a play to be well put together, more compact, drier in its dialogue. It likes that dryness offset by the kind of poetry we find in the choruses of Athenian drama; it reacts favourably to poetry which is intellectually more demanding, more complex in its imagery, less simply rhetorical.

To some extent, in short, and in certain circumstances, it is possible to give a rational account of a literary work, or a literary form, in terms of the circumstances in which it came into existence, the circumstances, we might almost say, which produced the work or the form, and ensured its vitality. In doing so we are not merely explaining literary success; we are, to some extent, and after the event, explaining the work or the form itself.

It works well for Homer. It works well for Athenian tragedy. It works excellently for Plautus. We can explain Plautus as the dramatist who wrote for a ready-made audience of ex-soldiers stimulated by their contact with Greek comedy (the comedy of manners of Menander and his contemporaries, not the old Attic comedy of Aristophanes) while campaigning in Greek-speaking southern Italy and Sicily. Hundreds of them, if not thousands, must have attended performances of Greek comedies, and been ready to respond enthusiastically to an appropriately Romanized version of the same thing in their own language. Plautus' audience cannot read, or isn't at any rate accustomed to read for pleasure, but it can listen. It is an audience which is not yet sophisticated enough to say, 'Why can't we have comedies of our own?' It is content to have Greek plays Latinized and to some extent Romanized, willing to accept Greek settings and Greeks behaving as Greeks, or as Romans liked to think Greeks behaved. Such an audience is not greatly concerned with plot, but can appreciate a comic situation. A love interest is almost essential, cynicism towards the great of this world desirable. One can easily imagine the *Miles Gloriosus* (the infantry officer who is always boasting of his non-existent feats of bravery in the field, but is easily made a fool of by an ordinary girl, or by his own batman) appealing to an ex-soldier audience. To such an audience Plautus' exuberant use of language can be imagined as having an instant appeal.

The plays of Plautus are entertainments, they are not works written to claim a permanent place in literature. The fact of the matter, however, is that they have won that place. For our explanation is only an explanation of the conditioning circumstances. There might still have been no Plautus. Or Plautus might have been a mediocre writer of indifferent plays that did not last and had no literary consequences. If Plautus' sense of comic situation went far beyond what his audience would have been content with, if his brilliant virtuosity with words was able to create something of permanent worth out of common Latin speech and such paraliterary forms as existed in Latin (popular songs, hymns perhaps, primitive dramatic forms like the Fescennine verses), that is a matter of individual genius. Plautus in this sense can no more be explained than Shakespeare. Both needed the right circumstances; both had it in them to give their audiences more than they bargained for.

It is equally possible to explain Catullus as the individualist retreating in a disintegrating society to the twin standards of artistic and personal integrity. His intimate acquaintance with Greek poetry (a natural enough possession in the milieu in which he moved) provided the former; the social environment of Rome in the time of Julius Caesar both provided and threatened the latter. It makes sense to speak of Catullus' contemporary Lucretius as reacting against the pressures, which in the case of the artist are also the stimuli, of contemporary society. That they reacted differently, we may say, is a matter of individual genius. What makes Catullus or Lucretius important isn't just the reaction, it is the result of that reaction in the case of a poet of genius. With Catullus the result is a new kind of personal poetry: direct, hard-hitting, urbanely ironic as long as things went well; vitriolically passionate in the statement of hatred or contempt. With Lucretius, the result is a poetic justification of his withdrawal from society, proclaimed with the passion of a convert.

Such explanations are not to be taken too seriously. Emphasis on the social context as a complex of determining factors is a healthy corrective to the habit of some modern criticism of examining a literary work in the laboratory isolation of a cultural vacuum that permits total concentration on analysis of the verbal structure. But explanation after the event is always something of an illusion. The determining factors can never be wholly or accurately described. We have to remember the reactions which interest us are those of highly individual, unusually sensitive and creative minds.

The socio-economic determinist naturally sees a literary work as a product produced for consumers. He admits it is produced by a special category of workers, but maintains it is a product none the less. The temptation exists, therefore, to assimilate description of what the artist produces to a general theory of production and consumption. The Marxist is aware of course of the active property of the work of literature, the impact of the work upon its contemporaries. But he tends to consider this aspect chiefly in the context of the socialist state, where the impact of literature, its capacity to generate ideas, to influence the awarenesses of the artist's contemporaries, is something which is regulated by the state, in the same way as the properties of more straightforward consumer products.

The fact of the matter is that the writer's audience is not the only standard by which to measure success or failure; the audience is no more than one component of a complex situation to which the writer feels himself drawn to react. There is another component, which is provided by the writer himself and his view of himself as not so much meeting requirements (responding as best he can to a determining social context) as seizing the opportunity provided by that context to exercise an active influence upon his audience.

Unless we understand both sides of the problem, the truly original work is likely to remain imperfectly apprehended, or even unintelligible. True, the great works of the past are good enough to excite and move us, however great, almost, the degree of our misunderstanding of them. But if we want to be at all fair to them, we must make a conscious effort of the historical imagination to improve our understanding. The point has been made very simply by Julien Green (Diary, 27 December 1946):

> Who is the Racine we read? Certainly not the seventeenth-
> century Racine, the wild, untamed Racine, but a domesticated
> Racine, a classic who lies around in all the schoolbooks of the
> secondary schools of France. Not the Racine who provoked
> raised eyebrows and startled exclamations from an embarrassed
> high-society audience decked out in wigs.

A similar warning is appropriate whether it is Virgil's *Aeneid* or Horace's *Odes* that we are reading. Like Racine's tragedies, these Roman classics have been domesticated by a kind of familiarity which has limited and distorted our response. It requires an effort of the imagination to think of them as works which must have seemed startlingly original to their contemporary audience.

At the beginning of this chapter I spoke of the deep-seated conservatism which is characteristic of all who concern themselves with literature. The writer's audience knows what it likes; the writer himself is conscious of working in a tradition whose conventions he respects because they permit the expression of what would otherwise remain crude, inchoate and unmemorable. But because tradition lends the writer eloquence, it does not have to stifle his originality. Every literary work which is good enough to last constitutes a challenge to the conservatism of the writer's audience. An artistic challenge, first of all: as a structure of words it is not quite like anything the writer's contemporaries have heard or read before. Then, because it is the special property of a literary work to be constructed of words which make statements, the work is likely to

46

be a challenge also to the thoughts of the writer's contemporaries. As long as the writer regards himself as little more than a craftsman, the challenge to the thinking of his audience will be modest and perhaps no more than implicit. Once he starts to think of himself as an individual, however, the assault upon the intellectual and emotional horizons of expectation of the writer's audience is likely to be more direct.

The challenge may be to men's ideas of what a poem should be about, or to their preconceptions about how a poem should behave: the layman tends always to have a narrower concept of what constitutes poetic etiquette than poets. Catullus' short, intensely personal, deliberately casual poems about love constitute such a challenge, as the opening poem of the collection acknowledges. Three generations later, the *Amores* in their turn challenge current ideas about how love should be treated in poetry: they do not simply reveal Ovid's frivolity, as is often supposed, his inability to treat love seriously. The frivolity is calculated in order to scandalize; for clearly the *Amores* did scandalize some; if they hadn't, it wouldn't have been necessary for the Emperor to be scandalized. A generation earlier, however, the challenge would have seemed simply outrageous and would have been impossible.

Take two other examples. Seneca's tragedies and Lucan's epic *On the Civil War,* instead of 'reflecting' (as is often stated) the current taste for rhetoric, are perhaps conscious attempts to scandalize by rhetorical flamboyance. What in different circumstances (in our day, for instance) would be pointless and intolerable was in its time a special kind of *tour de force.* At the same time Lucan's epic and Seneca's tragedies challenge the intellectual horizons of their contemporaries. *On the Civil War* is Lucan's passionate defence of the dignity of dissent from dictatorship in an age of the most arbitrary dictatorship the Roman world had known. Seneca's tragedies represent the great and powerful of the heroic world (Aristotle's tragic heroes) as morally sick; the grotesqueness and crudity of the action becomes a kind of oblique or disguised comment on the grotesqueness and crudity of the contemporary world. (We may compare Camus' play *Caligula,* produced in the Paris of 1944 in the shadow of the German occupation.)

It must be stressed that the artistic challenge and the intellectual or emotional challenge, though separable in discussion, are fused into a single entity in the literary work itself. The form embodies, and therefore expresses, the insight; the formal challenge permits the intellectual challenge. The work which is not somehow fresh in its form remains an inadequate embodiment of fresh insight.

CHAPTER 2

The Poet as Storyteller

The first requirement of a literary critic is a working knowledge of his material. His first task, once he has acquired that knowledge, is to classify his material. Like the historian or the biologist—like anyone who attempts systematic discussion of complex material—he must put his material in order.

The literary critic adopts the method of the historian when he arranges the authors he intends to discuss in their proper sequence, describes the works of each author, and then attempts to make some kind of historical sense of the material he has thus arranged, by isolating and assessing the influence of one writer on another, the complex influences brought to bear on the writer by the society in which he lived, and the influence each writer attempted in his turn to exert upon his contemporaries.

He can do all these things very adequately so long as he is content to talk about literature in terms of the ideas that a work contains, or in terms of paraphrase and summary of the writer's story—the things that make up what is usually called the 'content' of the work. To these may be added the verbal echoes, the 'quotations' from earlier works. Here he passes from abstraction of content (what is sometimes called 'content analysis') to lifting the writer's words from their context in order to compare them with the words of other writers, though the distinction between summary of content and consideration of the writer's actual words out of context is often blurred by those who deal in what are usually called the writer's 'sources'; but by and large the same method will serve, or has been pressed into service.

It is when the critic attempts to discuss a particular work in anything like its totality that he has forced upon him the method of the biologist. Directly he turns his attention to what is usually called the 'form' of the work, he finds himself classifying and distinguishing—not just writers and works and 'echoes' (verbal or conceptual) of one writer in another, but types of writing, particular ways of doing things which are distinct and which it is important to keep apart; ways that existed before the particular writer began to work with them; ways that are somehow transmitted from writer to writer, and somehow survive as palpable entities despite constant transformation of content and even some transmutation of the form itself (though the transmutation of form is less radical) in the course of what is usually called a particular 'literary tradition'.

Older critics tended to talk of categories—what Dr Johnson called the 'departments' of literature—and favoured abstractions such as 'epic' and 'lyric'. But it is more in accord with the modern concept of form to talk of 'the epic poem' and 'the lyric poem', meaning by that a formal reality evident in all particular epic poems or lyric poems (however much the individual poems differ from one another), rather as the biologist talks of 'the domestic cat', or the mathematician of 'the right-angled triangle', in preference to 'domestic felinity', or 'right-angled triangularity'. (Roman critics sometimes used abstractions, such as *iambi* and *hendecasyllabi*, meaning poems written in those metres; at other times they identified the writer by the form he used—for example, *lyricus*, a writer of lyric poems.)

The forms the critic has to deal with may be as general as 'the epic poem' or 'the lyric poem'; or they may be as narrow as 'the sonnet' or 'the ballade' or those forms which one finds much discussed by those who write on Roman poetry, 'the propemptikon' (or bon-voyage poem) and 'the paraclausithyron' (a special kind of serenade sung by the lover before his mistress's locked door). We enter now an area where the terms used are imprecise and confusing: clear-cut, generally accepted distinctions as the distinction the biologist makes between 'species' and 'genus' are not available to the literary critic. Some critics distinguish between 'genre' and 'form', some use both terms without any clear distinction between them; even to keep 'form' and 'content' apart is not easy since some at any rate of the forms of classical literature ('epic', for example) exercise a more or less rigid control over content, while in other cases a particular content (for example, a poem attacking a personal enemy) is by convention limited to certain metrical forms. Hence much confusion reigns. Whatever the terms used, they represent an attempt to grapple with the growing realization by modern critics that the originality of the individual writer is counterbalanced by an awareness, shared by all who make literature, that there are particular ways of doing things, and that each of these ways has its own traditions which have to be mastered and then manipulated. The choice of a form thus involves certain sacrifices on the part of a writer with regard to the manner of expression of his thoughts, and certain voluntarily accepted limitations on his originality. The sacrifices are made and the limitations accepted in the interest of artistic gain. For the finished work has form. And the true test of a writer is his ability to manipulate form to his own ends. Form is the means by which the individual writer liberates himself from the entanglement of inarticulate thought.

The most obvious distinction is that between prose and verse. In Roman literature, as in most periods of our own literature, the distinction is fundamental between forms whose basic structure is metrical and forms whose basic structure is syntactical. Take two fairly extreme instances. The first is the opening stanza of Horace's third book of *Odes*:

> Odi profanum vulgus et arceo.
> favete linguis: carmina non prius
> audita Musarum sacerdos
> virginibus puerisque canto.

> I exclude the uninitiated throng, have no time for such.
> Be silent, heed my words. Strains never before heard,
> I, the prophet of the Muses, proclaim
> to the Nation's youth.

The second is the opening sentence of a speech made by Cicero in 70 BC in which he defended his right to appear in court on behalf of the people of Sicily against their ex-governor Verres:

> Si quis vestrum, iudices, aut eorum qui adsunt, forte miratur me, qui tot annos in causis iudiciisque publicis ita sim versatus ut defenderim multos, laeserim neminem, subito nunc mutata voluntate ad accusandum descendere, is, si mei consili causam rationemque cognoverit, una et id quod facio probabit, et in hac causa profecto neminem praeponendum mihi esse actorem putabit.

> Gentlemen of the jury, if there is any man among you, or any man among those present in court, who is surprised, perhaps, that I, who have so conducted myself these many years in both civil and public cases as to appear many times as counsel for the defence and not once as counsel for the prosecution, should now change my mind and fall to appearing as prosecutor, when he has discovered the reason and the basis for my decision, he will both extend his approval to my action, and will be of opinion that in the present case there is absolutely no one who can be permitted to appear in preference to myself.

In both instances the speaker wishes to begin by making clear his claim upon his listeners' attention. But if the situations are comparable, they produce two quite different verbal organizations of what the speaker wishes to say. Horace speaks as the poet-prophet. What holds his opening stanza together is its metrical structure—a distinctive pattern of forty-one syllables, traditionally arranged as four lines of verse with a minimum of permissible variations. So long as the stanza remains incomplete, until we come to the end of the fourth line, we know there is more to come: the metrical structure creates an expectation that is not satisfied until the forty-first syllable slips into place. Without that structure to hold it together, Horace's statement of the role he is about to assume would fall apart into three disjointed statements of which only the third displayed any syntactical complexity. In Cicero's opening sentence, things are quite different: it is the syntactical structure which creates an expectation about the way the sentence must end. The anticipated goal, instead of approaching, keeps receding, as subordinate clause after subordinate clause intervenes, until the whole structure is finally locked into a single unit as the fifty-seventh word assumes its predetermined place.

Naturally, the distinction between verse and prose is not always so palpable. These are extreme cases. Horace does not always compose in short, simple sentences (nor does the end of a sentence always coincide, as here, with the end of a stanza). Cicero does not always speak in periods. Each of the two principles of verbal organization depends, moreover, to some extent on the other. Horace's stanza is something more than a sequence of long and short syllables; for the words to make sense, some syntactical organization is necessary. Cicero's period is something more than syntactical virtuosity; it depends in part for its success upon qualities (rhythm, balance) related to those required of metrical structure. As is well known, Cicero favours certain sequences of long and short syllables at the end of his periods, so that, most often, the syntactical climax is underpinned by a recognizable metrical pattern. As it happens, the closing sequence here ([ac]*tōrĕm pŭtābĭt*) is the same as in the opening five syllables of Horace's Alcaic stanza (*ōdī prŏfānŭm*); a commoner pattern (it occurs in *ārbĭtrārēntŭr* at the end of the second sentence in Cicero's speech) is the same as the opening five syllables of another four-line pattern much used by Horace, the Sapphic stanza.

Syntax, in other words, is needed to make sense, and syntactical structure must take account of the sound of words to be rhetorically successful. Indeed the penetration of verse form by the characteristic structures of prose becomes more subtle as the Roman poets learn more about their craft. The largest metrical units are relatively small (forty-one syllables in an Alcaic stanza, twenty-five to thirty-one in a normal elegiac couplet). Syntactical organization permits much larger structures: several

51

stanzas can be held together by syntax to form a clear-cut unit within a poem; in an extreme case a whole poem can consist of a single sentence. Similarly in narrative poetry, where the metrical unit is the single hexameter, there is a movement away from strictly end-stopped structure (coincidence of metrical structure and syntactical structure at the end of each line). Virgil in the *Aeneid* will often use syntax to make the verse paragraph, not the individual line, the unit of sense.

The fact that each kind of organization depends on the other does not invalidate the distinction. And that distinction carries with it a complex body of tradition by which are established, if not rules, at least very clearly felt expectations about what will be talked about. A decision about theme foreshadows a decision about form; a decision about form means respecting the style which that form imposes. Thus Horace can argue that a passage of poetry (the passage he chooses is from Ennius):

> Postquam Discordia taetra
> belli ferratos postis portasque refregit . . .

> After Discord foul
> tore open the iron-clad gates and portals of war . . .

will remain unmistakably poetry even if you scramble the order of the words; however much you dislocate the metre, the poet's dismembered corpse (the *disiecti membra poetae*) cannot be concealed. Contrariwise, suppose it were possible to rearrange the words of Cicero's period until they scanned as hexameters: so long as you did not break up the syntactical structure, any competent Latinist would sense that something was wrong; that behind the metrical form the dismembered corpse of Cicero was not far to seek.

In both Greek and Latin, verse comes before prose. The reason lies probably in the origin of literature as something that emerges from earlier useful forms of organized verbal statement—the ritual of religion, oracles (always quoted in hexameters, often indifferent ones)—and the guarantee metre provided of memorable formulation not easily tampered with. The organized statements of law come later, when man has learnt to think syntactically, from subordinate hypothesis to conclusion, or from generalization to particular instance. Already in Homer we find complex metrical structure giving form to relatively rudimentary syntax; much the same is true of Ennius or of many of the short poems of Catullus.

The technicalities of ancient metres can be made to sound very complicated, but they need hardly delay us long. Certain basic distinctions, however, which seem to have been accepted, or at any rate sensed, by Roman poets, are important and interesting.

All Roman metres, except for some early experiments with accentual metres, are Greek in origin and based on more or less fixed patterns of long and short syllables. The metres fall into two groups according to whether the syllable-count is strictly observed (in which case each line contains the same number of syllables) or not (in which case the number of syllables can vary within fixed limits). In the latter case, a principle of equivalence prevails, which permits a long syllable to count as two shorts.

The fixed-syllable-count metres form a mixed bag. The best known examples are the *Odes* and *Epodes* of Horace and the iambic and hendecasyllabic verse of Catullus and Martial. Generally speaking, the only permitted variation is the occasional substitution (normally at a single point in a line) of a long syllable for a short. The variable-syllable-count metres are commoner. The principle of equivalence is carried furthest in the dactylic hexameter; lines are possible in which only one foot is in fact a dactyl (the rest being spondees, two long syllables) while lines in which only two of the six feet are dactyls are frequent. The result is a line varying in length from thirteen to seventeen syllables (twelve-syllable lines are very rare and eighteen-syllable lines never occur; the last foot is never a dactyl).

The hexameter is the commonest Roman metre. It is, like the English iambic pentameter, something of a Jack of all trades: a metre which can be used for narrative poetry, for didactic poetry and for satire hardly carries with it any expectation with regard to subject or style, except in so far as all Roman verse styles are syntactically less elaborate than most prose styles. Most Roman verse is written, moreover, in a single poetic dialect: there is nothing like the diversity of styles and dialects which we find in Greek. Each Roman writer has his own style, but appreciation of differences in style calls for considerable familiarity with Latin.

Next in frequency after the hexameter comes the elegiac couplet, which consists of an ordinary hexameter followed by a line, known as a pentameter, which reproduces the ordinary hexameter pattern up to the normal caesura, and then continues in a repetition of that structure, except that in the second half-hexameter no equivalence is permitted. The result is an *a-b-a-a* structure, and indeed elegiac couplets were often successfully rendered into four-line stanzas until the English heroic couplet (two iambic pentameters) caught on in the eighteenth century, and was brought to a level of perfection by Pope that could claim to rival Ovid's elegiac couplets. This is the metre of the elegiac verse of Catullus, the metre used by Propertius and Tibullus, and by Ovid in all his surviving work apart from the *Metamorphoses*.

Since a line in which variety is secured on the basis of equivalent length sounds more sophisticated than a line in which variety is secured by straight substitution, it is possible to regard the hexameter as the most highly evolved Roman metrical form, though it is in fact the metre of the oldest surviving Greek poetry, the poems of Homer. It is tempting, however, to see the distinction as one between narrative and other types of verse where variety was desirable, and shorter verse-forms closer to song whose simpler syntactical structure encouraged adherence to the basic metrical pattern. We have, of course, to bear in mind that the uses to which the Romans put the metres they borrowed from Greek do not necessarily correspond to their original functions. For the Roman poet the distinction seems to have been more that between the formal style of epic and didactic poetry (what I shall call 'public poetry' in Chapter 4) and what I shall call 'personal poetry'. But it must be admitted that this is a distinction which does not account for Roman elegiac verse, or the practice of Roman dramatists (who adopt fixed-syllable-count metres with fairly free concessions to equivalence); nor does it account for the choice of the hexameter by Roman satirists.

One is left with the impression that, except in the case of the 'lyric' metres (where Horace consciously followed Greek models), choice of metre had for a Roman less influence upon the way he wrote than the way he thought about himself in relation to his poetry. The tendency of classical scholarship to allow itself to be bewitched by the twin idols of source criticism (which is apt to turn a Roman poem into a string of quotations from Greek poets) and criticism based on the study of inherited forms (which is apt to represent the Roman poet as engaged in an ineffectual struggle against inherited rules) easily leads to belittlement of the distinctiveness and artistic originality of the individual writer, or the individual work. What is usually ascribed to the constraints of formal tradition is often better ascribed to the moulding force of function. Already in the Hellenistic Age, when poetry no longer fulfilled a direct social purpose, the boundaries between the old forms had begun to break down. The Romans felt free to innovate within a framework of borrowed traditions because they were conscious of making a fresh start, doing their best in a language where no traditions existed until the different kinds of poetry that came to be written at Rome developed their own traditions.

II   ROMAN NARRATIVE POETRY

The oldest form of literature everywhere seems to be the poem that tells a story, much as a modern novelist tells his story, more or less from beginning to end. All long narrative poems, in Latin as in Greek, take the *Iliad* and the *Odyssey* as their models. Such poems are called epics (the name perhaps means poetry which is spoken, as opposed to poetry which is sung).

The rules for an epic poem were clear-cut and respected by all practitioners. An epic had to be written in dactylic hexameters (the only exception is Livius Andronicus' early experiment with the primitive Roman Saturnian metre in his translation of the *Odyssey*). It had to tell a story. But not just any kind of story: the poet's audience was entitled to feel they were being told about things that had happened; that were, as we should put it, part of history. Later, when history came to be written in prose, it became possible to draw a distinction (as Aristotle did) between history as a form dealing with particular historical events, and the narrative poem which, though recounting events that did perhaps happen, moulds those events into a fiction (*mimesis*) of more or less universal truth. Naturally, Homer and his contemporaries could not have seen the matter in that way. In the Hellenistic Age poets began to experiment with themes from the more recent, more strictly historical, past. Modern critics call the two kinds of epic 'mythological epic' and 'historical epic' respectively. In a highly sophisticated society with an efficient prose language at its disposal, attempts to beat prose history at its own game were doomed to failure; nor was there any longer much hope for traditional mythological epic: Apollonius' *Argonautica* is a brilliant *tour de force*, but it is also an almost perverse exercise in sham archaism. For large-scale fiction, as for history, the future lay with prose.

Transplanted into the neo-heroic society of Rome in the third and second centuries BC, historical epic enjoys a genuine revival. The more easily adapted conventions of epic form enabled Ennius to do something he could not have hoped to do in prose: moreover, he had an audience for whom the long narrative poem was something fresh and exciting. This early success gave both historical and mythological epic a status that blinded mediocre poets of the Classical and Postclassical periods to the sterility of a form that had by then lost its social function. Undoubtedly the prestige of epic retarded the development of Roman prose fiction. The only compensation is that in the hands of two poets of genius epic was transformed into something fresh and artistically viable.

The two masterpieces of Roman narrative poetry are Virgil's *Aeneid* (12 books, about 10,000 lines) and Ovid's *Metamorphoses* (15 books, about 12,000 lines). There is every indication (to judge not only from the immense reputation it enjoyed among later writers, but also from the fragments which have come down to us) that a third masterpiece, the *Annals* of Ennius (18 books, of which we possess about 500 lines), has been lost. Compared with the *Aeneid* and the *Metamorphoses*, Lucan's

On the Civil War (10 books, about 8,000 lines) must be judged a bad third. The rest are nowhere.

Because the *Aeneid* and the *Metamorphoses* are the only two Roman narrative poems the modern reader knows much about, he needs reminding that neither is a typical Roman epic. Epic poetry in Virgil's day was moribund. The *Annals* of Ennius had fulfilled a valid social function: his epic gave voice to genuine Roman feelings of simple patriotism about what the Romans had done in the world as they knew it in the only literary form available to a writer in Latin of the second century BC. But that kind of straightforward historical epic had been superseded by prose history: the legitimate successor of Ennius in the Augustan Age is Livy. Instead of attempting to resuscitate a dying form, one that had become not only socially useless but artistically sterile, Virgil went back to Homeric epic, and created a new synthesis of historical and mythological epic. Ovid's *Metamorphoses* is a superb parody of mythological epic. Epic after Virgil and Ovid reverted to the hands of those who were content to flog a dead horse.

Ovid is twenty-seven years younger than Virgil. The two thus belong to successive generations. But the two generations are separated by the Civil War, which destroyed the Republic and established Augustus as the master of the Roman world. Virgil lived through that war; Ovid was still a boy when it was over. Virgil is a republican who has had to come to terms with change and a new régime; Ovid is a product, in many ways a characteristic product, of the Augustan Age.

Lucan is more than eighty years younger than Ovid. His *On the Civil War* takes up the dead tradition of historical epic, not the broad annalistic sweep of Ennius, but the historical epic which concentrates on a single war or a single hero. We hear of such poems in late Republican and Augustan times, and the impression we get is of something closer to propaganda than to poetry. Lucan's poem is fiercely partisan (for Pompey and against Caesar), much, one imagines, the sort of partisan epic poem that some would have liked Virgil to write in praise of Augustus. But the propaganda is for a cause that was lost nearly a century before, when Caesar defeated the old republicans on the battlefield at Pharsalus (48 BC). Yet Lucan's poem is not negligible. Nor is it hackwork. The propaganda is for a moral ideal (Stoicism), only indirectly for a political system; it idolizes a hero (Pompey) only in so far as he embodies the Stoic ideal. Lucan's passionate support of Pompey (rhetorically more effective than his absurd vilification of Julius Caesar), far from being aimed at winning favour with an imperial patron (the poem was hardly calculated to please Nero), is the reaction of a highly emotional juvenile to tyranny in his own day. Lucan's reaction is not just rhetoric, moreover:

it drove him to join the conspiracy which cost him his life.

Chance has preserved four more epic poems for us, or rather, three and a bit. They are: Valerius Flaccus' *Voyage of the Argonauts* (8 books, unfinished, about 5,800 lines); Silius Italicus' *The Punic Wars* (17 books, over 12,000 lines, the longest poem in Latin, but still shorter than Homer's *Iliad*, which runs into something like 15,000 lines); Statius' *Theban War* (12 books, about 10,000 lines; its subject is the famous quarrel between Eteocles and Polynices, the two sons of Oedipus who fought one another for the kingdom of Thebes); and an unfinished *Achilles* by Statius (one book and only part, apparently, of a second completed, 627 lines; subject: Achilles' adventures while disguised as a girl at the court of Lycomedes and his military education by the centaur Chiron).

Silius is actually several years older than Lucan, and Statius only a few years younger; it is a reasonable guess that Valerius was much the same age as the other three. Silius and Statius lived on, however, until the turn of the century and Valerius till about AD 90: where Lucan is the contemporary of Nero and Seneca (the product of a period when the expression of passionate personal feeling seemed again temporarily possible), Silius, Statius and Valerius are the contemporaries of such writers as Martial, Quintilian and the younger Pliny. Their writing lives belong to the period of the Flavian emperors, Titus, Vespasian and Domitian (AD 69–96; hence the term 'Flavian epic' used by some literary historians). They are the product of a period when the only safe feeling to give expression to was cynicism, and the attitude predominated that on the whole it was wiser to leave one's personal feelings out of literature altogether. As Juvenal sardonically remarked (*Satires* 1. 162–4):

> It's safe to retell how Aeneas fought fierce Turnus.
> Nobody minds Achilles getting killed, or all those searches
> for Hylas, who tumbled in pitcher and all.

Juvenal, of course, like Tacitus, belonged to the next generation. Their writing lives fell in the reigns of Trajan and Hadrian (AD 98–138), a period when it was once again safe to say what one thought, at any rate about the past.

Thus, if one takes the six long Roman narrative poems which have survived complete (plus the two books of Statius' *Achilles*), the history of Roman epic seems one long decline. In fact, the picture is almost certainly distorted for us by the survival of Virgil's *Aeneid* and Ovid's *Metamorphoses* and the complete loss of the epic poetry of their contemporaries.

It is true that the fragments of Ennius give good ground for the opinion that already in the second century BC more significant narrative poetry was being written than 250 years later, at the end of the first century AD. Ennius' style is fresh and vigorous; he has a theme which interests him; it is reasonable to suppose he had an audience. One must not judge Silius, Statius and Valerius too harshly, however. The rot had set in much earlier. True, they are writing a century and a half and more after Virgil (the *Aeneid* falls almost exactly in the middle of the space of nearly three hundred years which separates the *Annals* of Ennius from Silius' *Punic Wars*) and are in a position to have learnt a good deal, therefore, about the minutiae of epic style from Virgil. There is every sign, however, that the typical historical epic in Virgil's day (as in Ovid's, or Lucan's) differed little from Silius' long and boring poem. Where Ennius' style had been full of vigour—the style of a writer of genius who has had to hammer out a way of writing from practically nothing—the style of these minor epic poets is bland and conventional, their themes trite and 'literary' (in the worse sense of that term). Ennius had had a subject that was fresh, on a scale not attempted before, a source of national pride.

The conventional mythological epic must likewise have remained for a century and a half pretty much like Valerius' *Voyage of the Argonauts*: the best that can be said is that it may be presumed to be an improvement on the lost version by Varro of Atax of Apollonius' Hellenistic rococo masterpiece, if only because Varro was not in a position to learn from Virgil's *Aeneid* and Valerius was. In the hands of Silius, Statius and Valerius epic was what it had been for the poetasters of the Augustan Age: a meaningless, precious exercise for essentially uncreative talent. Pliny's obituary of Silius (see Chapter 5, Section IX) is a clear indication that the long narrative poem counted for no more in his day than Pliny's own 'lyric' verse; true, Pliny was inordinately conceited about his verse, but he had the sense to realize it was nothing more than a sophisticated pastime, something to keep himself occupied and amuse his friends.

Epic poetry retained, no doubt, a claim to seriousness denied to occasional verse. In a period when poetry seemed to have left to it no social function whatever, the epic poet devoted to the stylistic perfection of his dinosaur could at least feel he had substituted craftsmanship for social function. W. H. Auden (speaking of the final dissolution a century or so later) has put the case for the writers of minor epic as favourably as it can be put ('The Epigoni', 2nd stanza):

> It would have been an excusable failing
> Had they broken out into womanish wailing
> Or, dramatising their doom, held forth
> In sonorous clap-trap about death;

To their credit, a reader will only perceive
That the language they loved was coming to grief,
Expiring in preposterous mechanical tricks,
Epanaleptics, rhopalics, anacyclic acrostics:
To their lasting honour, the stuff they wrote
Can safely be spanked in a scholar's foot-note,
Called shallow by a mechanised generation to whom
Haphazard oracular grunts are profound wisdom.

III   TRAGIC EPIC: VIRGIL'S *Aeneid*

Two epic poems, then, worth worrying about. At a pinch, a third; but it is hard to get involved in *On the Civil War*: though not devoid of imagination or of eloquence, Lucan resorts too freely to the bludgeons of rhetoric, the tortured one-line paradox and the purple patch; the tone is too shrill for the modern reader to want to read him for long. Ovid's tools are the kaleidoscope (colourful picture melting constantly into colourful picture) and a special dynamic suppleness and subtlety of syntax that lends his narrative its characteristic vitality. But Ovid has to be read quickly; his style is too slick and amusing to stimulate prolonged attention. It is a work to be taken up in an idle hour or so. One can't help admiring how Ovid, the author of the *Amores*, has turned his hand to an epic poem without any real change of style or attitude. It is a poem whose status as a major work is inevitably compromised by a lack of serious purpose, or even that breadth of comic vision which characterizes—to take a poem that owes much to Ovid—Chaucer's *Canterbury Tales*.

It does not take much familiarity, in short, with these three poems before Virgil's unchallengeable superiority becomes evident. Where Lucan is stridently rhetorical, Virgil can command, when the occasion calls for it, a smoothly articulated, sensitive, poetically suggestive sublimity, as in this description of Dido on the morning of the hunt that was to end in disaster (*Aeneid* 4. 129–50):

The dawn-goddess was up meantime and took her leave of Ocean.
From the city gates a selected company issued forth at sunrise:
coarse-meshed nets, fine nets, broad iron-bladed hunting spears,
Massylian horsemen at the gallop, a pack of keen-scented hounds.
Phoenician nobles attend at the door of the royal chamber,
waiting for the queen to emerge; her horse, all purple and gold,
stands, hoofs ringing, spirited, champing foam-flecked bit.
At last she advances, the great crowd packed round her,
clad in a Sidonian cloak with an embroidered hem.

Her quiver is of gold, her hair is tied in gold,
gold is the brooch that catches up her purple dress.
The Phrygian party, a happy Iulus accompanying them,
also advances. Aeneas, the handsomest figure among them by far,
takes position beside Dido, combines the two companies in one.
He looked like Apollo when, leaving Lycia and the river Xanthus
still in winter's grip, he visits his mother's home in Delos,
to start the dancing up—and crowding around the altar
Cretans, Dryopians and painted Agathyrsans raise their voices.
The god moves along the ridge of Cynthus, adjusting garland
of leaves and band of gold till they sit firm on flowing hair;
bow and arrows clatter, shoulder-slung. Just so, Aeneas
stepped out, his noble features stamped with an equal distinction.

This is the grand manner of epic, Homeric simile and all. But the grand manner is disciplined by a new intellectual control, which accurately notes every detail of the picture the poet has in his mind and then exercises a ruthless discipline over what is said and how it is said. As the passage begins, sharply observed detail ('broad iron-bladed hunting spears'), highly compressed syntax. Then a trace of irony in the contrast between the courtiers waiting for a queen who hesitates (as if in foreboding, before embarking on the day's adventure) and her horse, all excitement for the hunt, and not trained, like a well-bred courtier, to conceal his impatience. Then, when the queen emerges, evocative imprecision takes over from sharply observed detail. The heroic scene becomes a blaze of purple and gold. At the same time, the syntax begins to flow, as the narrator's eye moves back and forth: first the queen and her courtiers; then the Trojan party (Iulus with them); then Aeneas: he assumes command of both parties, with the assurance of the god Apollo, controlling the pageant and yet aloof from it, coolly adjusting the garland of leaves and the ring of gold upon his head as he watches. A hint of irony gently challenges the heroic sublimity at its climax.

It is understandable that Ovid should forgo sublimity and content himself with an affectation of the grand manner as a counterpoint for his wit, just as it is understandable that Virgil should forgo wit. But even Virgil reserves sublimity for special occasions. Where the occasion is more relaxed he will sometimes permit himself a poetic conceit, as when the reader is forced by a series of verbal ambiguities to entertain the picture of Mount Atlas as an actual giant supporting the heavens (*Aeneid* 4. 246–51):

And now as he flies Mercury sees the cap and broad flanks
of unyielding Atlas, Atlas who props up the sky with his head,

that wind-beaten, rain-beaten head, round which the black
clouds swirl, upon which the pine trees grow;
snow piled deep hides his shoulders, streams cascade from
the old man's chin, his unkempt beard is stiff with ice.

Take a comparable passage in Ovid (*Metamorphoses* 5. 572–6). First, the
Latin:

Exigit alma Ceres, nata secura recepta,
quae tibi causa fugae, cur sis, Arethusa, sacer fons.
conticuere undae, quarum dea sustulit alto
fonte caput viridesque manu siccata capillos
fluminis Elei veteres narravit amores.

Here is Arthur Golding's splendid, accurate version of 1567:

Then fruitfull *Ceres* voide of care in that she did recover
Hir daughter, prayde thee *Arethuse* the storie to discover
What caused thee to fleete so farre and wherefore thou became
A sacred spring, the waters whist. The Goddesse of the same
Did from the bottom of the Well hir goodly head up reare.
And having dried with hir hand hir faire greene hanging heare,
The River *Alpheys* auncient loves she thus began to tell.
[Translation: Golding]

Where Virgil is fanciful but poetic, Ovid's coolly rational picture of the
nymph Arethusa drying her hair as she emerges from the spring which
bears her name is instantly destructive of gravity. Ovid goes on
(*Metamorphoses* 5. 577–81):

'Pars ego nympharum quae sunt in Achaide,' dixit,
'una fui. nec me studiosius altera saltus
legit nec posuit studiosius altera casses.
sed quamvis formae numquam mihi fama petita est,
quamvis fortis eram, formosae nomen habebam.'

For once, Golding's simple dignity will not quite do:

I was (quoth she) a Nymph of them that in *Achaia* dwell.
There was not one that earnester the Lawndes and forests sought,
Or pitcht hir toyles more handsomly. And though that of my thought
It was no part, to seeke the fame of beautie: though I were
All courage: yet the pricke and prise of beautie I did beare.
[Translation: Golding]

Any translation which does not do something to recapture the sprightliness of Ovid's syntax misrepresents Ovid by suppressing a clear warning that Ovid has no wish to be taken seriously. A. E. Watts's version is an attempt at the impossible:

> 'One of Achaea's nymphs was I, not least
> Of them that set the snare, and trailed the beast.
> Yet athlete as I was, I bore a name
> For beauty, though desiring no such fame.'

[Translation: Watts]

The reader pauses to admire lines like these: they are clever, precise, concise; the line of statement is limpid, the meaning instantly apprehensible. But he quickly sees all that is admirable in the line and passes on. With Virgil the precise control of complex, continually expanding meaning in line after line is something that only yields itself up fully to intimate acquaintance.

Take these elegant, pointed lines from Ovid, written in a style that foreshadows the prose style of Seneca, except that where Seneca is formal and sententious, Ovid is effortless, witty, unable to repress the characteristic Ovidian gaiety even in the retelling of a tragic tale (*Metamorphoses* 7. 9–20: Medea in love):

> *Aeëtas* daughter in hir heart doth mightie flames conceyve.
> And after strugling verie long, when reason could not win
> The upper hand of rage: she thus did in hir selfe begin.
> 'In vaine *Media* doste thou strive: some God what ere he is
> Against thee bendes his force, for what a wondrous thing is this?
> Is any thing like this which men doe terme by name of Love?
> For why should I my fathers hestes esteeme so hard above
> All measure? sure in very deede they are too hard and sore.
> Why feare I least yon straunger whome I never saw before
> Should perish? what should be the cause of this my feare so great?
> Unhappie wench (and if thou canst) suppresse this uncouth heat
> That burneth in thy tender brest. And if so be I coulde,
> A happie turne it were, and more at ease then be I shoulde.
> And now an uncouth maladie perforce against my will ⎫
> Doth hale me. Love persuades me one, another thing my skill. ⎬
> The best I see and like: the worst I follow headlong still.' ⎭

[Translation: Golding]

Compare Virgil (*Aeneid* 4. 1–27: Dido in love):

> But the queen, long since crippled by love's blow,
> nourishes the wound with her veins, is torn at by a hidden fire.

Much the manliness of the man to her thoughts keeps coursing back,
much the honour of his line: in her mind his face, his words
stick fast, passion denies her limbs the peace of sleep.
Next day's dawn was ranging the earth with Phoebus' torch,
had pushed apart the damp darkness in the sky,
when, hardly sane, she addressed her sister (always like-minded) thus:
'Sister Anna, what dreams rack me with indecision!
What a man this stranger is who has come newly to our house.
What a countenance is his, what a chest and shoulders on him!
I do believe, it is no fancy, he is of the race of gods.
Ignoble spirits are by fear betrayed. Oh, how tossed
by fate, what wars drained to the last he told of!
If it were not settled in my mind, unshakable,
never again to bind myself with the marriage bond,
if I did not loathe marriage beds, marriage torches,
I might perhaps have surrendered and failed this once.
Anna, I will confess it, since my poor husband Sychaeus
died, his blood shed in his own house by a brother's hand,
this man alone has upset my feelings, sent my thoughts
tottering. I acknowledge the old fire. It smoulders still.
But I had sooner the earth opened up before me,
or that the all-powerful father blasted me to the deep
night of hell, hell that the pale shades inhabit,
than ravish honour or undo honour's laws.'

It is silly to say Ovid is not to be compared with Virgil. He invites comparison. He sets out to undercut the style of which Virgil is the supreme master. He avoids direct challenge. To pit a Dido of his own against Virgil's Dido would be too crude a confrontation. Ovid's Dido gets no more than a passing reference, therefore. His witty presentation of Medea in love is a challenge to Virgil's Dido in love, none the less. Where Virgil's Dido, her emotions bursting out and then brought under control again, is a figure of pathos, a genuinely poetic creation, Ovid's Medea is a witty, slightly cruel study in the veering emotions of a woman torn between love and duty to her father. The study is acute enough to stand on its own feet (this is not the kind of parody that subordinates itself to an original), but it is not meant to move or to convince.

Nor has Ovid the time for anything like the density of Virgil's verbal poetry. Note how the latent metaphor of the opening line of *Aeneid* 4:

> But the queen, long since crippled by love's blow,

is caught up and developed into a living metaphor in the line following:

63

vulnus alit venis et caeco carpitur igni

nourishes the wound with her veins, is torn at by a hidden fire.

The wound is now an actual wound which has become inflamed and infected. Note too how the heavy double alliteration in this second line suggests the throb of the infected, burning wound. In lines 3–4:

multa viri virtus animo multusque recursat
gentis honos

Much the manliness of the man to her mind, much the
honour of his line keeps coursing back,

the psychological study begins. She cannot keep him out of her thoughts. Another double alliteration rams the point home. In lines 4–5:

haerent infixi pectore vultus
verbaque, nec placidam membris dat cura quietem

fast rooted in her mind his looks,
his words, her love allows her limbs no rest,

Virgil presents the traditional picture of the woman in love who cannot sleep for thoughts of her lover; but the words are filled with weight and foreboding by the continued heavy alliteration. And at this point echoes begin to establish themselves of Lucretius' wrily ironical picture of the lover separated from his beloved, whose mind is filled with images of the beloved. The echoes are not there simply because Lucretius is available as part of the tradition; they prepare the reader to accept Dido, not just as a figure of pathos, but also in Lucretian terms, as a woman rendered foolish by passion.

Virgil is, in short, a more subtle, a more poetic poet than Ovid. He is also a poet who offers his readers, in addition to the complex pleasure great poetry brings, the more intense, if more disturbing, pleasure that great literature often offers by challenging the reader's attitudes and beliefs. Take the end of the poem (*Aeneid* 12. 919–52):

Turnus hangs back. Aeneas keeps eyes on him, waiting his chance,
then lashes out with the spear of death, hurls it at him
from afar, his whole weight behind it. Louder than crash of rock
hurled by catapult at city wall, or the crackle that radiates
out from a thunderbolt, like a black hurricane the spear flies
with its dread burden of death, unlocks the joints of
Turnus' corslet and the rim of his seven-ply shield,

64

and screams deep into the thigh. Turnus collapses,
a mighty figure, knee doubled, to the ground.
The Rutulians jump up groaning, there is an echoing groan from
the whole hill around, tall trees throw back the sound from afar.
Prostrate, a suppliant, Turnus looks up, extends right hand to
ask for mercy: 'I have my deserts,' he says, 'I make no dispute;
it is your chance, take it. But if any thought for a father's
misery can touch you—for you had such a father too
in Anchises—I pray you, have pity on Daunus and his ageing years,
and restore me, or my body stripped of life if you will,
to my people. You have won, the Italians have seen me raise
my hands, a beaten man. You have Lavinia as your wife.
Do not stretch the net of hatred wider.' Aeneas, fierce,
sword raised, stopped, looked him up and down, checked his right hand,
and gradually as he stood there, his opponent's words were
starting to tell, when high on one shoulder the ill-fated
belt caught his eye, as the light hit the familiar plaques:
it was Pallas' belt, the boy whom Turnus had struck down and killed,
and now he was wearing his enemy's gear on his shoulders.
Aeneas, after he had drunk in the looted belt and its reminder
of cruel grief, in a blaze of madness and terrible
with anger cried, 'Are you who are decked with the spoil of those
dear to me to escape my clutches? Pallas, yes, Pallas strikes
the avenging blow, spills in repayment a scoundrel's blood.'
So saying, blazing, he drives his sword into the chest
before him. Turnus' limbs relax in the chill of death,
and life, resentful, flees with a moan to the shades.

After much bitter fighting the Trojans and Italians agree to let the
outcome of the war between them be decided by a 'duel' between the
leaders on each side (a hand-to-hand fight in the tradition of Homeric
warfare, conducted according to a strict unwritten code of rules, the last
of several such contests in the poem). Virgil's narrative of the duel is
something of a *tour de force*. It began with an exchange of spears as the
two contestants advanced toward one another, and might have ended
then (as did the contest between Turnus and Pallas in *Aeneid* 10—Pallas
missed, Turnus' spear inflicted a mortal wound). This time, however,
both Aeneas and Turnus missed. In the hand-to-hand fighting which
followed, Turnus seized the initiative: seeing his opportunity, he brought
his sword crashing down on Aeneas' helmet; and the sword splintered
into fragments in his hand. The initiative passed to Aeneas: a man
without either spear or sword is helpless against a man with sword. But

Aeneas could not press his advantage home, for his opponent turned and fled, and Aeneas could not catch him because of a leg wound received in the fighting which interrupted the preparations for the duel. Turnus could not escape, however: the contestants were hemmed in by the onlookers on both sides. Then Turnus' sister handed him a sword (to do so was strictly against the rules, but she was half a goddess), and the contestants were once again evenly matched. Aeneas ran to where his spear had lodged in the trunk of a tree and wrenched it free with a superhuman effort, and the initiative passed a second time to Aeneas: a man with a sword cannot reach a man armed with a spear. All Aeneas had to do was await his opportunity, and then strike his opponent down from a safe distance. At this point, Jove intervened and sent down his messenger of death, an eerie invisible bird that beat with its wings in Turnus' face. Turnus, aware his time had come, in a last desperate effort grasped a huge rock to fling it at his opponent in a final act of defiance: his knees gave way beneath him and the rock fell short.

The final episode now begins, with Aeneas still confronting his helpless opponent. He sees his chance and strikes. That might have been the end, as it was for Pallas. But Turnus is not killed, only wounded. Aeneas might still have stepped forward and despatched Turnus with his sword after a short verbal exchange: a few taunts from the victor, a few words of defiance from the vanquished—it would have been wholly in the heroic tradition. That is how Mezentius died at the end of *Aeneid* 10. It is not that way with Turnus. When death stares him in the face, he weakens and asks for mercy. Aeneas is about to spare him. Then fate steps in. Aeneas catches sight of the belt that had belonged to Pallas; the belt brings back memories that tumble over reason, thrust compassion aside, and Aeneas kills the enemy he was about to spare in a mad blaze of terrible anger. As it flees to the world beneath, the soul of Turnus registers a protest.

Suppose, as seems perfectly possible and indeed probable, that the *Aeneid* was first presented to the world in a public reading organized by Virgil's literary executors shortly after his death, under the patronage of Augustus himself: a reading lasting three days, perhaps; we gather readings that length were not unusual a hundred years later, for works of much less importance. Imagine the reading is just over. Was there a loud round of applause as the reader read those last eight lines? Listen while the audience files out. What are the reactions you hear around you?

No doubt there are some members of the audience whose reaction is superficial and uncritical; they see only victory for the right side; for them Turnus' conduct when death stares him in the face, his final protest when the living soul of Turnus abandons the dead body and 'flees resentful to the shades', only confirm Turnus' weakness: he could not face death like a soldier, as Mezentius does. But surely, or so one likes to think, the more general reaction is puzzlement. Why did it have to end like this? That final sudden blaze of anger somehow discredits the victor. Victory of the just cause, victory that is to be followed by peaceful union of the two peoples who have been fighting against one another, should surely be more dispassionate. Shouldn't the poem have ended with proclamation of the victor, congratulation of Aeneas, a solemn declaration of peace between the two peoples, instead of this uneasy, inconclusive conclusion? I find it hard to imagine that thoughts similar to these were not present in the minds of many of the members of that original audience.

We must remember that, if the poem ends the way it does, it is because Virgil wants it to end that way. He has complete say in how he ends his story. True, Turnus must be got rid of: however humane the gesture if Aeneas had spared his life, it would be dramatically and poetically intolerable for Turnus to survive to fight another day. Aeneas' victory leaves no place for Turnus. But Aeneas does not have to kill his enemy in a mad blaze of anger. He kills Turnus in revenge, as the agent of a personal vendetta, not as the agent of the destined victory of his people. Fate springs a trap on Turnus; Aeneas sees the belt, is reminded of Pallas; the pressure of emotion is too great; mad, unreasoning anger wells up and he kills him. That would do as an end for the poem if Aeneas were just any hero in the traditional heroic mould. But he isn't. He is the man who is always straining after a higher ideal, a more civilized standard of conduct, than the rest. It is because he and the Trojans stand for civilization against mere uncivilized personal courage that Aeneas deserves to win—*must* win, in order that fate's purpose can be accomplished.

But, as it turns out, the manner of his final victory degrades all he stands for. The duel upon which we saw him embark in a mood of serene detachment as the agent of fate's purpose becomes, as his opponent keeps slipping through his clutches, a fight like any other fight; the point is reached where Aeneas' only thought is to catch his man and kill him. True, when the fight is over, Turnus' plea not to widen the net of hatred further takes instant effect. Aeneas' humanity reasserts itself. And then fate springs its trap upon Aeneas as well as upon Turnus. The sight of Pallas' belt, the sudden surrender to the impulse for revenge: it is all entirely understandable, entirely true to human nature. But it is the final stage in the demotion of Aeneas from the detached agent of fate's purpose to the mere instrument of fate: the man who does the right thing for the wrong reason; or, if not quite the wrong reason (for that is to oversimplify Virgil), for reasons that must to some extent discredit the cause.

I think this is the reaction Virgil planned: not simply enthusiasm for a story well told, but a fresh understanding that one cannot become involved in the horror of war, and remain detached. The critics, the students of Greek tragedy, the philosophers in that original audience, would have had no difficulty, one imagines, in seeing what Virgil was driving at. Others less sophisticated were perhaps exasperated at being denied the simple heroics they had expected. But one likes to think there were many who felt impelled to sort out the rights and wrongs of it all in their minds as they filed out of the room where the reading had taken place.

For them, one likes to think, it meant a new ordering of their own experience, a more complete understanding of what had happened in the great Civil War, now twelve years and more over and beginning to take up its place in history as something that could be thought and talked about more honestly and more compassionately than in the hour of final victory. For in that struggle, too, victory came only at the cost of lives destroyed; things were done in the heat of battle, or in the angry pursuit of revenge, that one could now wish undone. Instead of asking them to criticize Aeneas, was not Virgil asking his audience to admit to themselves that by the time final victory comes, no man, least of all perhaps the leader on the winning side, can hope to count his hands or his conscience clean?

IV IRONIC EPIC: OVID'S *Metamorphoses*

In Virgil's *Aeneid*, the challenge the poet extends to the expectations of his audience is, first of all, an artistic challenge: his epic is unexpectedly traditional; it follows Homeric conventions more strictly than any other Roman epic poem. But at the same time the *Aeneid* challenges unquestioning acceptance of the heroic ideal: to people who had lived through the Civil War the old heroic stories could no longer appear in the same light; their own experience had prepared them for a less shallow understanding of what victory costs. The *Aeneid* is Virgil's attempt to formulate, through art, that new awareness; it challenges his contemporaries to see heroism in a new light.

In the *Metamorphoses*, the challenge is an artistic challenge only. If Ovid's heroes and heroines are less heroic, that is because his poem is lighter in tone, more relaxed, not because Ovid is questioning traditional concepts of heroism; it is not Ovid's intention to question his contemporaries' beliefs about anything. He offers them instead a poem that is startlingly fresh, like no poem they have read before.

Ovid lacks Virgil's acute dramatic sense, as he lacks Virgil's reticence.

His narrative style is crisp, fast-moving, economical. But he has not Virgil's power to make the reader feel that every word counts, and conveys more than it is in the power of words normally to convey. Nor has he the creative imagination of a Petronius or an Apuleius: he chooses at any rate to accept the limitations imposed on the imagination that result from confining himself to an inherited body of legend, the myths, familiar and unfamiliar, handed down from ancient Greece and from pre-historic Italy. But he is the best storyteller in Latin. No writer can spin a tale as deftly, as wittily as Ovid; no other writer can bring to bear upon the world of legend the same easy, sure insight into human nature. In all classical antiquity his only rival is the poet of the *Odyssey*. To this gift for telling a story he adds a quite remarkable narrative lucidity and a deft verbal wit.

By conventional standards, Ovid's *Metamorphoses* must rank as an epic poem. It meets the basic requirements: it is a long narrative poem in dactylic hexameters, divided into books. Ovid's status as an epic poet cannot be denied. At the same time one feels he wishes to do no more than just qualify.

The feeling is prompted first of all by Ovid's style. One can hardly speak of mock-heroic: the word suggests too openly satirical, too frivolous, a purpose—an open admission on the writer's part that he is not claiming for his work a place in the front rank of literature. Yet no reader can miss the way Ovid consistently undercuts the grand manner of epic. It is, so to speak, the difference between grand opera and *opera buffa*. The best label, perhaps, is 'ironic heroic'. We are made to feel that the man who tells the story is too sophisticated, too intelligent, to take the story quite seriously, and expects his readers to be no less sophisticated and intelligent. The tales are told with a display of earnestness which never quite convinces, and does not ever seem meant wholly to convince. Having fulfilled the basic requirements for an epic poem, Ovid is patently anxious to leave the impression that he takes his chosen theme and the conventions that go with it lightly. At the same time the *Metamorphoses* isn't just a series of tales casually tossed off. For there is a theme which connects the tales: the theme of *metamorphosis*. The Latin word which corresponds to the Greek word *metamorphosis* is *transformatio*, and transformation is what the poem is ostensibly about: a change of shape, usually sudden transformation, from human shape to animal, vegetable or divine shape.

Thanks to this ostensible continuity of theme, the *Metamorphoses* qualifies also as a didactic poem.

It begins indeed with a clear statement of didactic purposes (*Metamorphoses* 1. 19):

Of shapes transformde to bodies straunge, I purpose to entreate;
Ye gods vouchsafe (for you are they that wrought this wondrous feate)
To further this mine enterprise. And from the world begunne,
Graunt that my verse may to my time, his course directly runne.
Before the Sea and Land were made, and Heaven that all doth hide,
In all the worlde one onely face of nature did abide,
Which *Chaos* hight, a huge rude heape, and nothing else but even
A heavie lump and clottred clod of seedes togither driven
Of things at strife among themselves for want of order due.

[Translation: Golding]

As the long introductory section proceeds, this note of rational exposition and inquiry becomes increasingly apparent (*Metamorphoses* 1. 76–81):

Howbeit yet of all this while the creature wanting was,
Farre more devine, of nobler minde, which should the residue passe
In depth of knowledge, reason, wit, and high capacitie,
And which of all the residue should the Lord and ruler bee.
Then eyther he that made the worlde, and things in order set,
Of heavenly seede engendred Man: or else the earth as yet
Yong, lustie, fresh, and in hir floures, and parted from the skie,
But late before, the seede thereof as yet held inwardlie.

[Translation: Golding]

The didactic tone is not kept up, of course. But even in the great body of the poem—that part that most people would describe as written in the epic tradition—the *Metamorphoses* differs from other epics in the mass of detail recounted, as it were, by a writer who is expounding the results of research to an audience eager for information and speaking with a note of authority which it is as impossible to miss as it is to take seriously. In the final book of the poem, the note of philosophical seriousness is resumed for a long disquisition on the Pythagorean doctrine of vegetarianism, metempsychosis and the universality of change (15. 50–478; it occupies nearly half the book). This time, discarding the persona of the poet as teacher, Ovid puts the lesson on Pythagoreanism on the lips of Pythagoras himself.

It is this element of apparent didactic seriousness (coupled with the fact that the poem is one of the most graceful expressions of civilized sensibility ever written) that made the *Metamorphoses* the secular Bible of the Middle Ages. Even some modern scholars have taken Ovid's didacticism seriously. Yet it is precisely the quality of seriousness which is lacking in this poem, no less in its ironic pretence of didacticism than in its ironic pretence of the grand manner of epic. No writer who seriously wished to develop the doctrine of the universality of change would choose the examples Ovid chooses. Nor would he string his examples together in so palpably disingenuous a manner, however dazzlingly ingenious the transition effected from one tale of metamorphosis to the next. The fact is that, just as Ovid coolly, elegantly, detaches himself from the tales he tells with such an urbane, witty affectation of earnestness, so too is his detachment discernible from the moral precepts he enjoins and the philosophy which he expounds with such effortless clarity. Take the following lines (15. 143–64):

> And forasmuch as God this instant howre
> Dooth move my toong too speake, I will obey his heavenly powre.
> My God *Apollos* temple I will set you open, and
> Disclose the woondrous heavens themselves, and make you understand
> The Oracles and secrets of the Godly majestye.
> Greate things, and such as wit of man could never yit espye,
> And such as have beene hidden long, I purpose too descrye.
> I mynd too leave the earth, and up among the starres too stye,
> I mynd too leave this grosser place, and in the clowdes too flye,
> And on stowt *Atlas* shoulders strong too rest my self on hye,
> And looking downe from heaven on men that wander heere and there
> In dreadfull feare of death as though they voyd of reason were,
> Too give them exhortation thus, and playnely too unwynd
> The whole discourse of destinie as nature hath assignd.
> O men amaazd with dread of death, why feare yee *Limbo Styx*,
> And other names of vanitie, which are but *Poets* tricks?
> And perrills of another world, all false surmysed geere?
> For whither fyre or length of tyme consume the bodyes heere,
> Yee well may thinke that further harmes they cannot suffer more.
> For soules are free from death. Howbeet, they leaving evermore
> Theyr former dwellings, are receyvd and live ageine in new.
> For I myself (ryght well in mynd I beare it too be trew)
> Was in the tyme of Trojan warre *Euphorbus*, *Panthewes* sonne,
> Quyght through whoose hart the deathfull speare of *Menelay* did ronne.
> I late ago in *Junos* Church at *Agros* did behold
> And knew the target which I in my left hand there did hold.
>
> [Translation: Golding]

The dry, lofty manner of Lucretius is delicately echoed. Compare the opening lines of Book 4 of *On the Universe* (4. 1–5 [=1. 926–30]):

> I range the Muses' pathless tracts that none has trod
> before. I am minded to drink deep from springs where none

has drunk, minded to pluck flowers none has plucked,
and weave from them a glorious garland for my head
like none the Muses placed till now on poet's brow.

Or the opening lines of Book 2 (2. 7–11):

But nothing sweeter is there than to hold the citadel serene,
high placed, by the teachings of the wise firmly fortified,
and from there to be able to look down on men aimlessly
wandering on all sides, seeking the path of life, each
struggling to beat the others in wit and rank.

And that death is not to be feared is of course one of the fundamental
tenets of Lucretius. In Ovid, however, the doctrine is not expounded for
the Lucretian reason that death means complete extinction, but for the
Pythagorean reason that death means reincarnation.

The Lucretian echoes are even more evident in these lines
(*Metamorphoses* 15. 237–57):

And theis that wee call Elements doo never stand at stay. ⎫
The enterchaunging course of them I will before yee lay. ⎬
Give heede thertoo. This endlesse world conteynes therin I say ⎭
Fowre substances of which all things are gendred. Of theis fower
The Earth and Water for theyr masse and weyght are sunken lower.
The other cowple Aire and Fyre the purer of the twayne
Mount up, and nought can keepe them downe. And though there doo
[remayne
A space betweene eche one of them: yit every thing is made
Of themsame fowre, and intoo them at length ageine doo fade.
The earth resolving leysurely dooth melt too water sheere,
The water fyned turnes too aire. The aire eeke purged cleere
From grossenesse, spyreth up aloft, and there becommeth fyre.
From thence in order contrary they backe ageine retyre.
Fyre thickening passeth intoo Aire, and Ayër wexing grosse
Returnes to water: Water eeke congealing intoo drosse,
Becommeth earth. No kind of thing keepes ay his shape and hew.
For nature loving ever chaunge repayres one shape a new
Uppon another, neyther dooth there perrish aught (trust mee) ⎫
In all the world, but altring takes new shape. For that which wee ⎬
Doo terme by name of being borne, is for too gin too bee ⎭
Another thing than that it was: And likewise for too dye.

[Translation: Golding]

This witty contamination for Ovid's own poetic ends of Lucretius' doctrine of the indestructibility of matter with more or less respectable Pythagorean lore approaches philosophical nonsense. As in Ovid's *The Art of Love*, the role of teacher is a pose. True, it is possible in both cases, and even legitimate, to sense an element of social satire or even a moral purpose: the follies of mankind derided by Pythagoras are real enough; the single-minded pursuit of love which Ovid takes for granted (the only question for the lover is how most efficiently to attain his object) is not fantasy but a playfully ironic simplification of the lifestyle of a society committed to the belief that seduction was the chief occupation of civilized man. In both cases, however, Ovid's first object is to entertain.

Both the epic tradition, in short, and the didactic tradition are made sport of in a poem which is patently neither an epic (it lacks seriousness of tone) nor a didactic poem (it lacks a serious subject). The fact is that by the time we come to Ovid the social function from which the traditional genres derived meaning or validity has been lost. Already in Lucretius' day, or Virgil's, the structure of society which gave the poet a specialized view of his function as a teacher or a teller of tales was a thing of the past. Lucretius and Virgil retained an artistic respect for the forms they adopted: though the *Aeneid* is a poem filled with bold invention, though Virgil's concept of his social function is very different from Homer's, his poem remains innovatory within the epic spirit. Ovid mixes traditions he feels no craftsman's obligation to respect. He is having a last fling at ways of writing which have had their day. Only irony can make them viable. To write an ironic epic means recourse to desperate measures; but the desperate measures are taken by a writer of genius.

There is a third element in the mixture. The *Metamorphoses* is something more than a contamination of epic and didactic, something more than an elegantly witty expression of irreverence for forms Ovid felt outmoded. The wealth of detail which Ovid builds into his stories, the philosophical tone which from time to time asserts itself, the parade of learning, are the demonstration of a special kind of wit. His models here are not the old Greek poets, but the more recent poets of Alexandria: Callimachus, for example, who wrote elegies on mythological themes so replete with learned detail and allusion, his poetry would have been insufferably dull if he had been serious (it is touch and go, as it is). Like Callimachus, Ovid makes it a point of honour to know all the unusual details of this story (to get the facts right, so to speak), only to mock the legends he has made the object of his research. Fortunately, he made no attempt to imitate Callimachus' tortuously complicated style: Ovid's Latin is invariably a model of urbane lucidity.

Structurally, the *Metamorphoses* owes its inspiration to another typically Hellenistic innovation, the miniature epic or 'epyllion', a poem which retells a known story, but retells it with a new elegant selectivity and compactness. The only example to survive is Catullus' *Marriage of Peleus and Thetis*, but we hear of others (Cinna's *Zmyrna*, for example, whose wealth of recondite detail made it a standing challenge to commentators of the following generation). The *Metamorphoses* is really a series of such epyllia, an almost inexhaustible repertoire of tales in a scintillating, ever-changing pageant that resists, if it does not defeat, the attempts of those who try to reduce the poem to a rational plan. The line of narrative is, as it were, constantly metamorphosed. One tale melts into another; or a character within one tale begins to talk, and in a moment we are off in a new direction, into a new tale, only to be brought back to where we were, and then whisked off afresh. The only continuity is the pseudo-philosophical theme of a poem that purports to study change of form in all its aspects, in all ages and contexts. Also in the tradition of the epyllion is the emphasis on love, though in Ovid the pathetic style is more tongue-in-cheek than in Catullus. Ovid possesses one of the surest instincts for pathos in all literature. He has a subtle understanding of character and a real talent for description, but empathy is never allowed to stand in the way when the impulse asserts itself to pen a witty line or to pull the reader's leg.

The structure of the *Metamorphoses* is in itself a demonstration of Ovidian wit. To string together so complicated a series of tales is a *tour de force*. Each time the transition is effected in the space of a few lines. What is remarkable is, not the perfection of the joints, but the effrontery with which the joints are papered over. It is an aspect of the poem that can be illustrated only by taking a sequence of tales. The easiest way is to take a whole book.

Metamorphoses 6 contains 721 lines. It provides a very fair random specimen of Ovid's slick, superbly nonchalant, supremely competent technique. The theme is jealousy and vengeance as well as metamorphosis. It begins (lines 1–312) with two cautionary tales illustrating the dangers for mortals in thinking themselves the equals (or the betters) of gods: the tale of Arachne, who challenged the goddess Minerva to a weaving contest and was transformed into a spider for her pains; and the tale of Niobe, who offended the goddess Latona by boasting of her numerous progeny (she had seven sons and seven daughters, Latona had only one son and one daughter, the god Apollo and the goddess Diana), and was transformed, after the destruction of her children and her husband, into a weeping pillar of stone. A pair of shorter and lighter tales follow (lines 313–400): the tale of the Lycian peasants who became frogs; and the grimmer but briefly and lightly recounted story of the fate of the satyr Marsyas (he attempted to rival

74

Phoebus in playing the pipe, and when he was mercilessly destroyed, all nature wept for him, and the tears were transformed into the river in Phrygia which bears his name). A bridge-passage (401–23) follows this interlude, to prepare the way for the bizarre, cruel, moving tale of the seduction by Tereus of his sister-in-law Philomela (lines 424–674). A short excursus (lines 675–721) on the myth of Orithyia concludes the book.

The transitions are instantaneously rather than smoothly or elaborately contrived: where logical continuity is plainly deficient, terse, deft editorial intervention is resorted to in a way that would be intolerable if serious continuity of exposition were being attempted, and shamelessly transparent assertion of continuity not all part of the fun. As the book opens, Minerva has been sitting in the shade listening to the Muses telling the tale of how the Pierides were defeated by them in a singing contest and turned into magpies. She is aroused by this tale to an act of revenge of her own, and thus the transition is manipulated to the tale of Arachne. The transition to Niobe is more casual: she had heard of Arachne, we are told, and failed to take the hint that in dealings with the gods humility is called for (147–50). But the fact that the two tales form an obvious pair excuses the casualness. The transition to the following tale is more carefully manipulated. Latona's vengeance, Ovid tells us, reminds all who witnessed it of an earlier case of vengeance exacted by Latona (316: *a facto propiore priora renarrant*) on some obscure Lycian peasants for their inhospitality to her (they would not let her drink from their pond when she came among them as an exile with her children parched with thirst, and were turned into frogs); the tale is told by an unnamed narrator who had got it, he said, from a guide he had once had in that part of the country. The explanatory bridge-passage is an outstanding example of the extraordinary concision which Ovid can command when he is in a hurry to sketch in details (6. 319–24). Ovid's ablest modern translator, A. E. Watts, gets left behind; his almost word-for-word version requires eight lines for Ovid's five and a half:

> A striking story, yet of little fame,
> Being told of peasants, men without a name.
> A lake there was—these eyes the place have seen,
> Where local memory keeps the marvel green;
> For there I traveled, by my father sent
> (When now, with age, his traveling powers were spent)
> To fetch picked bulls for breeding, and for guide
> Was given some native of the countryside.
>
> [Translation: Watts]

This story in its turn reminds another speaker of the satyr Marsyas, and in the space of three and a half lines that story is already in motion (382–6):

> The story ended; and in one who heard
> The Lycians' fate, another memory stirred,
> Of Marsyas, and the price the satyr paid,
> By Phoebus on Minerva's pipe outplayed.

[Translation: Watts]

A longer bridge-passage now brings us back to Niobe, whom we abandoned at the climax of her story not quite a hundred lines earlier (at line 312). The scene now is the mass funeral of Niobe, her husband and her children. All the neighbouring nobles came to the funeral with one exception; there were no representatives of the Athenians, who were engaged in a war. After the war was over, says Ovid, this time in his own person as the omniscient narrator, Pandion of Athens gave his daughter Procne in marriage to King Tereus of Thrace who had been his ally in the war: it was to prove an ill-omened marriage. The story of Tereus and Procne and her sister Philomela which follows is the longest in the book (lines 437–674). The fantasy of Boreas and Orithyia forms a short tail-piece. Their twin sons, Zetes and Calais, Ovid reminds us, joined the expedition of the Argonauts; the fact is mentioned in the last three lines, and the way thus prepared for the story of Medea and Jason in *Metamorphoses* 7.

As he passes from one story to another, Ovid frequently pauses to describe a particular telling of the tale, thus establishing a neat contrast between the simple, garrulous world of the distant past, in which one good story leads to another as men and women sit around and spin yarns, and Ovid's own elegant, clipped, ironic evocation of that primitive world. At the same time, with almost impudent casualness, Ovid is able to create the illusion that each tale arises naturally out of the tale just told. There is a kind of sleight of hand involved which depends for its success upon not passing entirely unobserved: we are meant to spot that we are being tricked, but we are not left the time to work out just how before being caught up afresh in the next fast-moving narrative.

Ovid constantly varies, moreover, the appeal of his stories. The story of Arachne is virtuoso writing. It begins with something close to epic parody; the best part, however, the part Ovid clearly enjoyed most, is the description of the rival tapestries: Minerva's depicts the gods proudly contending for Athens (four examples of divine vengeance upon human beings), while Arachne's tapestry is a breathtaking list of Jove's adulteries in different animal and bird disguises, Neptune's amorous adventures, Apollo in various disguises, Bacchus, Saturn, a border of flowers and ivy—all in the space of 26 lines. The story of Niobe descends almost to tragicomedy as the corpses pile up. The story of the Lycian peasants who become frogs is high-speed comedy. Who except Ovid would dare to write such a line as this (6. 376)?

Quamvis sint sub aqua, sub aqua maledicere temptant.

Though beneath the water, beneath the water they keep their depraved
[talk up.

The metrical technique (a chiasmus built round the principal caesura, so that the first half runs up to the phrase *sub aqua*, and then the second half retreats from the caesura in a repetition of the key phrase) is beyond reproach. But the repeated phrase echoes of course the croak of the frogs and *maledicere* is a calculated ambiguity ('speak with difficulty' and 'speak maliciously').

The story of Tereus and Philomela on the other hand is both horrible and truly pathetic. A properly moral stance is adopted from the opening lines and maintained throughout. The narrative of the ill-omened marriage, with its echoes of the strange, wild marriage of Dido and Aeneas, is in the best tradition of epic. Compare Ovid's lines, however (*Metamorphoses* 6. 428–34):

> At this match (as after will appeare)
> Was neyther *Juno*, President of mariage wont to bee,
> Nor *Hymen*, no nor any one of all the graces three.
> The Furies snatching Tapers up that on some Herce did stande
> Did light them, and before the Bride did beare them in their hande.
> The Furies made the Bridegroomes bed. And on the house did rucke
> A cursed Owle the messenger of yll successe and lucke.
> And all the night time while that they were lying in their beds,
> She sate upon the bedsteds top right over both their heds.
> Such handsell *Progne* had the day that *Tereus* did hir wed:
> Such handsell had they when that she was brought of childe a bed.
> [Translation: Golding]

with Virgil's (*Aeneid* 4. 166–70):

> Earth supreme and Juno, whose province marriage is,
> give signal. The sky connived, the lightning flared
> when these two joined, on mountain-top the nymphs howled out.
> That day was first entered on an unhappy road that led
> to death.

Even the owl comes from Virgil. It is inspired partly by the sinister figure of Rumour in the lines which immediately follow (*Aeneid* 4. 186–7):

> By day she sits on guard, either on rooftop, or on tall towers.

and partly by the owl which troubled Dido as she lay torturing herself with thoughts of death (*Aeneid* 4. 462–3):

> And often from a rooftop would some lonely owl
> sound her long drawn-out prophecy of grief.

Ovid cannot match Virgil's perfect rhythmic control, or his power to evoke the eerie and the sinister with a few well-chosen, well-placed words. But then, tragic serenity is not his object. For Ovid, the high style is an attitude to be struck; it has not become a natural mould for the poet's thoughts.

In the story of Philomela the note of something overdone, something close to parody is indeed essential: the tautly stylized diction and syntax are undercut continually by the carefully planned thrust of wit. A first hint follows shortly. After a brilliant passage of high-speed narrative in which Ovid flashes over five years of marriage and sketches in the story of Tereus' journey to Athens at his wife's urgent request to beg her father to allow her sister to visit her, Ovid relates how Tereus fell in love with his sister-in-law at first sight (451–60):

> When (see the chaunce) came *Philomele* in raiment very rich,
> And yet in beautie farre more rich, even like the Fairies which
> Reported are the pleasant woods and water springs to haunt,
> So that the like apparell and attire to them you graunt.
> King *Tereus* at the sight of hir did burne in his desire,
> As if a man should chaunce to set a gulfe of corne on fire,
> Or burne a stacke of hay. Hir face in deede deserved love. |
> But as for him, to fleshy lust even nature him did move. |
> For of those countries commonly the people are above |
> All measure prone to lecherie. And therefore both by kinde
> His flame encreast, and by his owne default of vicious minde.
>
> [Translation: Golding]

As it happens, we can place alongside Ovid's witty expansion the sombre, simple lines of the tragedian Accius, written perhaps a century earlier:

> Tereus, a man of ways untamable, and a barbarian at heart,
> turned his gaze upon her; out of his mind with flaming love,
> utterly overcome, he plans in his madness a deed most foul.

From this point onwards the narrative assumes a dry, witty note.

78

Anything like the plangency of the true high style is avoided. Instead we have something closer to tragicomedy: an ostensibly pathetic narrative enlivened with flashes of verbal ingenuity, backed by shrewd, cynical observation of human nature, such as (467–8):

> Iamque moras male fert cupidoque revertitur ore
> ad mandata Procnes et agit sua vota sub illa.

> [Tereus can scarcely] brook delay, but with fond speech recurs
> To Procne's plans, and masks his hopes with hers.
> > [Translation: Watts]

or (471):

> Addidit et lacrimas, tamquam mandasset et illas.

> Tears too he sheds, as if she [Procne] bade them flow.
> > [Translation: Watts]

Or this typically Ovidian line when Philomela, whom Procne mourns as dead, has been raped and mutilated by Procne's husband—he tore her tongue out so that she could not denounce him (570):

> Et luget non sic lugendae fata sororis.

> And tears of mourning for her sister shed,
> Who might indeed be mourned, though not as dead.
> > [Translation: Watts]

The role of Ovid's elegant, efficient syntax as an instrument of wit is worth pondering: its function isn't just to give momentum to the narrative; somehow, it simultaneously creates the flash of wit and condones it; more crudely structured, the wit would appear crude.

As the first climax of his story approaches Ovid slackens the tempo of the narrative and reapplies the colouring of the high style without denying himself the quick, cynical, witty thrust (486–93):

> To endward of his daily race and travell *Phebus* drew,
> And on the shoring side of Heaven his horses downeward flew.
> A princely supper was prepaarde, and wine in golde was set:
> And after meate to take their rest the Princes did them get.
> But though the King of *Thrace* that while were absent from hir sight,
> Yet swelted he: and in his minde revolving all the night
> Hir face, hir gesture, and hir hands, imaginde all the rest
> (The which as yet he had not seene) as likte his fancie best.

He feedes his flames himselfe. No winke could come within his eyes,
For thinking ay on hir.

[Translation: Golding]

Again the echoes of Virgil are easily caught: Dido and Aeneas drank
from golden cups at the end of *Aeneid* 1; Dido cannot sleep, her thoughts
are filled with Aeneas' appearance at the beginning of *Aeneid* 4.
Substituting only an epic cliché for the end of day for Virgil's epic cliché
for the beginning of day (*Aeneid* 4. 6–7), Ovid reformulates his material
in an affectation of the high style that is at the same time an expression of
Ovid's cool, witty detachment from the pathetic story his lines relate.

With the ground prepared in this fashion, Ovid sends the pair off on
their ill-fated journey with a crisp sentence that is almost boisterous in its
simple, brisk, expression of eager, gay lust (511–14):

As soone as *Tereus* and the Maide togither were a boord,
And that their ship from land with Ores was haled on the foord,
The fielde is ours he cride aloude, I have the thing I sought
And up he skipt, so barbrous and so beastly was his thought,
That scarce even there he could forbeare his pleasure to have wrought.

[Translation: Golding]

The narrative of the rape and its barbarous outcome follow. Here, as a
sample, are the lines which describe the cruel mutilation to which Tereus
is driven by anger at Philomela's reproaches and by fear of discovery
(549–62):

The cruell tyrant being chaaft, and also put in feare
With these and other such hir wordes both causes so him stung,
That drawing out his naked sworde that at his girdle hung,
He tooke hir rudely by the haire, and wrung hir hands behind hir,
Compelling hir to holde them there while he himselfe did binde hir.
When *Philomela* sawe the sworde she hoapt she should have dide,
And for the same hir naked throte she gladly did provide.
But as she yirnde and called ay upon hir fathers name,
And strived to have spoken still, the cruell tyrant came,
And with a paire of pinsons fast did catch hir by the tung,
And with his sword did cut it off. The stumpe whereon it hung
Did patter still. The tip fell downe, and quivering on the ground
As though that it had murmured it made a certaine sound,
And as an Adders tayle cut off doth skip a while: even so
The tip of *Philomelaas* tongue did wriggle to and fro,
And nearer to hir mistresseward in dying still did go.
And after this most cruell act, for certaine men report

That he (I scarcely dare beleve) did oftentimes resort
To maymed *Philomela* and abusde hir at his will.

[Translation: Golding]

One of Ovid's commentators remarks: 'This exaggerated, detailed, tasteless description corresponds to Ovid's Alexandrian weakness for the shocking and the grisly.' It is easy to see what prompts the observation. But 'tasteless' assumes that Ovid tried to write epic and lapsed into something unworthy of the epic manner. In fact, his object is a witty entertainment, and it is in the nature of that entertainment to carry the reader or the listener to the point of protest—and then disarm him by sheer genius and an incredible sureness of touch. One is reminded of the 'obscene' poems of Catullus: the reader who thinks he knows just how far the etiquette of the short personal poem allows a poet to go in such matters is about to protest that Catullus goes too far—and then understands that these are not just obscene poems, but poems that play with obscenity at a new level of urbanity and wit. Ovid is a gifted storyteller with a genuine sense of pathos always at his command to mitigate the horror and to add a fresh dimension to the wit. He offers an entertainment which makes a genuine claim upon our emotional sensibility. We are invited to accept the piling on of the horror and the slick manner in which the horror is related as a legitimate literary experience akin to tragicomedy. The climax brings, not catharsis, but a resolution via metamorphosis into something like a happy ending.

Catullus can play this kind of trick in a society where a taste for the prurient was common and not held utterly shocking, criminal, or an offence against God. Similarly Ovid needs a public whose appetite for the macabre has got a little out of control. If the detailed realism is Hellenistic in origin, the extension of that technique of detailed realism to the description of wanton cruelty must be symptomatic of a depravity of taste in contemporary society. Ovid finds it amusing to titillate that appetite; half a century after Ovid, Lucan and Seneca pander to it openly.

V   RHETORICAL EPIC: LUCAN's *On the Civil War*

The *Aeneid* and the *Metamorphoses* are outstandingly good poems. Their very excellence had unfortunate results. If it had not been for them, it might not have taken the Romans another hundred years to realize that, except in the hands of an original genius, epic was as good as dead. The *Aeneid* and the *Metamorphoses* are not only good poems: they are unique. Though each is made out of traditional elements, each is made

81

into something quite unlike any poem previously written: an artistic challenge to the poet who wrote it; a challenge to the poet's audience to adjust to an exciting, fresh synthesis, the new that had been made out of old.

Both poems are good enough to have survived into modern times as poems which are read upon the printed page; both, however, were designed to be heard, not read. Hence the intensely dramatic quality of the *Aeneid*, the showiness of the *Metamorphoses*. During the first century AD the public performance of literary works became a flourishing social institution. While it killed the short, complex, intensely personal poem, it gave a final lease of life to epic. To us, who read a poem on the printed page, first-century epic is almost unreadable: either because it is so stridently rhetorical it cloys, or because it is just too boring. We cannot easily appreciate how stylishness of a kind was imparted to mediocre sense by rhythm and the sound of words; missing, as we must, the excitement injected into the occasion by the skill of the professional interpreter, what was good enough to get by becomes for us unendurable.

After the *Aeneid* and the *Metamorphoses*, Lucan's *On the Civil War* is something of a surprise to the modern reader. Yet Lucan is more in the old Roman tradition than Virgil or Ovid. Apart from Livius' *Odyssey* (a translation, not an original work), Roman narrative poetry began in the real world of Roman experience. The first Roman epic took up the story of what most Romans must have regarded as the greatest single event in history: the struggle of Rome against Carthage. Following in Naevius' footsteps, Ennius had set out in his *Annals* the whole pageant of Roman history down 'to his own day, leaving out only the First Punic War in deference to his illustrious predecessor. True, Naevius had begun his poem, we gather, by bringing Aeneas to Italy, thus establishing the connexion with Homer's Troy. But Livy, two centuries later, did much the same. Naevius' real theme, like Livy's, was history. Not what had happened to Greeks, not the imaginary or at any rate legendary world of Greek mythology, but what the Romans themselves had done.

It was only when Roman poets became more concerned with rivalling the Greeks than with making poetry about the real world of contemporary experience or national memory, that they turned to mythological epic. Neither the *Aeneid* nor the *Metamorphoses* is really representative of this relatively minor genre. Both are wholly exceptional poems: the *Aeneid*, in the extent of its challenge to Homer (the poem is, as far as we can tell, an unprecedented attempt to write a Roman poem strictly within the conventions of Homeric epic); the *Metamorphoses*, in its break with the traditionally flaccid structure of mythological epic (a whole poem devoted to a single tale), in favour of a brilliant virtuoso

82

structure, in which epyllion grows out of epyllion in an apparently unending metamorphosis. The typical mythological epic seems to have been the work of coterie poets, like Propertius' friend Ponticus (whose *Thebaid* was perhaps an imitation of Antimachus' *Thebaid*); or else scholarly exercises, like the *Argonautica* of Varro of Atax (a Roman version of Apollonius' *Argonautica*). The only surviving example of mythological epic proper is the competent, but long and wholly unoriginal *Voyage of the Argonauts* of Valerius Flaccus. Similarly, though tragedy on Roman themes had been written from the second century BC onwards, only one example survives, the *Octavia* attributed to Seneca. It is one more reminder that much of Roman literature has gone for good. We have, however, considerable fragments of Republican tragedy, just as we have considerable fragments of the historical epics of Naevius and Ennius. Where Republican mythological epic is concerned we have next to nothing. It is perhaps an indication that, though the form flourished in the Classical period, it flourished at the level of mediocrity. All the signs are that Roman mythological epic never cut much ice. As far as theme is concerned, Lucan represents the true Roman tradition of historical epic.

Lucan's raw material, then, like that of Naevius and Ennius, is Roman history. The dissimilarities are instructive. Naevius and Ennius wrote for a public which had virtually no native prose literature; it was the business of the poet to recover and give shape to the great events of the past, to appeal to the sense of pride of a whole people in its struggle against foreign foes and in its own destiny. Partisanship, both national partisanship and partisanship in favour of individuals (the poet's patron, for example), was excusable, indeed only to be expected, provided it remained discreet. Lucan writes for a public to whom the facts of the great Civil War of the previous century are familiar and readily accessible; if history was what was wanted, prose histories were available. As an historian Lucan is shamelessly, even boringly, partisan: he belongs to that special tradition of Roman historical writing which caters for the anti-patriotism of those who like to believe that the system is corrupt. In prose the great exponents of this kind of history are Sallust and Tacitus: both write for upper-class reactionaries. Lucan is a reactionary too, but with a slant. Pompey is cast in the role of the Stoic saint; his overthrow by the unscrupulous pragmatist Julius Caesar attains cosmic significance. Such one-sided preaching is only for the converted— and indeed only for the recent convert. Lucan's uncle, the veteran Stoic, primly reproves Cato (another of Lucan's heroes) for his lack of philosophical detachment and shows no particular enthusiasm, or even sympathy, for Pompey.

One can't help wondering who Lucan's audience were and how they took the parallels which are plainly to be drawn with their own day. The picture, for example, of the young Ptolemy swayed by unscrupulous advisers to accept a policy of cynical expediency (8. 536–8):

> All assented to the crime. The boy-king was pleased at the unaccustomed deference shown him by his slaves in allowing him to give orders for such a deed.

Or take Pothinus' words (8. 484–7):

> 'Ius et fas multos faciunt, Ptolemaee, nocentes;
> dat poenas laudata fides, cum sustinet,' inquit
> 'quos fortuna premit. fatis accede deisque,
> et cole felices, miseros fuge.'

> 'Doing what is right in the eyes of the gods and the law gets many into trouble, Ptolemy,' he said. 'Men find loyalty admirable, but when it means supporting those who have fortune against them, there is a penalty to be paid for loyalty. Side with fate and the gods, keep in with those whose luck is in, have nothing to do with those who are in trouble.'

And he goes on (8. 489–92):

> 'The power of kings is completely destroyed if they begin to take justice into account. Respect for what is right destroys the power of cities. It is his freedom to commit crimes, unrestrained resort to the sword which keeps the ruler who is hated safe.'

It is as impossible to believe that these shafts were not directed against Nero (who was seventeen when he came to power) and his hated advisers as it is to see no allusion to Seneca in the picture of the ineffectual Acoreus ('made mild by age and taught moderation by decrepitude') whose moderating influence is rejected. One would like to know what the elderly Seneca (who had tried indirect comment on the absolute corruption of absolute power himself in his tragedies) made of Lucan's youthful lack of caution.

All totalitarian regimes expose themselves, by the pretence of high moral principle which they affect, to counter-propaganda cloaked as censure of another age. Denunciation, open or implicit, of moral turpitude is not easily denied lip-service by those in power, so long as those who do the denouncing are careful to make it clear that their denunciation is directed against the universally recognized villains of mythology, or at least against those decently dead and buried. We have to remember, too, that no age sees itself as quite as wicked as it is. Its wickedness is after all only apparent to a few: to those who exercise power and their initiates (who easily delude themselves on the score of their own wickedness); to well-informed opponents of the regime; to the eyes of history when these are opened by historians whom indignation or detachment has aroused to candour. All the same, *On the Civil War* was clearly dangerous talk, and it can hardly be a matter for surprise that it destroyed its author. The poem belongs to the period between his first favour with Nero which secured his reception as a court poet (in AD 60 he won a prize for a poem on Nero) and his denunciation and suicide five years later for membership of the conspiracy of Piso. Three books only of *On the Civil War* were published, it seems, in Lucan's lifetime.

The features of Lucan's poem which irk the modern reader most are the shallowness and onesidedness of his characterization, and the long screeds of purple rhetoric, some of which he puts on the lips of his characters (in speeches which are often intolerably long), while others adorn the frequent outbursts of moral indignation to which Lucan gives vent in his own person. As a storyteller Lucan is by no means to be despised. One wishes indeed he had indulged his talent for narrative more.

Take *On the Civil War* 8, which tells the story of Pompey's flight after his defeat at Pharsalus in Thessaly (9 August 48 BC) and his murder in Egypt (some six weeks later, on 28 September 48) by the minions of the young Ptolemy. The structure of the final tragedy is roughly Virgilian, in that it can easily be regarded as falling into three acts: the flight to Lesbos and the reunion there of Pompey and his wife Cornelia (8. 1–202); the council of war in Cilicia (203–471); and the murder in Egypt. The three acts form an increasing triad. The first, brief and relatively subdued, stresses the relationship of affection between Pompey and his wife Cornelia. The second is an extended rhetorical exercise: a 65-line speech by Pompey defending his plans for enlisting the aid of the Parthians, and a speech nearly twice the length of Pompey's by Lentulus opposing Pompey, as a result of which the plan is rejected and they head for Egypt. In the third act, which occupies the last four hundred lines (472–872) the narrative is fuller; first comes the scene at the Egyptian court, then the murder and the burial of Pompey's truncated body.

In the two acts which form the first half of Book 8 Lucan's interest seems to be in writing speeches. The narrative tends to be confined to short, not very sharply visualized sections, almost extended bridge-passages, chiefly concerned with getting Lucan's hero from one place to another, and apt to turn aside into description of emotion at the expense of description of scene. The opening lines provide a typical example (8.

1–33; the translation is Nicholas Rowe's dignified, if somewhat free, version of 1718, described by Johnson as 'one of the greatest productions of English poetry'):

Now through the vale, by great Alcides made,
And the sweet maze of Tempe's pleasing shade,
Cheerless, the flying chief renew'd his speed,
And urg'd, with gory spurs, his fainting steed.
Fall'n from the former greatness of his mind,
He turns where doubtful paths obscurely wind.
The fellows of his flight increase his dread,
While hard behind the trampling horsemen tread;
He starts at every rustling of the trees,
And fears the whispers of each murmuring breeze.
He feels not yet, alas! his lost estate;
And though he flies, believes himself still great;
Imagines millions for his life are bid,
And rates his own, as he would Caesar's head.
Where'er his fear explores untrodden ways,
His well-known visage still his flight betrays.
Many he meets unknowing of his chance,
Whose gathering forces to his aid advance.
With gaze astonish'd, these their chief behold,
And scarce believe what by himself is told.
In vain to covert, from the world he flies,
Fortune still grieves him with pursuing eyes:
Still aggravates, still urges his disgrace,
And galls him with the thoughts of what he was.
His youthful triumph sadly now returns,
His Pontic and piratic wars he mourns,
While stung with secret shame and anxious care he burns.
Thus age to sorrows oft the great betrays,
When loss of empire comes with length of days.
Life and enjoyment still one end shall have,
Lest early misery prevent the grave.
The good that lasts not, was in vain bestow'd,
And ease, once past, becomes the present load:
Then let the wise, in fortune's kindest hour,
Still keep one safe retreat within his pow'r;
Let death be near, to guard him from surprise,
And free him, when the fickle goddess flies.

[Translation: Rowe]

One's first impression is of simple sense coded into the stock artificialities of epic style. Take the opening lines: they lack the sober gravity and the simple, strong rhythms of Ennius, as they lack Ovid's sinewy, sparkling liveliness or the subtle, graceful complexity of Virgil. Worst of all, they take a long time to say not much and the detail of what is said still remains unclear. Line 3:

> cornipedem exhaustum cursu stimulisque negantem

> urging on a horse exhausted by flight, to the spur unresponsive

aims at the grand manner, both in vocabulary (*cornipes*, 'horny-footed one', for horse) and in syntax (noun and agreeing participle form a frame round the line, two participles and two nouns chiastically arranged, but the chiasmus 'exhausted by flight, to the spur unresponsive' is both forced and flat). One feels Lucan is trying too hard; the context does not justify the claims asserted by vocabulary and syntax. The grand manner has been too consciously sought.

The same striving after effect is seen in such absurd phrases as (10–12):

> Seque, memor fati, tantae mercedis habere
> credit adhuc iugulum, quantam pro Caesaris ipse
> avolsa cervice daret.

> Mindful of his fate, he believes his throat worth no less a price
> than he himself would give for Caesar's severed neck.

Moreover, if Lucan is on Pompey's side, the talk of severed necks is unfortunate.

When he isn't straining after effect, Lucan tends to lapse into historical prose done into hexameters (14–18):

> Multi, Pharsalica castra
> cum peterent nondum fama prodente ruinas,
> occursu stupuere ducis, vertigine rerum
> attoniti, cladisque suae vix ipse fidelis
> auctor erat.

> Many, on their way to the fighting at Pharsalia, the report of the
> disaster not having reached them, were startled to encounter
> their leader, taken aback at the sudden change of fortune, and
> Pompey was hardly accepted as a reliable witness to his own
> defeat.

This kind of sentence, which climbs up to the key phrase (*occursu stupuere ducis*, 'were startled to encounter their leader'), then subsides in a series of explanatory amplifications, is good Livy, just as the dry irony of the final phrase (*cladisque suae vix ipse fidelis auctor erat*, 'and Pompey was hardly accepted as a reliable witness to his own defeat') is good Livy. But rather bad poetry. Virgil and Ovid avoid elaborately balanced prose syntax. In their long sentences, they build instead upon the simple gravity of Ennius; they distribute the emphasis more, so that the sentence does not turn on, or lead up to, a single phrase. The result is a complex sentence that retains the vitality which the tradition of epic narrative requires. The prose historian records the past: balance, static structure, are his tools of expression, enabling him to stand back from the events he records and fit them into an intellectual frame that stresses his detachment. The poet's task is to create the illusion of involvement, the flow of narrative scarce keeping pace with the events described as they occur in all their immediacy.

Nobody expects Lucan simply to model himself on Virgil. One can understand that a different personality and a different audience require a different technique. But one is entitled to complain that Lucan tries too hard with too little success. Sometimes, he hits the target, as in (27–29):

> Sic longius aevum
> destruit ingentes animos et vita superstes
> imperio.

> Thus length of days and life surviving power humble the proudest heart.

Too often, however, there is a wilfully obscure coding of simple sense that reminds us of bad Propertius. Line 25, for example:

> actaque lauriferae damnat Sullana iuventae.

Literally, 'he damns the Sullan deeds of a laurel-bestowing youth'. But Lucan means something like 'he curses the achievements which brought him the glory of a triumph as a young man in the days of Sulla' (a reference to Pompey's first triumph in 81–80 BC). Too often, too, we are given an ancient equivalent of the more heavy-handed, moralizing psychological insight with which a bad modern writer loads down his narrative, as in (29–31):

> Nisi summa dies cum fine bonorum
> adfuit et celeri praevertit tristia leto,
> dedecori est fortuna prior.

(literally, something like:

88

Unless our final day and end of happiness coincide and sorrow
is anticipated by speedy death, past greatness shames.)

Or take the next sentence (31–32):

> Quisquamne secundis
> tradere se fatis audet nisi morte parata?

Who dares to trust prosperity, unless preparations for death are
already made?

Unfortunately, this kind of forced paradox just does not stand up to
scrutiny. Lucan is no doubt intrigued by the idea that prosperity turns
sour after a crushing defeat. But this is not the immediate reaction of a
man fleeing from his pursuers. The abject figure of fear of lines 5–8 is
followed too closely by the embittered failure of lines 19–29 to be
psychologically convincing. A better poet would have put a narrative
interval between the two states of mind, and provided each with its own
objective correlative—a description, perhaps, of the end of the day would
have relaxed the tension and given Pompey time to recover his calm and
sink into embittered despondency. Lucan lacks the capacity to think
himself into the situation he is describing. Remaining outside it, he
substitues rhetoric for empathy. No doubt his fondness for paradox, his
straining to turn traditional wisdom upside down are morbid symptoms of
the time in which Lucan lived. Nor is it poetically illegitimate to project
the sensibility of the writer's present into a past age (Pompey had been
dead for about a hundred years); a poet is not after all writing history.
One's complaint is that it is not better done.

Lucan can do better, however. In the last four hundred lines of Book 8
the technique changes. The narrative of the murder (560–636) is stirring,
even dramatic. It is followed by the bizarre episode of the improvised
secret funeral under cover of darkness of the headless body of Pompey by
one of his former officers, a man called Cordus (lines 712–93). The
episode is too long to quote in full, but here is a specimen (743–58):

> Thus while he spoke, he saw where through the shade
> A slender flame its gleamy light display'd;
> There, as it chanc'd, abandon'd and unmourn'd,
> A poor neglected body lonely burn'd.
> He seiz'd the kindled brands; and 'Oh! (he said)
> Whoe'er thou art, forgive me, friendless shade;
> And though unpitied and forlorn thou lie,
> Thyself a better office shalt supply.
> If there be sense in souls departed, thine

To my great leader shall her rites resign:
With humble joy shall quit her meaner claim,
And blush to burn when Pompey wants the flame.'
He said; and, gathering in his garment, bore
The glowing fragments to the neighbouring shore.
There soon arriv'd, the noble trunk he found,
Half wash'd into the flood, half resting on the ground.
With diligence his hands a trench prepare,
Fit it around, and place the body there.
No cloven oaks in lofty order lie,
To lift the great patrician to the sky:
By chance a few poor planks were hard at hand,
By some late shipwreck cast upon the strand;
These pious Cordus gathers where they lay,
And plants about the chief, as best he may.

[Translation: Rowe]

For the modern reader the burial episode has an instant appeal. It is easy to regard it as the highlight of the book, but that is perhaps to rate the lines higher than they deserve. The episode shows Lucan capable, like Apuleius, of a kind of imaginative realism: the sardonic description of events that fall within the framework of the world as we know it (they aren't imagined and expressed, that is to say, within the traditional heroic or mythical framework) and are yet made to transcend the everyday. It is a talent any modern writer is expected to demonstrate and we are surprised by its rarity in ancient literature. There is the occasional flash of an eloquence that is more than rhetoric (721–3):

> Lucis maesta parum per densas Cynthia nubes
> praebebat, cano sed discolor aequore truncus
> conspicitur.

> A sad moon shed a too scanty light through thick clouds; but the headless body was visible by its different colour in the foaming waves.

But in the main the style is jejune, almost monotonous, as though it were important for the words not to stand in the way of the sordid fantasy of the scene which is being described.

How Lucan intended the burial episode is hard to say. Even before the narrative is complete, he breaks off to taunt Cordus for the timidity and stealth with which he completes the burial (778–92):

Now 'gan the glittering stars to fade away
Before the rosy promise of the day,
When the pale youth th'unfinish'd rites forsook,
And to the covert of his cave betook.
Ah! why thus rashly would thy fears disclaim
That only deed which must record thy name?
Ev'n Caesar's self shall just applause bestow,
And praise the Roman that inters his foe.
Securely tell him where his son is laid,
And he shall give thee back his mangled head.
But soon behold! the bolder youth returns,
While, half consum'd, the smouldering carcase burns;
Ere yet the cleansing fire had melted down
The fleshy muscles from the firmer bone,
He quench'd the relics in the briny wave,
And hid them hasty in a narrow grave:
Then with a stone the sacred dust he binds,
To guard it from the breath of scattering winds:
And lest some heedless mariner should come,
And violate the warrior's humble tomb,
Thus with a line the monument he keeps,
'Beneath this stone the once great Pompey sleeps!'

[Translation: Rowe]

And then, when the narrative is complete, it is followed immediately in mid-line by an angry denunciation of Cordus for confining to so mean and contemptible a resting place one whose achievements entitled him to claim the whole world as his tomb. How are we to take this final rhetorical flourish? Can Lucan just not help himself? Or is the burial episode composed tongue-in-cheek? Has Lucan taken a passage which evokes one of the most memorable themes from Greek legend (burial in defiance of authority as an act of obedience to a higher authority), famous from Sophocles' dramatization of it in his *Antigone*, and then turned that passage into an exercise in bizarre realism? Or does he challenge the reader to reflect that, when Antigone acted in open defiance without thought of the consequences, Cordus acts in abject terror and thus demeans the piety which has prompted his action?

VI   ROMAN DRAMA

Roman drama means for us thirty-seven plays, all in verse. Comedy is represented by Plautus (twenty-one plays, some incomplete) and

Terence (six plays); tragedy by the ten tragedies ascribed to Seneca (the *Octavia* may not be by him). It is a natural assumption that these were the great names in antiquity. Yet Aulus Gellius quotes a set of verses from the *De Poetis* of Vulcacius Sedigitus (late second century BC) listing in order of merit ten Roman comic writers: first comes Caecilius Statius; Plautus is second, Terence sixth. The twenty-seven comedies all belong to the Preclassical period (they were all produced, roughly speaking, during the fifty years 210–160 BC). The surviving tragedies belong to the middle of the first century AD and are thus some 200 to 250 years later than the comedies. We have in addition a large number of fragments from scores of other plays, comedies and tragedies, chiefly by dramatists of the Preclassical period.

That neither comedies nor tragedies survive from the Classical period seems to be explained by the fact that no plays of consequence were written. But that only comedies survive from the Preclassical period and only tragedies from the Postclassical period seems more like accident. Tragedy was as popular, apparently, with Roman audiences of the second century BC as comedy. Both comedies and tragedies continued to be written throughout the Classical and Postclassical periods.

The status of the drama changes completely, however. At the beginning of the Classical period it almost ceases to exist as a living form. No new tragedies seem to have been written for performance in the theatre after the death of Accius (about 90 BC), and few new comedies. The old plays continued to be performed throughout the Classical period. But clearly the drama did not occupy the place in the social life of the first century BC that it had occupied in the previous century.

Under Augustus and during the first century AD, the growth of private readings to invited audiences brought about a renewal of interest of a kind. The new plays were not performed in the theatre. The general public was more interested in what were called 'mimes' (a kind of music-hall show ranging from striptease to political satire) and in what we call 'shows'; later these were supplanted in their turn, and in the Postclassical period the popular entertainment *par excellence* became the gladiatorial contest in the Circus. The writer of plays is now little more than a dilettante. His plays are praised by his friends, but are written without thought that they will be staged, or even of how they might be staged. Pliny in a letter to his friend Caninius praises warmly a new comedy by a certain Vergilius Romanus, which he has just heard at a private reading: Vergilius had already written comedies, Pliny tells us, that rivalled those of Plautus and Terence. To listen to what he has to say about Vergilius' latest play, you would think Vergilius was a second Aristophanes. And then Pliny concludes his letter by saying he really must persuade the author to lend him the script so that Caninius can read the play: in other words, not even publication of the script seems to have been contemplated. Seneca was perhaps the one writer of the Postclassical period who took the writing of plays seriously.

With one exception, all the plays which have come down to us have a Greek, not a Roman setting. The human characters in all the Roman comedies we have (leaving out of account, that is, the occasional god) are Greeks, or at any rate inhabitants of the Hellenistic Greek-speaking world; the plays are in fact Roman adaptations of Greek plays, the successes of the previous hundred years. Seneca in his tragedies takes over the myths and legends used by the writers of Athenian tragedy 400 to 500 years before; and these are, of course, the myths and legends used by Homer and his contemporaries from the eighth century BC onwards. Clearly in doing so Seneca was following a well-established tradition. The exception is the *Octavia*, which is set in Rome at the court of Nero.

We hear of both comedies and tragedies with Roman characters in Roman settings (the tragedies based on episodes from Roman history) almost from the very beginnings of drama at Rome, though they never seem to have been as numerous as the Greek plays. We have titles and some fragments (the most significant from a *Brutus* by Accius). The position at Rome in the Preclassical period seems to have been much as it is with Shakespeare or the French classical theatre: plays on the old themes (Shakespeare's *Julius Caesar*, the Roman plays of Racine) continue to be written, but their supremacy is challenged by plays whose setting is England or France. How it came about that the *Octavia* is the only play with a Roman theme to survive is anybody's guess. Were the Roman plays just not as good? Or did the Roman literary public feel that history was better done in a narrative poem than in a play, and contemporary life just not the stuff for literature, but only for such non-poetic themes as satire and the mime? The thing is odd. If during the early period of provincialism there had been no plays on Roman themes, if such plays had come only later as Roman literature became more independent, it would have been easier to understand.

In the typical modern drawing-room comedy, such as has dominated the western stage from Molière, if not Shakespeare, until recent times, everything happens indoors. The typical device for bringing the characters together is the visit, usually with a change of set from act to act, since to have all the characters continuing to call on one character taxes plausibility. In the typical Roman comedy everything happens out of doors. Whereas in modern comedy the movement has been toward increasing naturalism of set, the typical Roman set is highly stylized (as in Racinian tragedy). The audience is asked to think of the set as representing a street. At the back are doors representing different houses, usually two houses, each belonging to a key character in the play. There is no reason to suppose the Roman stage had painted scenery, or realistic props of any kind. The characters meet in their comings and goings to and from the houses, and to and from town (conventionally represented by the exit on one side of the stage) or 'abroad' (conventionally represented by the exit on the other side of the stage). Occasionally characters fail to notice one another so that a twin action takes place on the stage, as often in Shakespeare. Dramatic asides and in Plautus non-dramatic asides (in which a character steps out of his part to take the audience into his confidence) are frequent. The actors wore masks. Female parts were played by men.

In a large open-air theatre, the illusion of intimacy possible in the small European theatre of the nineteenth and twentieth centuries (the typical London theatre holds only a few hundred people, all in relatively close proximity to the stage) is naturally impossible. The masks preclude facial expression in any case. As at Athens, Roman plays were normally presented only on special occasions—festivals (i.e., public holidays) and the like. There were no long runs and apparently only occasional repeat performances. If it sounds primitive, we should remember the same conditions of performance at Athens in the fifth and fourth centuries resulted in some of the greatest masterpieces of the western comic and tragic stage. The main difference at Rome was that the plays were produced throughout the Preclassical period in temporary theatres set up for the occasion (rather perhaps like the booths in a modern exhibition, or agricultural show).

VII   COMEDY AS ENTERTAINMENT: PLAUTUS'
The Brothers Menaechmus

Plautus (born about 250 BC) and the Roman theatre grew up together. He was some kind of stage carpenter, presumably an artisan who was called upon to get the stage ready when a festival was approaching. From that he graduated, it seems, to writing plays—comedies only, but a prodigious number of comedies (over 130 were attributed to him in antiquity).

The Latin word for a 'play' (*fabula*) is the word we also translate as 'story', as in Horace's well-known saying *de te fabula narratur* ('the story is told about you'). A play after all tells a story. In modern times the term 'plot' is also used, especially of plays, and it is convenient to make a distinction between the two words: 'story' stresses the yarn itself, the raw material, so to speak, before the writer has got to work on it; 'plot' stresses the way he puts his story together.

The stories Plautus chooses for his plays show considerable variety and individuality; he goes in for unusual settings, unconventional stories. His interest in plot—the plausibility and coherence of his story once he has put it together as a play—is slight. Comparison with Terence is instructive. Terence's plots are better constructed, more ingenious. Writing for an audience that was interested in plot-construction, he perhaps found it only sensible to borrow a good plot from a Greek play, or to make a new plot out of two Greek plays that had used the same basic plot. Plautus is content to get his plot out of the way as soon as he can. More than half his plays begin with a prologue in which the audience is told what has happened up to the point where the play begins, and given some idea of what is about to happen.

The Brothers Menaechmus is typical. It begins with a long prologue (76 lines) spoken in character (i.e., not in the author's persona, or impersonally on his behalf, as in Terence, but in the persona of an unnamed character). After some opening persiflage, the background to the plot is set out. Some further banter follows, then explanation of who is who is resumed, and in the concluding lines of the prologue the one detail of the coming action that it is important and safe to implant in the audience's mind at this point is disclosed (69–76):

> This, for the duration of the play, is the city of Epidamnus. When
> there's a different play, it'll be a different town. The people who
> live in the houses change in the same way: one day a pimp lives
> here, another a young man, another an old man—poor man,
> beggar, rich man, hanger-on, soothsayer, that's the way it
> goes.
>   Now the twin who lives in Syracuse is in Epidamnus today
> along with his servant, trying to track down that twin brother
> of his.

Before we accuse Plautus of dramatic naïveté it is as well to remember that this is a way of doing things which appealed also to Euripides. For both writers the function of plot is to generate dramatically effective situations. The plot of *The Brothers Menaechmus* does not bear a moment's serious reflection. It turns on a case of mistaken identity. For something like two-thirds of the action, nobody on stage is in any doubt which brother is which. Everybody except Sosicles' slave Messenio takes it for granted that Sosicles is his long-lost brother Menaechmus; for everybody except Messenio there is only one Menaechmus, and that is the Menaechmus who lives in Epidamnus. For Messenio too there is only one Menaechmus, and that is his master Sosicles (also known as Menaechmus), who has never till today set foot in Epidamnus. Nobody ever suspects for a moment that the person he is speaking to can't be the person he takes him for; even to Messenio and Menaechmus II (i.e., Sosicles), who are supposed to be looking for Menaechmus I, the possibility never occurs that the people who are acting so strangely all round them have mistaken one brother for the other. That Menaechmus I's wife, his mistress, his personal friend Peniculus, as well as Menaechmus II's personal slave Messenio, should all mistake one brother for another strains credulity beyond what is tolerable if one stops to consider the point outside the structure of the play; but that does not worry Plautus, any more than Shakespeare allows himself to be worried by similar implausibilities in *The Comedy of Errors* or in *Twelfth Night*. It is upon such conventions that the pseudo-naturalism of comedy depends. All that is required of the plot is an excuse for involving first one brother and then the other in a series of confrontations with different characters all of whom make the same mistake.

The plot is as complicated as it is improbable. It would need pages to get it straight, and would hardly be worth the trouble. The audience is not expected to keep the plot straight. What makes a Plautine comedy often hilarious and never less than lively is the way in which contrasted characters are thrown together at high speed. Since the Menaechmus brothers are to be mistaken for each other, the two characters cannot of course be too dissimilar, and yet it is desirable that the audience should feel that they are behaving differently. Plautus solves the problem by making both equally bewildered (that is what they have in common); and by giving Menaechmus I a bad conscience (he is deceiving his wife) while Menaechmus II is a model of good-humoured innocence, nothing loath to seize an opportunity when it presents itself (so that he passes a most agreeable afternoon in the company of his twin brother's mistress without ever comprehending why he has been so lucky), but not afraid to answer back sharply or to take extreme measures when provoked beyond endurance.

Plautus' interest in character, in short, is not our interest. He is interested in types rather than what we should call development of character. Here too he shows more independence than Terence, who concentrates on what was to pass in the Augustan Age for the stock formula for a Roman comedy: the honest (within limits), hard-headed father who has made a success of life and is determined to prevent his son from making a mess of his; the honest (within limits), soft-headed young man desperately in love with a girl he has no hope apparently of marrying; the more or less honest girl who has known better days in another part of the world and turns out in the end to have a heart of gold—and what is even better, a long-lost father who is willing to put up a dowry; the completely dishonest, clever, witty slave with a weakness for reaching simple objectives by the most devious routes, who proceeds from critical situation to critical situation and eventually manages (more by luck, or a sudden twist of the plot, than by good management) to bring the play to a happy ending.

Plautus clearly found it hard to take the elegant craftsmanship of the Athenian comedy of manners very seriously. His *Pseudolus* is a *reductio ad absurdum* of the romantic love plot that turns with bewildering speed on the ingenuity of the unscrupulous but resourceful household slave. Mostly he prefers simpler, more striking plots more calculated to appeal to the audience he had before him in the theatre. To introduce novelty it is sufficient to change one of the characters. In *The Pot of Gold* the love intrigue remains, but the centre of interest shifts to the girl's father, who is worried out of his wits at the thought of losing a treasure he had found concealed in his house; unlike Molière's *L'Avare*, this is not a play about a miser, but a kind of satire on the theme that riches bring more worry than they are worth. In *The Braggart Warrior* (*Miles Gloriosus*) the passionate lover is that stock military type, the professional army officer who fancies himself as a ladies' man and bores everybody to ill-repressed mirth by boasting of his non-existent campaigns: he is to crop up again many times in western literature from Shakespeare and Molière to Eugene O'Neill. It is not likely that Plautus invented him: the braggart warrior is cited in the prologue to *The Prisoners* (a comedy in which the love interest is eliminated altogether—there are no female parts at all) along with the lying pimp and the unscrupulous *meretrix* as types which Plautus has eliminated from his new play; but that the type was an instant success with a largely soldier audience can hardly be doubted.

In *The Brothers Menaechmus* the lover becomes a respectable bourgeois (still young, but a successful, shrewd businessman) who seeks consolation from his sharp-tongued wife with a fashionable mistress (terms like 'harlot' and 'whore' misrepresent the sophistication of Plautus' *meretrices*). Naturally he cuts a ridiculous figure, and the dramatic interest has to be sustained by another time-honoured theme, that of the long-lost brother; and the whole is then wound up tightly by the non-stop near-farce of a series of cases of mistaken identity.

Another way in which Plautus' unconcern with plot shows itself is in his trick of stopping the play while one of the characters delivers a long monologue to the audience. Though the action is set in some part of the Greek world, more often than not the monologue is a comment for the benefit of a Roman audience upon life at Rome. Here is an example.

Peniculus, believing himself tricked by his friend Menaechmus I (in reality it was Menaechmus II, who acted in all innocence), has tipped off Menaechmus I's wife about a dress Menaechmus I gave his mistress. The two are now lying in wait for Menaechmus I on his return from town (*The Brothers Menaechmus* 559–601):

WIFE

Why do I have to waste time putting up with being married
to a man who ransacks my house behind my back
and takes everything off to his mistress?

PENICULUS

Look, he's on his way back—couldn't be better.
He hasn't got the dress, though.

WIFE

What do I do with him?

PENICULUS

Same as usual. Get into a temper, that's my suggestion.
Let's go over here, you can hear what he says without being
spotted.

MENAECHMUS

What a stupid custom this is of ours,
such a nuisance, too, and yet the more important
we are, the more we cling to it!
Everybody wants to have lots of clients;
nobody asks whether they're honest men or rogues.
What the fellow's worth—that's what we ask;
not whether he's a reputation for keeping his word.
Nobody wants anything to do with a decent pauper;
a wealthy rogue, now—he's your model client.
Yet these fellows have no respect for law or anything else.
They only make trouble for their patrons.
They swear they never got what they've received, they're all the time in court,
greedy rogues, crooked as you make them,
get their money by usury and perjury.
They land up in court, so does their patron—
we've got to speak for the scoundrels,
whether it's a public hearing or one for judge and jury.
Today, for instance: client of mine gave me no end of trouble,
haven't been able to do what I wanted (or with whom),
couldn't get away from the fellow.

Had to put up a case to the aediles for all his rotten crimes—
whole string of them—proposed complicated, tricky settlements,
had argued my case as far as was necessary to get
a satisfactory agreement . . . fellow asks for a surety!
All the evidence against him—never saw a clearer case:
three witnesses keen as mustard for every one of his misdeeds.
Damnation on the fellow, the way
he's spoilt my day for me,
damnation take me too for ever setting
eyes on the Forum today.
Wasted a perfect day I have.
Had lunch all arranged.
My girl friend has been expecting me, I'll be bound.
Just as soon as I could I rushed
away from the Forum.
Suppose she's in a temper now with me.
The dress I gave her will calm her down a bit—
stole it from my wife and gave it to Erotion here.

By itself, Menaechmus' monologue is a witty, cynical cut at one of the most characteristic of Roman institutions, the patron–client relationship, based in typical Roman fashion upon mutual interest: the influential man of business or the man of assured social standing recognizes an obligation to protect the interests, before the courts and in other everyday dealings, of a group of men who depend on him for financial support and protection; in return they offer him their support in politics, or in the event of an outbreak of violence. It has remained a very typical Italian institution. But the monologue has really no place in a play which is supposed to be set in Greece. Plautus, one assumes, hardly cared: he knew it would arouse the interest of his audience to hear a character in a supposedly Greek play talk like a Roman about what the audience knew to be a typically Roman institution. Many in that audience had recently served in the campaigns in the south of Italy and Sicily. They would understand that what Menaechmus was describing was a Roman institution: an emerging awareness in his audience of their own identity as Romans enables Plautus to exploit the incongruity.

But the passage is more than a virtuoso cadenza, a clever monologue to dazzle the audience while the play stands still. True, Plautus is interested, almost more than in anything else, in language. A translation cannot convey the rapidity and sprightliness of the original. Almost any translation, moreover, will turn out to be half as long again as the original; Plautus' racy Latin is extraordinarily economical. Add to that his metrical virtuosity: as Menaechmus' excitement mounts (as he passes from the boring day he has had to thoughts of what he has missed), the metrical structure becomes lighter and more fast-moving, building up to a tempo that unwinds only in the last line of the scene, in which we come back to the plot. But the plot, though suspended, has not been forgotten. Menaechmus' monologue is overheard by his angry wife and by his equally angry friend Peniculus. We know they are there, Menaechmus does not. We listen to Menaechmus' complacent irritability at having his plans for an agreeable day with his mistress interfered with by an obligation, which Menaechmus recognizes and discharges while remaining agreeably cynical about the way his time has been wasted and the merits of his client, in full awareness of the trouble which is brewing. The longer he talks the more we wait for the storm to break. And then Plautus plays a trick on us: the storm does not break after all; it breaks instead two scenes later when Menaechmus' wife thinks she has caught her husband with the incriminating evidence in his hand. But she is wrong too: it is not her husband she has caught but his twin brother.

Plautine comedy is excellent entertainment. Though strictly a practical man of the theatre (a dramatist who writes 130 plays in a relatively short life—Plautus was about sixty when he died—has no time to be a perfectionist), he is a practical dramatist of genius. Nobody else is going to be quite as good at entertaining a Roman audience with a suitably cynical (but not too cynical) picture of the foibles of human nature for a long time, perhaps not until Ovid. Certainly it is not till we come to Ovid that we find again so deft and witty a stylist, or a writer who has so spontaneous a sense of fun. Entertainment is not everything. But for a long time after Plautus Roman literature is going to take itself rather more seriously than was good for it.

VIII   COMEDY AS PLOT: TERENCE'S *Phormio*

Plautus is said to have died in 184 BC, Terence to have been born in Carthage in either 195 or 185 BC. His first play was produced in Rome in 166. He wrote six plays altogether in the space of as many years; and then about 160 BC 'the African', as he was called (Publius Terentius Afer), disappeared from the Roman scene as abruptly and as mysteriously as he had appeared upon it.

If we know little about Plautus, we are told a good deal about Terence by his ancient biographer, but much of it is confused or suspect. How did it come about that a young African (a Numidian, perhaps—not, presumably, a Phoenician, and not of course a black), from Carthage of all places (the second great war which Rome fought against Carthage had ended only in 202, the third was to break out in 151) became the leading playwright in Latin and the leading Latin stylist of his day? True, there was already a tradition upon which to build: Terence is the successor, not merely to Plautus, but also to Ennius, who died in 169, three years or thereabouts before Terence's first comedy was performed: for as well as his great narrative poem on the history of Rome, Ennius wrote plays, mainly tragedies (including a Roman tragedy on the rape of the Sabine women), but also a couple of comedies. But, where Plautus and Ennius can be explained, Terence remains a mystery. Perhaps that accounts for the story which circulated in antiquity that the plays were actually the work of members of a group of Roman nobles, friends of Scipio Aemilianus (the man who was to destroy Carthage in 146 BC). Was somebody needed with some connexion with the theatre to lend his name to the plays when they were produced because it was not respectable for a Roman noble to stage plays? The dates do not fit very well, and Suetonius seems to have got his facts wrong. But that is not a reason for rejecting the story out of hand.

In time, Terence stands half-way between Livius' first play, or plays, in 240 BC and the Ciceronian age. Comedy has become a good deal more sophisticated. It is written with a different audience in mind. It perhaps takes its moral function a little more seriously—Terence certainly moralizes where Plautus is content to be funny. But some of the moral comment is well directed: for example, a thrust that marriage has nothing to do with love (*Phormio* 799–800):

CHREMES
Impossible to get her away.

DEMIPHO
How do you mean, impossible?

CHREMES
Because they are in love with one another.

DEMIPHO
What's that to do with us?

The plays show a new elegant purism of style. They are also duller. The only concession to fun is strictly stage comedy (Phormio forgets the name of the girl at a critical moment, Demipho's friends, appealed to for advice, resort to buck-passing and evasion). Terence is scrupulous about plot. A play by Plautus is of course something more than a sequence of comic situations strung together to entertain a popular audience (a sort of

101

ancient equivalent of the modern variety programme). But not much more. Terence's plots seem at first like the plots of Mozart's operas, meant to bewilder more than to be understood. Nobody in the audience, one imagines, took the trouble to get the plot straight in his head. But if one does take the trouble, the plots do work. A properly constructed plot was clearly for Terence a guarantee of artistic respectability: the more impossibly complicated, the better. Moreover, where Plautus was content to implant the facts his audience needed before the fun could start, Terence's prologues are real prologues, brief explanations from the author of where he got his play from, sharp answers to criticisms by rival dramatists, defences of his practice of departing from his originals. The tone is that of a man who takes his business too seriously to clown.

The reason for the difference in plot structure can hardly be simply that Terence translated different plays; the difference in technique must tell us something about the two dramatists. It is a sign also of a new kind of audience. Terence's prefaces are evidence that serious dramatic criticism is beginning; comedy is being treated as something more than popular entertainment.

We have to remember that between Plautus and Terence fall the last very active fifteen years of Ennius' poetic career, the period during which he wrote his verse history of Rome and established himself as the respected client of an important Roman nobleman, with whom he could claim to associate on easy terms. The position Ennius (and others too, no doubt) had won for poetry makes it easier to believe that Terence could become the protégé of a man like Scipio Aemilianus. Scipio was one of the first of the new line of Roman nobles to open his mind to new ideas and, in the modern phrase, take an active interest in the arts. From such a patron and his friends Terence could expect, not merely support, but informed criticism: it may have been this new, more intimate, better-informed relationship between wealthy patron and poet-protégé which led to the story, intended perhaps more as a joke than anything else, that Scipio and his friends had written Terence's plays for him.

Terence sets himself the rule that his plays must start from scratch: everything the audience needs to know has to emerge, as if naturally, from dialogue; from these data woven into the dramatic fabric itself, an intelligible, if complicated, plot must proceed through graspable complication after graspable complication to its final dénouement. The art of telling a story has become more self-conscious. Short of a prologue which tells us all we need to know before the play begins, the simplest device for putting the audience in possession of the state of affairs when the curtain rises is for one character to tell another what the situation is. The device works best if the character told is outside the main action.

Since he does not know what is going on, it is reasonable for somebody who does know to tell him.

In the *Phormio*, for example, Geta, who is very much part of the plot, waxes eloquent on the carryings-on of his master Antipho and his cousin Phaedria to a fellow-slave, Davos, who has called to pay the final instalment of a loan Geta had made to him. The two slaves form the first of a series of contrasting pairs in the play: they will be followed by the two cousins Antipho and Phaedria, the two brothers Demipho and Chremes, and (with a regrouping) the two schemers, the slave Geta and the parasite Phormio. It is a simple but effective recipe for securing a complex but coherent plot and also a set of sharply opposed characters. Conscious, perhaps, that the second slave has no place in his play except as Geta's confidant (he does not reappear after this opening scene), Terence almost overdoes the explanation for their meeting. Anyway, the two fall to gossiping, as slaves will, and Geta is only too eager for an opportunity to tell the story of all that has been going on while his young master's father has been on a business trip to Cilicia (*Phormio* 80–111):

GETA
No trouble with our man to begin with. Phaedria here
goes off at once and gets himself a girl—
plays the lyre, she does—and falls head over heels in love.
A slave girl, owned by a real dirty crook of a pimp.
Wasn't any money to buy her with—the boys' fathers
had seen to that.
Only thing to do was to feast our eyes,
follow her around, escort her to school and back again.
I wasn't busy, so I kept an eye on Phaedria.
Just opposite the school the girl went to
there was a barber's shop. We'd usually
wait for her there to come out and go home.
One day we're sitting there, a young fellow
comes along in tears. We were interested at once,
ask what's up. 'Never before today,' says he,
'have I known what a terrible business it is to be poor.
I saw a girl just now, close to where we are,
all in tears for her poor, dead mother.
There the mother was, laid out in front of us: not
a friend or relative or well-wisher in sight
to help with the funeral, apart from one old girl.
A rotten business.
The girl was a beauty, the sort that stands out in a crowd.'

103

Need I say more? He had us all curious. Antipho speaks up,
'Suppose we go and have a look?' Somebody says, 'Yes,
let's; show us the way, will you?' We go, we arrive,
we look her over. Pretty girl—all the more so, one
had to admit, for not having anything to
help her look attractive.
Hair undone, no shoes, in a mess,
all tears, dress dirty; if she hadn't been
a natural beauty, her looks would have been ruined.
'Not bad!' says our friend who had just fallen for
the lyre-player. My young master, though . . .

DAVOS
Don't tell me! He's fallen in love.

One sees at once how much is gained by making the groundwork of the plot a story in its own right instead of a quick summary sketched in by the speaker of the prologue. The fact that the girl Geta's young master has fallen in love with isn't just any girl is graphically impressed upon us; we learn something about Geta himself. The narrative also works well as narrative.

There is another barber's shop in Roman literature, and it is interesting to turn aside for a comparison of the two. The second is in an epistle which Horace wrote to his patron Maecenas about 20 BC. The setting this time is Rome (Terence's play is set in Athens); the actors are a successful lawyer and an auctioneer (the typical Roman small-time businessman); the time, if the lawyer, whose name is given as Philippus, is rightly identified with the consul of 91 BC, must be some sixty years after Terence set his narrative in a barber's shop. As Horace tells the story, however, it might have happened the other day: the barber's shop is the scene of a moral anecdote, an illustration of the point that Horace wishes to make to his patron: that sudden translation to material prosperity can be a mixed blessing for a man unaccustomed to the cares and responsibilities of material possessions. The goal aimed at, then, is different, but in both cases the barber's shop is the starting point: a scene from everyday life—the setting typical, but in that setting something occurs worth describing. It is one more instance of the curious continuity, despite the difference of place and time, between the picture of social life evoked in Roman comedy (set ostensibly in the Greek world of the second or third century BC) and the ostensibly real world evoked by the poetry of Catullus and Horace. Perhaps the Hellenistic world possessed the kind of stability which an ancient civilization past its prime sometimes does possess; perhaps it represented for the Romans an ideal to aim at from the

comparative crudity of social life in Rome, an ideal to be first created in
literature and then lived out in reality (Horace, *Epistles* 1. 7. 46–61):

Strenuus et fortis causisque Philippus agendis
clarus ab officiis octavam circiter horam
dum redit atque foro nimium distare Carinas
iam grandis natu queritur, conspexit, ut aiunt,
adrasum quendam vacua tonsoris in umbra
cultello proprios purgantem leniter unguis.
'Demetri'—puer hic non laeve iussa Philippi
accipiebat—'abi, quaere et refer, unde domo, quis,
cuius fortunae, quo sit patre quove patrono.'
it, redit et narrat, Volteium nomine Menam,
praeconem, tenui censu, sine crimine, notum
et properare loco et cessare et quaerere et uti,
gaudentem parvisque sodalibus et lare certo
et ludis et post decisa negotia campo.
'scitari libet ex ipso quodcumque refers: dic
ad cenam veniat.' non sane credere Mena.

Hard-working Philippus, well known for his appearances
in court, was on his way home one afternoon, his labours
over, grumbling that the Carinae were too far from the
Forum (for he was getting on in years) when he caught sight,
they say, of a fellow sitting in the shade of a barber's shop,
quietly doing his own nails after he'd had his shave.
'Demetrius'—this was the lad who attended, with some skill,
to Philippus' commands—'go, find out for me who that is, where
he lives, how he's doing, who's his father or his patron.'
He goes, returns, reports: Volteius Mena is the name,
auctioneer, modest circumstances, clean record, known
to work by fits and starts—makes his bit and spends it—
content with a few old friends, happy to have a roof over
his head, likes the games, enjoys a work-out in the Campus
when the day's business is over.
'I'd like to hear all this from the man himself. Tell him
to come to dinner.' Mena doesn't believe his ears.

The modern reader cannot fail to be struck by the social continuity
between the two anecdotes. Despite the century and a half which
separates Terence and Horace, the same easy, sure Roman tradition of
economy in telling a story is apparent. Compare Terence's *intus,
venimus, videmus* ('we set out, arrived and saw her') with Horace's *it,*

redit et narrat ('he went, returned and explained'): both are as authentically Roman in their terse, eloquent simplicity as Julius Caesar's famous *veni, vidi, vici* ('I came, I saw, I conquered').

Terence can give literary structure to a deep-seated Roman instinct for effective, incisive aphorism in anecdote. He is already something of a master of syntactical economy. But if he does not waste words in saying what he wants to say, he lacks Horace's mature, apparently artless grace; he is not, like Horace, a master of the easy flow of anecdote. The run of Terence's lines, like the run of his thought, is jerky. Nor has he Horace's dramatic economy, the gift for the single phrase that will evoke a whole scene.

But on the whole the job is well done, much better done than it could be done in a prologue. The mystery girl Antipho has fallen in love with, though she never appears on stage, is well on her way to becoming one of the main centres of interest in the play. The other girl, Phaedria's girl (for the plot is a double plot), is not allowed to steal her thunder: *she* remains a completely stock character, a run-of-the-mill member of the establishment of a high-class pimp. Or so we must presume, for she never appears either. The only female characters to appear on stage are the nurse of Antipho's girl and the wife of his uncle, both minor characters, though Chremes' wife has an important function in the dénouement of the play. Terence's usual practice is to keep his *jeunes premières* off the stage; in *The Girl from Andros*, for example, the heroine never appears; the women who do appear tend to be either servants or figures of fun (nagging wives, harlots assigned non-romantic parts); perhaps he felt that sympathetic female parts should not be played by male actors.

Like Plautus' *The Brothers Menaechmus*, the *Phormio* is the story of two brothers. Both are by conventional standards respectable businessmen in late middle age. Both are absent from Athens when the play opens. Chremes, who has rather nobler instincts than Demipho but is in the weaker situation morally, has been on a visit to Lemnos, to re-establish contact with a former mistress there; he has in mind to marry the daughter she bore him to the son of his brother Demipho; he finds, however, that mother and daughter have moved to Athens. It is reasonable to assume that Terence relied on his audience to put two and two together and conclude that the daughter is the beautiful mystery girl Demipho's son has fallen in love with. And he hasn't just fallen in love with her; as Geta goes on to tell Davos, in next to no time the two were married, thanks to Antipho's friend Phormio, who has thought up a story that Antipho was related to the girl and was thus obliged under Athenian law, as her nearest surviving kin, to marry her or find a husband for her.

The play is off to a promising start: the more alert in the audience have twigged that when Chremes returns, disappointed in his hopes of arranging a marriage, it will be to find his nephew already married, though he doesn't know it, to just the girl he wanted him to marry. Phormio's trumped-up story is actually true: Antipho *is* the girl's nearest unmarried kinsman. At line 485 a fresh emergency shifts the attention from Antipho and his girl to Phaedria and his girl, and the sub-plot gets under way: if Phaedria is to keep her, he will have to buy her from the pimp who owns her. Geta realizes it is another case for Phormio.

Back now to Antipho. Chremes has returned. Like his brother he takes it for granted that the girl his nephew has married is the sort of designing hussy that young men left on their own always fall into the clutches of. The brothers' only thoughts are to undo the marriage as quickly as possible. Rather than wriggle out of it by recourse to the courts in an action of doubtful legality and propriety, they are to bribe Phormio to take the girl back and marry her himself. The money will come from rents collected by Chremes on behalf of his (legal) wife on properties she owns in Lemnos. (Chremes thus adds embezzlement of his wife's money to bigamy.) Phormio (who has, of course, put Geta up to the deal) says he is willing to marry the girl if he is covered financially (he represents himself as being about to marry a girl with means). He has in fact no intention of doing so: his only reason for agreeing is that he wants to get his hands on the money so that he can do a second good turn (ably abetted as before by Geta), this time to Chremes' son, who needs three thousand drachmas to buy the girl *he* is in love with from the pimp who owns her.

It takes two-thirds of the play (four of the five acts into which it was divided in the Renaissance) to intertwine the threads of this double plot. The audience can see that Phormio will have to talk fast if Antipho is to keep the girl he has married and Phaedria to keep the girl whose freedom he has bought with the money his father has paid Phormio to take Antipho's girl back and marry her himself. Nobody, we may be sure, in Terence's audience was in much doubt that Phormio would pull off his double coup. But they would have been curious to see how he would manage it.

The resolution of the plot begins at line 728 with that most classical of dénouements, the recognition scene (what Aristotle called an *anagnorismos*). Here it takes the form of a chance encounter between Chremes and his daughter, accompanied by her old nurse. Naturally, it is the nurse that Chremes recognizes; she quickly spills the beans about the real identity of the girl whom Chremes and his brother are trying to get Phormio to take off their hands. Chremes' first thought on finding the marriage he had been hoping to arrange has already taken place is to call off the deal with Phormio.

A splendid piece of theatre begins at line 796. Chremes bursts on stage to tell Demipho the news and finds Demipho talking to Chremes' wife (the brothers have enlisted her aid in persuading the girl to go back to Phormio). He is thus confronted with the problem of explaining to his brother why Phormio must not be allowed to take the girl back, without giving the game away about his past indiscretions in Lemnos or the money he has subtracted from his wife's rents to pay Phormio.

The centre of the stage passes to Phormio, fresh from his double triumph: Antipho has married the girl he loves, and, thanks to the proceeds of the deal with the two fathers, Phaedria has been able to buy his girl from the pimp. And now that the two fathers are all anxiety to back out of the deal (having discovered the girl is Chremes' daughter after all), Phormio is freed from the problem of how to wriggle out of it himself. The only catch is that they want their money back. Phormio solves that problem by adding blackmail to sharp practice—as before, with the best of motives. He threatens to tell Chremes' wife all about the affair in Lemnos. His bluff is called. Phormio tells all. And then suddenly everything falls into place with no more sleight of hand than the comic dramatist is traditionally permitted when he has got all he wants out of his plot. Demipho talks his sister-in-law into forgiving Chremes. Phormio seizes the opportunity to explain the use to which he has put the three thousand drachmas. Chremes' wife instantly takes the side of her son—and Phormio—against her husband, and agrees to Phormio's suggestion to round everything off by inviting Phormio to dinner.

What the prevailing attitude was in second-century Roman society to the sowing of wild oats is hard to say. A century later, a Roman court was sufficiently indulgent of youthful folly for Cicero to be able to argue, on behalf of a client who was notoriously the ex-lover of a consul's widow, that youth must have its fling. (The widow was Clodia; Cicero's client, M. Caelius Rufus.) One suspects that Terence is writing primarily for the younger members of his audience, and that any admission that they had had their fling too in their day could have been only grudgingly wrung out of the fathers of family present; even more grudgingly, it is to be presumed, any admission that respectable elderly businessmen have affairs about which their wives know nothing; or that, when in a fix, they are as ready as their juniors in age or their social inferiors to resort to sharp practice.

Like all good comedy of manners, the plays of Terence derive their impact, not from the plausibility of the action (for it is wildly implausible), but from the universality of their social criticism. The characters are in the main stock characters, though well-drawn and well-contrasted stock characters, and the situations stock situations; but that only enhances the universality instead of diminishing it. It is hardly profound or penetrating social criticism. Terence's object is not to disturb his audience, to make them uneasily aware of things they would prefer to keep hidden even from themselves, or to force on them fresh insights about the human condition. It is the kind of social criticism which teases out into the open things that your own bad conscience makes you indulgent about in others; not the kind of social criticism which harangues, or forces into an emotional corner.

But there is one character who cannot be dismissed as stock, and that is the hero of the play. As Terence says in his prologue, 'It is the *parasitus* Phormio who will play the leading role and serve as the principal agent of the intrigue' (*primas partis qui aget, is erit Phormio parasitus, per quem res geretur maxume*). The modern reader finds it hard to decide what to make of Phormio. It would be nice to know how much he is already there as a fully developed character in Terence's model (a play by Apollodorus, called *The Claimant*, a title which suggests the habitual litigant rather than the *bon viveur*). One sign that Terence may have done a good deal to make a stock character his own is that, though Phormio is the mainspring throughout the double plot, the part is a comparatively short one. In the first two-thirds of the play he is on stage for only a hundred lines (315–440, a short scene with Geta, and then a scene in which Phormio pulls the leg of an increasingly furious Demipho, with Geta pretending to back up his master, but taking his lead all the time from Phormio). For much of the play he operates behind the scenes. He does not come into his own until the dénouement: from 829 till the play ends he is on the stage continuously.

The word *parasitus* means strictly 'one who eats at the same table', that is to say, a man who specializes in eating out at the tables of the well-to-do. (One has to remember the central role the dinner party played in Roman upper-class society.) In Greek comedy the 'parasite' is a stock type, the man who lives by his wits—a familiar type, clearly, in Athenian society. In Roman comedy the usual role of the *parasitus* seems to have been a minor and quite inglorious one (like Peniculus in Plautus' *The Brothers Menaechmus*). Perhaps when he came to write the *Phormio* (his last play but one, most probably) Terence saw the possibilities of the part.

It is a reasonable guess too that he made out of Phormio a personality more common in Roman society than in Greek. The Latin word corresponding to *parasitus* is *scurra*, for which one can ask no better definition than the admittedly biased definition put on the lips of Callicles in Plautus' *Trinummus* (199–211, 2 lines omitted):

There's no getting away from it: there's nothing stupider,
nothing more oafish, nothing more full of lies, nothing sharper,

nothing quicker to blurt out a secret or to break an oath than all
these smart men about town—these 'wits', as they call them.
They pretend to know everything, and don't know anything.
They know what everybody's thinking, or is going to think. They
know what His Majesty whispered in Her Majesty's ear, they
know what Juno was gossiping about with Jove. Things that
won't happen, things that aren't happening, they know about
them just the same. Whether they butter their informants up
with false praise or true, whether they get any man they care
into trouble, doesn't matter two hoots to them, so long as
they find out what they want to know.

We hear a lot about *scurrae* in Plautus. The type becomes a familiar one
in the pages of both poets and prose writers of the Classical period. But
Terence's Phormio is an interesting and distinctive development of the
type. Terence makes him an irreverent, witty, shameless defender of the
young against the narrow-minded moral hypocrisy of their elders. We
have to remember that in Roman society young men were completely in
the power of their fathers. Phormio delights in intrigue for the sake of
intrigue, confident he will be able to extricate himself from any scrape,
not just by ingenuity, like a witty slave, but with the bare-faced effrontery
of a free man. It is an interesting character, even if the apparently
motiveless pleasure in risk and intrigue is not made convincing. How
seriously, for example, are we to take the cynicism of the following lines
(327–35)?

PHORMIO
How many men do you reckon I've thrashed
within an inch of their lives: foreigners, citizens too?
The better I know 'em, the oftener. Well, tell me,
ever heard of anybody taking out an action against me?

GETA
How's that?

PHORMIO
Because you don't go setting a net for a hawk or a kite,
birds that do harm. It's the harmless birds people catch,
because there's money in it: nothing to be got out
of hawks and kites, always a chance, one way
or another, of squeezing something out of the rest.
People know I've got nothing. You'll say, 'They'll get a
conviction, hale you off to work for them.'
They don't want to feed a glutton. Sensible of them, I'd say.

110

The picture Phormio paints of himself a few lines later is more attractive, or more conventional (337–43):

GETA

Non pote satis pro merito ab illo tibi referri gratia.

PHORMIO

Immo enim nemo satis pro merito gratiam regi refert,
tene asymbolum venire unctum atque lautum e balineis,
otiosum ab animo, quom ille et cura et sumptu absumitur!
dum tibi fit quod placeat, ille ringitur; tu rideas,
prior bibas, prior decumbas; cena dubia adponitur.

GETA

Quid istuc verbist?

PHORMIO

Ubi tu dubites quid sumas potissimum.

GETA

My master can never repay you properly.

PHORMIO

No, it's a man's patron you never can repay.
You come empty-handed, fresh and scented from the baths,
nothing to worry about, while he's eaten up with worry
and expense. You do as you like, he makes a wry face.
You laugh, drink before he does, take your place
before he does. A problematic dinner is put in front of you.

GETA

How do you mean?

PHORMIO

The problem is to decide what to eat first.

Terence's Phormio is, of course, a larger-than-life *scurra*, a kind of cross between that charming fiction of P. G. Wodehouse, the lounge-lizard, and Robin Hood. It would be a mistake to suppose that in the best Roman society of the second century BC a Phormio was to be found at every dinner table. The implicit approval extended to him is extended to a dramatic fiction. But it is hard to believe that the most original of Terence's characters (though not, I think, the most successful—Phormio must have been a hard part to play convincingly) was not smiled on indulgently by his creator, and perhaps smiled at by the smart young noblemen who supported Terence and discussed his plays, as a version

111

larger than life of a type they recognized. Perhaps as a kind of *scurra* himself, Terence is to be pardoned for idealizing the part.

IX   RHETORICAL TRAGEDY: SENECA

In passing from Terence to Seneca we step across two centuries, from the middle of the second century BC to the middle of the first century AD (Seneca committed suicide in 65 AD). In between lies the whole of classical Roman literature. The technique of telling a story in verse has been studied and refined by the great masters of Roman storytelling, Virgil and Ovid, by Catullus, whose contribution to serious narrative technique, though confined to two poems (his *Attis* and his *Marriage of Peleus and Thetis*), is far from negligible, and by a score of lesser writers of verse, most of them known to us only as names, of from the paltriest fragments.

It would have been exciting to see what Virgil, a poet of the very first rank endowed with a keen dramatic sense and a genuine tragic insight, could have made of Roman tragedy. Or what Ovid, the cleverest and the wittiest of all Roman writers, did with tragedy (his *Medea* has not survived). But this is to speculate about what might have happened if the whole course of Roman literature had been different. Already by Virgil's day the old professional Roman drama (plays written for performance by men who made writing for the stage their business) had ceased to exist as a living form. The writing of plays for the stage came to an end, to all intents and purposes, about the close of the Preclassical period. The last of the old comic writers was Turpilius, who died as an old man in 103 BC; the last tragedian was Accius, who died about 90 BC—Cicero (born 106 BC) boasts that he heard him reminiscing more than once about his contemporaries; of the forty-five tragedies attributed to Accius, some 750 lines of fragments remain.

The state of the Roman stage during the first half of the Classical period seems to have been rather like that of grand opera, or even the symphony orchestra, in our own day. The old classics continued to be performed, and the performances were increasingly elaborate. Leading actors enjoyed great reputations, though by the middle of the century it seems that all the greatest Roman actors were already old men. A permanent theatre in stone on the Greek model, the gift to Rome of Pompey (Lucan's hero), was opened in 55 BC. Such theatres were to spread gradually all over the Roman world. But they were little used for the performance of plays. Drama as a creative act of communication between writer and audience had ceased to exist. It was not to be the only occasion in the western world when lavish conditions of performance came too late to save a form that had outlived its social usefulness. The only writers for the stage in the Classical period are the writers of mime, a sort of variety show with political overtones, still in verse, but essentially popular in its appeal, the medium, it seems, for a new class of performer in the Roman theatre, the glamorous female actress. Those who thought of themselves as poets preferred to attach themselves to a wealthy patron whose achievements they could make the subject of an historical epic. Those who took poetry more seriously (poets like Catullus, Virgil and Horace) were struggling to win a new status for poets and poetry, even if that meant losing all contact with a popular audience.

In the Augustan Age the drama undergoes a kind of revival. But it is drama of a different kind. The explanation lies once again in a change in the status of those who write. The dilettante noble in the Augustan Age who wrote plays was not interested in having them staged in the old way. It was not respectable to put plays on the stage; to do so meant you were a professional, at the beck and call of those who organized performances, subject to the whim of a popular audience.

The dilettante dramatists included, it is true, several distinguished men of letters. One was Asinius Pollio, a young contemporary and acquaintance of Catullus, afterwards a friend of Virgil and Horace, and an historian of some consequence, who established the first public library in Rome; he also wrote tragedies, about which both Virgil and Horace are politely complimentary; Horace even talks of their being staged, but probably that is part of the compliment. Another amateur tragedian was Varius, the leading epic poet of the generation before Virgil, and Virgil's literary executor; he wrote one play, a *Thyestes*, which was actually performed, it seems, at the games in celebration of the battle of Actium (clearly a prestige occasion). Then there is Ovid's *Medea*—presumably never performed, since later in life Ovid boasted he had never written for the stage. Horace took the writing of plays seriously enough to express his views on the subject, along with his views on how to write epic (the two forms treated by Aristotle in the *Poetics*, but also two forms practised by dilettanti in Horace's day), in a verse epistle which acquired more authority than it deserved. The custom of writing plays for reading to a small audience continued throughout the first century AD. One is left with the impression that to try your hand at tragedy (tragedy rather than comedy) was the done thing if you fancied yourself as a writer. Seneca was thus in good company when, having established his reputation as a man of letters in another field, he turned his attention to tragedy.

It is strange that a writer who did not even have the stage in mind should have had so immense an effect upon the English Elizabethan and the French seventeenth-century stage. The paradox was stated by T. S. Eliot in an introduction, which has since become famous, to a 1927 reprint of a volume of Elizabethan translations of Seneca:

> No author exercised a wider or a deeper influence upon the Elizabethan mind or upon the Elizabethan form of tragedy than did Seneca. . . . In the Renaissance, no Latin author was more highly esteemed than Seneca; in modern times, few Latin authors have been more consistently damned. The prose Seneca . . . still enjoys a measure of tepid praise. . .; but the poet and tragedian receives from the historians and critics of Latin literature the most universal reprobation. . . . Yet this is a dramatist whom Scaliger preferred to Euripides, and whom the whole of Europe in the Renaissance delighted to honour.

If one has to give a short explanation, it is presumably that the Renaissance saw Seneca as a tragic equivalent of Plautus, a Latin poet to provide inspiration and a starting point. They had to start from Seneca because the much greater Greek models were not generally accessible: not accessible, certainly, to Shakespeare; not even thoroughly familiar, it seems, to a Greek scholar of some standing such as Racine. But as far as the Elizabethans are concerned, that is not the whole explanation. Clearly, Seneca's insight into the crazed mind (the absolute, maniacal power of the tyrant, the mad lust for revenge) aroused a sympathetic response in a world in which violence was everywhere present as one of the realities of life.

Since Seneca's plays were not written for performance in the theatre, so that pursuit of the dramatic experience in what most would regard as its purest form (the involvement of the spectator in the spectacle enacted before his eyes) is abandoned, it is reasonable to ask what goals Seneca set himself. He seems to have been little concerned to create the illusion of dramatic enactment in his listeners' minds: his plays are only casually dramatic in structure—a series of scenes (mainly very long speeches with the barest minimum of dialogue sketched in almost casually) spaced out by longish choral interludes. In strictly dramatic terms, the tragedies are hard to defend. Nor are they much easier to defend as poetry: they are, of course, in verse, like all ancient plays; but there is very little of the imaginative spontaneity, or even of the eloquence of poetry. Though at times attractive in its simplicity (Seneca seems to have set out to recapture the simple diction of his Athenian models), the style is more often jejune and staccato.

The most distinctive quality of the tragedies is the pursuit of the macabre. It sounds perhaps a back-handed compliment, but there is a place in literature for the macabre, and Seneca's experiments with the genre are not uniformly grotesque; or rather there are occasions when the grotesqueness is not inappropriate. It offers opportunities for the particular kind of rhetoric which Seneca is able to command. Not the splendid, exuberant, boyish rhetoric of Lucan that lets no occasion slip, and packs more verbal fireworks into each line than most occasions can justify. Not the angry, hectoring, table-beating rhetoric of Juvenal. Seneca's rhetoric is the pointed, forced, barbed rhetoric of a man whose real medium is the witty, analytic, quick-stabbing prose of the *Moral Epistles*. True, the iambic trimeter and the other metres at the disposal of the Roman dramatist (even the anapaestic metres) lack the surging flow of the hexameter. But that alone does not account for the curious frigidity of Seneca. (It is one of the ways in which the tragedies on traditional themes differ from the *Octavia*.) The lack of flow is in the thought as well as in the metrical line. Seneca is not dull like Statius, whose *Thebaid* is a curious anachronism, a century and a half out of date, the sort of thing, it is to be supposed, people were writing in Virgil's youth. But Seneca's imagination is ingenious, contriving, rather than poetic. His style lacks passion, and therefore eloquence. He needs an argument, a long speech (his plays are filled with insufferably long speeches) to build up the kind of momentum of thought (the vacillation of a character between successive moods, for example) that Ovid could create in a few lines, apparently without effort. He is at his best in the long purple patch of narrative.

Given his limitations, Seneca's instinct was sound to make his messengers' speeches (or their equivalent on the lips of other characters) something more than a dramatically effective springing of the plot. In his hands they attain something like the sustained showiness of the epyllion, or those special showpieces in the epyllion tradition which Virgil occasionally incorporated into the *Aeneid* (the Cacus episode, for example, in *Aeneid* 8), or of which Ovid made much freer use in the *Metamorphoses* (as in the story of Tereus and Philomela). Take these lines from Theseus' long narrative to Amphitryon of Hercules' descent to Hell (*Hercules Furens* 762–81: Hercules is crossing the Styx); Jasper Heywood's version is slow-moving but truthful to the Latin:

THESEUS

A dyre and dredfull stone there is the slouthfull foordes fast bye,
Where sluggish freat with wave aston'd full dull and slowe doth lye:
This lake a dredfull fellow keepes both of attire and sight,
And quaking Ghosts doth over beare an aged ugly wyght:
His Bearde unkempt, his bosome foule deform'de in filthy wyse

A knot byndes in, full lothesome stand in head his hollowe eyes:
He Feary man doth steare about his Boate with his long Ore.
He driving nowe his lightned Ship of burden towarde the Shore,
Repayres to waves: and then his way Alcides doth requyre,
The flocke of Ghosts all geving place: alowde cryes Charon dyre,
What way attemptest thou so bolde? thy hastening pace here stay.
But Nathales Alcmenaes sonne abyding no delay,
Even with his owne poale bet he dothe full tame the shipman make,
And clymes the ship: the barke that coulde full many peoples take,
Did yelde to one: he sat, the boate more heavy like to breake
With shyvering joyntes on eyther syde the lethey floud doth leake.
Then tremble all the monsters huge, the Centaures fierce of myght,
And Lapithes, kindled with much wyne to warres and bloudy fight,
The lowest Chanelles seeking out of Stygian poole a downe,
His Lerney labour sore affright his fertile heads doth drowne.

[Translation: Heywood]

Not only the conception of Charon as the filthy, ill-kempt boatman who ferries his charges across the repulsive waters of the river of death, but also detail after detail of the description is lifted from Virgil's ironically stylized portrait of Charon in *Aeneid* 6. But in Virgil Charon earns his keep: he is an integral part of the fantasy-world of horror that Virgil creates in the first half of *Aeneid* 6. In Seneca, Charon is incidental embellishment. And in *Aeneid* 6 Virgil makes out of Charon two passages of fresh, sinewy, vivid, ironical verbal poetry. Seneca's narrative is dull, forced, pointless, except as a challenge to a greater poet, comparison with whom can only tell against Seneca.

When we talk of the macabre in Seneca, however, we mean (and these are the passages which stimulated the imagination and the pens of the Elizabethan dramatists) the detailed descriptions of murder and mangled corpses: the messenger's speech in the *Thyestes*, for example, which describes how Atreus sacrificed his brother's sons and then prepared the bodies for a banquet. Or these lines, which tell how Thyestes, having feasted upon the banquet prepared for him by his brother to celebrate his return, falls into a strange foreboding (*Thyestes* 965–1005):

THYESTES

I wretch would not so feare, but yet me drawes
A trembling terrour: downe myne eyes do shed
Their sodayne teares and yet I know no cause.
It is a greefe, or feare? or els hath teares great joy it
    selfe.

116

ATREUS

Lette us this daye with one consente (O brother celebrate)
This daye my sceptors may confyrme, and stablish my estate,
And faythfull bonde of peace and love betwene us ratifye.

THYESTES

Enough with meate and eke with wyne, now satisfyed am I.
But yet of all my joyes it were a great encrease to mee,
If now about my syde I might my litle children see.

ATREUS

Beleeve that here even in thyne armes thy children present be.
For here they are, and shalbe here, no part of them fro thee
Sal be withhelde: their loved lookes now geve to thee I wil,
And with the heape of all his babes, the father fully fyll.
Thou shalt be glutted feare thou not: they with my boyes as yet
The joyful sacrifyces make at borde where children sit.
They shalbe cald, the frendly cup now take of curtesy
With wyne upfylde.

THYESTES

Of brothers feast I take ful willingly
The fynal gyft, shed some to gods of this our fathers lande,
Then let the rest be dronke, what's this? in no wyse wil my hand
Obeye: the payse increaseth sore, and downe myne arme doth
    sway.
And from my lippes the wasting wyne it selfe doth flye away,
And in deceived mouth, about my jawes it runneth rounde.
The table to, it selfe doth shake and leape from trembling ground.
Scant burnes the fyre: the ayre it selfe with heavy chere to sight
Forsooke of sonne amased is betweene the day and night.
What meaneth this? yet more and more of backward beaten skye
The compas falles, and thicker myst the world doth overly
Then blackest darkenes, and the night in night it selfe doth hyde.
All starres be fled, what so it bee my brother God provyde
And soones to spare: the Gods so graunt that all this tempest fall
On this vyle head: but now restore to me my children all.

ATREUS

I wil, and never day agayne shal them from thee withdraw.

THYESTES

What tumult tumbleth so my guttes, and doth my bowels
    gnaw?

117

What quakes within? with heavy payse I feele my selfe opprest,
And with an other voyce then myne bewayles my doleful brest:
Come nere my sonnes, for you now doth thunhappy father call:
Come nere, for you once seene, this griefe would soone asswage and
    fall.
Whence murmure they?

ATREUS

With fathers armes embrace them
quickly now

For here they are loe come to thee: dost thou they children know?

[Translation: Heywood]

Once again comparison is instructive, this time with Ovid. The story of
Thyestes is not told in the *Metamorphoses*; but let us return to the story of
how Philomela, having been raped by her brother-in-law and her tongue
torn out, escapes and joins forces with her sister Procne to prepare a
banquet for Tereus of the flesh of his (and Procne's) son Itys. The
banquet is served by Procne, with Philomela present but concealed
(*Metamorphoses* 6. 644–60):

And while some life and soule was in his members yit,
In gobbits they them rent: whereof were some in Pipkins boyld,
And other some on hissing spits against the fire were broyld:
And with the gellied bloud of him was all the chamber foyld.
To this same banket *Progne* bade hir husband, knowing nought,
Nor nought mistrusting of the harme and lewdnesse she had wrought.
And feyning a solemnitie according to the guise
Of *Athens*, at the which there might be none in any wise
Besides hir husband and hir selfe, she banist from the same
Hir householde folke and sojourners, and such as guestwise came.
King *Tereus* sitting in the throne of his forefathers, fed
And swallowed downe the selfe same flesh that of his bowels bred.
And he (so blinded was his heart) fetch *Itys* hither, sed.
No lenger hir most cruell joy dissemble could the Queene,
But of hir murther coveting the messenger to beene,
She said: the thing thou askest for, thou hast within. About
He looked round, and asked where? To put him out of dout,
As he was yet demaunding where, and calling for him: out
Lept *Philomele* with scattred haire aflaight like one that fled
Had from some fray where slaughter was, and threw the bloudy head
Of *Itys* in his fathers face. And never more was shee
Desirous to have had hir speache, that able she might be
Hir inward joy with worthie wordes to witnesse franke and free.

[Translation: Golding]

118

In Ovid, we are insulated from the shock by the form; in Seneca, the form enhances the horror. True, the comparison is not altogether fair: though Atreus, like Philomela, is motivated by revenge—and revenge for a similar crime (Thyestes has raped Atreus' wife Aerope)—Atreus is in no sense an attractive figure, whereas Ovid wants the reader on the side of Philomela and her sister. Seneca's subject is how one act of madness leads to another in the working out of a curse; Ovid's subject is, as usual, a *tour de force*, a sentimental story set in a context of horror, in which, despite the horror of her acts, the beautiful victim of the king's lust remains a heroine who can arouse our pity. Seneca has to cope with something approaching moral earnestness; his story is not just the narrative of horror for its own sake; the horror is an illustration of how power corrupts the moral sense. Ovid can relate the horror with gusto and at the same time underplay it by the context of elegant irony which his complex of stories collectively creates for each individual story. But this is only to explain failure on the one hand, and success on the other. The storyteller-moralist does not have to pile on horror quite so clumsily as Seneca does; a narrative of events calculated to inspire horror (moral or otherwise) does not have to be so pedestrian.

CHAPTER 3

The Poet as Teacher

I TEACHER OR CRAFTSMAN?

In ancient Greece the notion of the poet as a teacher was a familiar one. When in the *Frogs* Aristophanes makes Dionysus, the god of poetry, appeal first to Euripides and then to Aeschylus for advice on what Athens should do, he provides a comic context for a deep-seated, traditional attitude: that the man who has a special power over words must also have a special insight into things. Naturally, with time, the poet's authority came to be contested. The debate between those who grant him no more than a technical competence and those who claim that he possesses, through personal experience or through study, a special revelation of truth continues to the present day. But for the Greeks poets were important people.

It is true that the poem which deals expressly in information, whose sole purpose is to give a true account of something, is a special case. To our eyes a poem on such a subject seems closer to paraliterature than to literature proper. But that is to take a somewhat sophisticated view of the matter. The first poetic storytellers—Homer and the other writers of early epic—hardly thought of themselves as making their stories up. Homer, like Virgil after him, claims to be reporting what the Muse has told him. If Virgil could distinguish (like Aristotle) between history and fiction, or (like Livy) between history and legend, it is by no means clear that Homer would have understood these distinctions. He might have admitted that he put words on his characters' lips that were appropriate to the dramatic situation. But then the historian Thucydides was to do much the same, quite openly, several centuries later. Nor is Homer above dealing openly in information. He will pause to set the facts right about a place, a man, an event: he is assumed to have special, expert knowledge of the things he writes about; to be able to inform his readers, in passing, if the information is out of the way or intrinsically interesting.

This double role of the poet as craftsman and as teacher is challenged first by the emergence of specialists: the philosopher, the historian, the antiquarian or literary scholar. Thus Plato makes Socrates deny poets a rational understanding of their own work, and in the *Republic* he banishes poets from his commonwealth as mischievous, while continuing in other dialogues (the *Ion,* the *Protagoras*) to acknowledge the validity of the poet's moral insight, even if it takes a philosopher to interpret the poet's inspired utterance.

At Rome the poet began strictly as a craftsman. His only function in society was to tell a story. That function, moreover, was a novel one in Roman society, and for a long time the Roman poet had to face the fact that at Rome poetry cut little ice: poetry was not, indeed it was never to become, what it had long been in the more advanced Greek city-states—an activity central to social life. If the story the Roman poet-storyteller told was to express social criticism, it had to do so indirectly and circumspectly.

The role of teacher, openly claimed and acknowledged as such, at any rate by intellectuals, arises in two distinct contexts. We may call them the 'public' context and the 'personal' context. (These terms will be discussed more fully in Chapter 4.) In his public context, the poet's role is, at any rate ostensibly, impersonal, to communicate information: we call such poetry 'didactic' poetry. In the context of personal poetry the role of the poet as teacher is to communicate insight (the moral insight, say, of Horace in his *Odes*), or to take a personal stand against contemporary society, to castigate its foibles and its vices in satire. The contexts are distinct, even if in practice the lines of demarcation are not as rigid as I make them sound. In this chapter, the discussion will be confined to didactic poetry proper; the role of the personal poet as teacher will be considered in Chapter 4.

II DIDACTIC POETRY

Everyone knows what a didactic poem is. It is (to take the leading Roman examples) a poem like Lucretius' *On the Universe,* Virgil's *Georgics* and Ovid's *Art of Love.* We may add to our short list Manilius' *On the Stars,* that dull erudite poem on which A. E. Housman squandered half a lifetime. And there were others (something will be said about them in the next section). But these three are the poems which spring first to the mind.

One can see that Ovid's *Metamorphoses* has some claim to rank as a didactic poem: it belongs in fact to that particular offshoot of the didactic tradition, the aetiological poem, of which the *Aetia* of Callimachus was the best-known model and the fourth book of Propertius a thoroughly Callimachean Roman example, and perhaps Ovid's immediate precedent in the *Fasti*. But where the *Metamorphoses* and the *Fasti* are concerned, it is clear that the assertion of a didactic purpose is no more than casually affected; it is not backed up by the structure of the poems in question, but serves merely as an excuse for a string of legendary tales and is constantly lost sight of while the tales are told. To treat the *Fasti* as a kind of Roman prototype of modern studies in cultural anthropology would be absurd. The poem may be a rich source of material for the modern cultural anthropologist, as Frazer's great edition of the *Fasti* demonstrates, but what may be found in the poem, if one cares to look, is another matter.

Essential to the notion of the didactic poem is that its primary object is to instruct; or rather, that the primary assertion of the poetic structure is that instruction is taking place. The primary assertion may not (to come now to the writer's attitude to his subject) be one we are expected to take seriously. It is evident that, though Ovid's *Art of Love* purports to instruct, the instruction is imparted tongue-in-cheek. But instruction tongue-in-cheek is instruction none the less.

The distinction between structure and intention is important and, where Ovid's *Art of Love* is concerned, easily understood. It is its irreproachable adherence to didactic structure which makes the poem a mockery of didacticism. At the same time the *Art of Love* makes plainer an element which all three of our leading examples of the Roman didactic poem have in common. The common element is an air of eccentricity. One wonders in each case why the poem was written at all. Where the *Art of Love* is concerned one need hardly wonder for long: a handbook on seduction is an obvious mockery of an established genre, though in itself some indication, perhaps, that the genre laid itself open to mockery. But when we read the others, too, the feeling that they can't be just what they pretend to be cannot be thrust aside. Some explanation seems called for. In the Rome of Julius Caesar and Augustus, the proper medium for such subjects, we tell ourselves, is prose; to write a handbook on physics or on farming in verse seems odd, even perverse: surely the thing is easier done in prose.

As a matter of fact, the contrary appears to be the case: verse of a kind actually seems easier than prose. George Bernard Shaw, we are told, having to put his novel *Cashel Byron's Profession* together in a hurry, claimed that he had tossed off a first version in heroic couplets, because it was quicker. (Quiller Couch, quoting Shaw, observed that Shaw might perhaps have found his story even more ductile in the medium of *Hiawatha*.) Verse, so long as you leave out all the things that justify verse, is easy to write. Lucretius may well have found those long technical discussions of his atomic theory easier to manipulate in the conventions of hexameter verse than we might have supposed. All the same, that can hardly be why he, or Virgil, or Ovid, chose verse in preference to prose.

The fact is that the didactic poem is a survival. If Lucretius, Virgil and Ovid had a choice, and exercised it in favour of verse, Hesiod (whose *Works and Days* must be reckoned the first didactic poem), or the early Greek philosophers Parmenides and Empedocles (who used verse to express their ideas about the physical nature of the universe), had little choice. The only medium available to them for sustained organized statement was verse. If Anaximander and Heraclitus turned to prose, the writings of the former were not extensive, while Heraclitus was notoriously obscure. We need not doubt that in the seventh, sixth and early fifth centuries BC prose of a kind existed, that even then politicians made speeches (though one remembers Aristotle's dry observation at the beginning of the *Politics* that the nature of politics changed when states passed out of the hands of generals into the hands of people who were good talkers). But for centuries the medium for all organized, structured statement intended to last was verse: hexameter verse (unless you had some kind of song in mind) cast in the standard Ionic verse dialect which became the literary lingua franca of the post-Homeric Greek world.

To call this early didactic verse 'prose that scanned' is to be guilty of an anachronism: prose able to cope with that kind of intellectual sophistication did not exist. If one can't exactly say the thing was impossible in prose, one can see that it would have been difficult and eccentric to attempt it: such prose as did exist lacked the dignity, the authority of verse. It was not unreasonable, however, for Aristotle to deny this didactic verse the status of poetry; in his view of the matter, the essence of poetry (unless you were talking about song, but there was no risk of confusing didactic verse with song) was plot. Hexameter verse, if it was to count as poetry, had to tell a story; it had, to use Aristotle's term, to be a *mimesis*. Didactic verse obviously didn't qualify.

By the time Lucretius came to write *On the Universe,* the situation was quite different. Didactic prose at Rome was almost as old as the beginnings of Roman literature. Already in the Preclassical period we can point to Cato's treatise *On Agriculture*; in the Classical period there is a whole string of prose treatises, works such as Varro's *On the Latin Language,* or Vitruvius' *On Architecture.*

The treatises of Cato, Varro, Vitruvius and the rest are not literature. They must be classed as paraliterature; their objective is to be useful in a practical context. No reader expects of such works more than that they will be clear and not offensively illiterate. If many modern writers of textbooks fall rather shorter of this requirement than Cato, Varro and

Vitruvius, it is because, though experts in their subject, they have had no rhetorical training. But the fact that you are a competent writer does not mean that what you write is literature. That depends on what you write about, and how.

At Rome in the Classical period *verse* treatises like *On the Universe* and the *Georgics,* though not isolated cases, are the exception, therefore, not the rule; they are in some degree anomalous. The fact that they are in verse calls for an explanation. The explanation is not far to seek. It is that the author thinks of his treatise as something more than a handbook; he expects it to be taken as literature too; perhaps more as literature than as a handbook. The practical objective is in some measure overshadowed, or concealed, or has vanished altogether. If, in other words, a writer in the last century BC chooses to write a treatise on physics or on farming in verse, it is a fair assumption that considerations other than practical necessity dictated his choice.

Once again, a look at our own day can help. Alongside the textbook pure and simple there exists today the kind of work that is intended to arouse natural curiosity about a subject (primitive art, say, or modern French music) which is generally agreed to be important, but which is not of immediate practical concern. In a literate, civilized society there is a demand for books on such subjects. Because they are not read as textbooks, but out of little more than mild curiosity about the subject, they have to be decently written. Collections like the *Pelican* books, the French *Que Sais-je?* series, are examples; in modern times books like these form a large part of the non-fiction list of most publishers.

Such books approach the frontier which separates paraliterature from literature. Some cross that frontier. They cross it because they possess, in a marked degree, some of the qualities (wit, intellectual strength, sensitivity of insight into the human condition, imagination) which we do not require of the author of a textbook, and do not expect, in more than a modest degree, of the general run of writers of books which are something more than textbooks. If those who cross the frontier are good enough to last, whatever doubt existed about their status ceases with the passage of time. But the number of those who cross the frontier is not large.

There exists, however, within this group of didactic works which are something more than textbooks a class of work whose status is less easily settled. The best contemporary examples are perhaps those very large biographical works which are written by professional writers of biographies to cater for the appetite of a reading public jaded by a surfeit of fiction at a time when the typical modern form of story (or *mimesis*), the novel, is coming to be felt as a dying genre. Take Michael Holroyd's life of Lytton Strachey. One imagines that the typical reader's curiosity about Strachey could be satisfied much more quickly and more efficiently by the kind of book described in the previous paragraph. The reader who takes up Michael Holroyd's two large volumes is responding to the author's challenge to participate in a sophisticated intellectual entertainment. Naturally, he is presented in the course of that entertainment with a great deal of information about Lytton Strachey; if he is to read the book intelligently, he must acquire as he goes along some kind of working knowledge of who is who, much as he would if he were reading a large historical novel. But most readers of such biographies make no serious attempt to master the information; they expect information in abundance as a kind of guarantee that the author has done his homework. They are prepared to makes some effort to keep the facts presented straight. But they read these biographies very much in the same frame of mind as they read novels. Often the author is in no sense an expert and makes no claim to have known the subject of his biography intimately. He may not have known him (or her) at all: he may simply have selected a suitable subject for his biography, and got up the information in order to write the book. Nor is this something which is peculiar to biography. It applies to much of what is described in the reading lists of bestsellers as 'non-fiction'. For, though not fiction, such books rank essentially as literature, and sometimes attract the huge audiences once reserved for works of fiction.

We shall come to didactic prose in Chapter 5. Our present concern is with that kind of didactic treatise in verse which is something more than a treatise in verse: the treatise which has crossed the frontier between paraliterature and literature, which ranks, despite its subject, as a poem, not as a treatise.

The didactic *poem*, as opposed to the verse treatise, seems to have become popular at Alexandria at a time when the traditional form of fiction, the long epic poem, was recognized as a dying genre. The old tricks of the storyteller's trade no longer worked; familiarity made the old stories seem threadbare. They might continue to provide interesting plots for plays (where the emphasis was on situation rather than telling a story), but the dramatic poet needed an audience, and the only audience available to the poet at Alexandria was the highly sophisticated audience of his fellow-poets and the members of an intellectual élite keenly interested in and knowledgeable about literature. To the poets of Alexandria and their audience, style, the sophisticated presentation of one's material, began to seem more important than telling a story.

With a less sophisticated audience at Rome, one less easily repelled by rhetoric (poetry in his own language was still something exciting for a Roman), one more willing to believe in its own historical destiny, epic poetry on themes from Roman history was to become a successful substitute for stories from the old heroic tales. At Alexandria, however, historical epic enjoyed no more than an indifferent success; the events of recent history proved recalcitrant, or poetically uninteresting. It was under such circumstances that the long didactic poem, a revival in a sense of Hesiod, came into its own. Aristotle's objection, that didactic verse was not poetry since it dealt with what we should call non-fiction, seemed less important to poets and a public that had become blasé about fiction.

The favourite subject seems to have been an account in immense detail of some aspect of what we should today call man's environment in the universe. The information had to be presented in polished, sophisticated, pleasurable form. But it was not presented for readers whose primary concern was with information. For such readers there existed more straightforward, more authoritative, duller prose works by experts. It was from these experts that the didactic poets got their facts. If sometimes they got the details wrong, only pedants were upset. The learned poem in hexameters became, in short, a fashionable form at Alexandria. Fashionable that is to say among poets, or those who were knowledgeable about literature: the poems were too technical to appeal to a wide audience, and indeed the Alexandrian poets had no wide audience to appeal to; their only public was a cultured élite. For such an audience difficulty of subject matter, like difficulty of style, seems to have been an added attraction.

The best-known didactic poem of this period is the *Phaenomena* of Aratus: its subject is astronomy, or, to be more precise, the rising and the setting of the stars and what we call meteorology (it is one of Virgil's sources for the *Georgics*). The style, though literary and artificial, is relatively straightforward; understandably, given the topic, the content is technical and abstruse. What Aratus offers us is a transposition into the conventions of Hesiodic didactic verse of prose treatises by Eudoxus of Cnidos. There is no reason to suppose that his intention was to make Eudoxus' ideas more palatable, or more accessible to potential readers who wished to know something of the subject. Such readers would have done better to consult Eudoxus, since Aratus' command of his subject was imperfect, as contemporary scholars were quick to complain. One finds it hard, in short, to see any real didactic purpose. The poem seems pretty clearly to have been written for an audience which could appreciate the technical virtuosity of a highbrow *tour de force*.

Aratus' *Phaenomena* was translated into Latin by Cicero (469 lines survive; the section on meteorology, though referred to by Cicero as completed, has been lost). It is a reasonable assumption that Cicero in his turn tackled the task in a spirit of technical virtuosity, to extend and demonstrate his command of words, to show what could be done—what

Cicero in particular could do—with Latin. His version belongs, as far as we can gather, to the 60s BC; that is to say, it was probably published about the time Lucretius was working on *On the Universe*. During the next two generations, the didactic poem became fashionable at Rome also. In addition to the poems which survive (Virgil's *Georgics*, Ovid's *Art of Love*, Manilius' *On the Stars*), we hear of a number of others (by Varro of Atax, by Macer of Verona, to cite two names). Didactic poetry seems indeed to have become, like mythological epic, a genre for the dilettante poet, something that a man who was of a bookish turn of mind and possessed of modest talent for verse could work away at happily for a long time. The favourite themes are sketched out by Virgil in a passage he puts on the lips of the Silenus in the sixth *Eclogue* (6. 31–40), before passing to a review of themes for epics and epyllia.

III   LUCRETIUS ON THE UNIVERSE

Lucretius' *On the Universe* consists of six long books: the shortest is Book 3 (1,094 lines), the longest is Book 5 (1,457 lines). Books 1 and 2 posit a universe made up of atoms (tiny, indivisible particles, the ultimate constituents of matter) in constant movement in infinite space and time. The process by which everything in the world and all who dwell in it come into existence and are then dissolved again into their constituent atoms is largely a random process, but not entirely so. Lucretius would no doubt have allowed the rightness of the favourite modern illustration of random process: the team of monkeys seated at a battery of typewriters, one of whom eventually types a complete Shakespearean sonnet. But his process has certain controls or restrictions built into it, in order to reconcile his theory with the world as we know it, of which the theory purports to be the true explanation.

The major limitation (and a serious limitation to the neatness of the theory) is that atoms are of different kinds. Thus not all combinations are possible: Lucretius allows ghosts (while rejecting the usual beliefs about them) but monsters such as Centaurs are impossible, since this would mean a combination of atoms of fundamentally different types (man-atoms plus horse-atoms). (This is explained in Book 2, lines 700–709; he reverts to the subject in Book 5 and adds the more sophisticated argument that each creature has its own lifespan and its own tempo of existence; Centaurs are also impossible because man's lifespan is incompatible with that of a horse. Hence William Empson's lines:

> Lucretius could not credit Centaurs,
> Such bicycle he deemed asynchronous.)

The fundamentals of matter and space settled, Book 3 applies the basic principles to mental processes and what is usually called man's 'soul' (his *anima*), whose individual immortality Lucretius firmly rejects; indeed, one of his primary objectives is to rid his readers of the fear of death and punishment in an afterlife by persuading them to accept that death does not mean annihilation, but a resolution of mind and body into their constituent atoms. Book 4 sets out to reconcile the theory with sense perception, turning aside near the end for the famous passage in which Lucretius derides those who make sex their chief pursuit instead of detachment from the world and its anguishes. Book 5, after dealing with cosmology, traces the development of human institutions and outlines Lucretius' social-contract theory of civilization. Book 6 treats a number of aspects of what we should call meteorology and geology (including an excursus on epidemics).

On the Universe has to be set against the background of Rome in the late 60s and early 50s. The 450-year-old Republic was in its death agonies. Though on the surface the forms of government survived, the rule of constitutional law and order, after being strained to its limits by Marius and Sulla and openly challenged by the conspiracy of Catiline, had virtually come to a halt. Shameless exercise of personal power, constitutional prevarication, and organized mob violence when these failed, were the order of the day. Though participation in political affairs was a traditional obligation on all who could claim to belong to the ruling class, it was a time to turn any honest man in disgust from politics, to reduce all men to despair for the future.

Lucretius' explanation of how he came to write his poem is as follows (1. 921–50):

> Take in now what follows, hear me more plainly:
> I am aware how obscure this is, but a great hope of fame
> has struck my heart with its sharp goad,
> and at the same time inspired me with sweet love
> of poetry, driven on now by which, my mind alert,
> I range the Muses' pathless tracks that none has trod
> before. I am minded to drink deep from springs where none
> has drunk, minded to pluck flowers none has plucked,
> and weave from them a glorious garland for my head
> like none the Muses placed till now on poet's brow.
> First, because I teach great things and seek
> to loose the mind from tight bonds of superstition.
> Next, because on a subject that is dark my poem sheds
> such clear light, endowing all with the Muses' grace.

I do this, moreover, from no idle motive:
for just as doctors, when they want to give children
a draught of foul wormwood, first smear the cup-rim
round with a film of sweet, yellow honey,
so that the unsuspecting child is tricked,
his lips conspiring, into drinking the whole
bitter potion by this innocent deception,
being thus restored in fact to health,
so now, since my subject too often seems
somewhat unattractive to those unacquainted with it
and people ordinarily are repelled, I plan
to expound it in the beguiling accents of poetry,
overlaying it, as it were, with sweet poetic honey,
in the hope this way to hold your attention
by my verses while you take in the whole
nature of the universe and the structure of it.

The explanation is repeated (less the bridge-passage 1. 921–5) as an introduction to Book 4 (with one interesting change: instead of the concluding phrase *qua constet compta figura*, 'and the pattern of its architecture', we have *ac persentis utilitatem*, 'and learn to appreciate the profit you are reaping'). Briefly, the explanation is that by choosing verse Lucretius hoped to achieve his moral purpose better.

It is usually assumed that the sugaring of the pill consisted in transposing into verse a text which Lucretius might have published in its prose form if he had not feared that the prose version would be too dull, or too difficult. It is equally usual to assume that that text was, except for the transposition into metrical form and the conventions of the high style, pretty much the text we have. Really, all Lucretius did, according to the common view, was to follow the precedent of Parmenides (late sixth century) and Empedocles (early fifth century); if by the first century BC to write such a treatise in verse was somewhat behind the times, that only goes to show that Lucretius was of a conservative cast of mind.

It is certainly a natural way to read Lucretius' words, but not one that does credit to his common sense. For the odd thing is that his poem has more to say about the physical universe (it is indeed our sole extensive authority for Epicurean theory on the subject) than it does about the Epicurean philosophy of opting out of a world where participation involved intolerable anguish and frustration. Given his moral objective, how did it come about that so much of his poem is devoted to the exposition of physical theory and so little to the problems of human conduct? If he had not made his treatise so technical, the bitter cup of theory would not have needed so much sugar.

The usual answer is that Lucretius found the atomic theory so fascinating he kept losing sight of his moral objective. It may seem a plausible answer, but it hardly takes account of the impressively methodical structure of his poem (it does not read like the work of a man who had lost track of what he wanted to talk about), to say nothing of the poem's title. True, Epicurus himself wrote a great deal about physics (thirty-seven books on the subject are attributed to him). But with Epicurus there can be no question but that his primary concern was with preaching and practising a way of life. Did Lucretius become so caught up in the exposition of physical speculation that he ended up with his priorities reversed?

There is a simpler explanation. Like any other writer, Lucretius had to choose from the forms available to him. No writer of genius hopes or attempts to write a work that is wholly original. He chooses a congenial form which he can revitalize and make his own. Complete originality is the dream of the artistically naive, or the refuge of the artistically incompetent. Their reward is to be not understood. Moreover, choice is not just a matter of choosing that form which expresses best what you want to say. If you want to be read, you have to give thought as well to your audience. In the case of the highly introspective personal poet this may not be a factor which bulks large in the poet's thoughts. But in the case of the propagandist or missionary, close attention to his audience is essential: if the form of his message does not attract the audience he has in mind, if his readers do not recognize his work as something they can feel they want to read, the chances are it will stay unread.

The audience with which Lucretius wished to communicate was not a large audience; he is concerned with a small group of intellectuals: those gathered around his patron Memmius, and the members of similar groups. The philosophy of withdrawal from the anguishes of contemporary society assumes that contemporary society will continue: not everybody can opt out; not everybody, fortunately for the Epicurean, will want to.

For such an audience the physical exposition need be little more than a sophisticated entertainment, like that offered by Aratus in the *Phaenomena*; Lucretius' readers, we may suspect, were less interested in mastering the detail than in appreciating the adroit manipulation of it. *On the Universe* was read as a poetic *tour de force*. But in providing this entertainment Lucretius had, unlike Aratus, an ulterior motive: to get his audience emotionally committed to the fundamentals of Epicureanism, to persuade them of their importance and their truth.

Epicurus' ideas about religion, death, love and the rest were very likely already familiar at an intellectual level to Lucretius' readers, in the sense that they knew about them as they knew about the teachings of other schools. No doubt Lucretius hoped to leave the impression that a massive physical basis existed for Epicureanism. But his procedure is very much adapted to the particular tastes and sophistications of his audience. We are not so very far from the modern writer of *littérature engagée* who writes a novel, or a play, not to argue with his audience about the rights and wrongs of a particular political or religious point of view, but to bring his audience into more intimate familiarity with that point of view, and then leave the idea to go on working in their minds. The difference is more in the nature of the entertainment offered than in the goal aimed at.

The moral use of fiction, except in the most rudimentary sense, was a possibility Roman writers in Lucretius' day had yet to grasp, though it had long been familiar to the Greeks (to the writers of Greek tragedy, for example). It is largely the achievement of Virgil in the next generation. Lucretius turned instead to a familiar Hellenistic form (recently domesticated in Latin by Cicero), one more easily bent to his moral purpose. Far from being possessed of a naturally conservative cast of mind, Lucretius, I suggest, determined to try his hand at the most fashionable verse form of his day. If he sounds old-fashioned, it is because we judge his style against the norm of the Augustan Age. No doubt the poem, once conceived, was worked at in a spirit of rivalry with such early writers of didactic verse as Empedocles. But that was not the starting point. The starting point was to use literature for a moral purpose.

An even more eloquent statement of Lucretius' moral objective is contained in his introduction to Book 2 (2. 1–33):

It is agreeable, when on the wide sea the winds throw the waves
in confusion, to watch from land another's desperate efforts,
not because there is joy or pleasure in any man's discomfort,
but it is agreeable to witness misfortunes you yourself
are free from. It is no less agreeable to watch great armies
drawn up on the field of battle when you have no share in the danger.
But nothing is as agreeable as to be lodged in the well-fortified,
serene citadel erected by the wisdom of philosophers,
from where you can look down on others all around
wandering in quest of the path of life from which
they have strayed, pitting their wits, exploiting rank,
struggling night and day with might and main
to reach the summit of material wealth and power.
O unhappy minds of men, O blind hearts!
Amid what darkness, amid what dangers your lives,
your few, brief days, are spent! Do you not see

nature cries out for these things only,
that our bodies be free from pain, our minds
free to experience pleasure without anxiety or fear?
   We see, then, the things we need for our bodily pleasure
are few indeed, those that rid us from pain,
that provide also all manner of pleasures.
There are times when it pleases us more if there are not
(as nature herself in no way demands) golden statues of youths
in our houses, grasping fiery torches in their right hands
so that we can see to feast at night;
if the house does not shine with silver, smile with gold;
if no lyres echo among the gilded ceiling recesses.
Instead, men stretch out together on the soft grass
of a river bank beneath a tall tree's boughs,
tending their bodies' needs at no great cost,
especially if the weather smiles and the time of year
sprinkles the green grass with flowers.

But the decision taken, the obligation to write a didactic poem according to the accepted rules is met squarely, though Lucretius complains of the inadequacy of the Latin language (1. 136–45):

   I am aware how hard it is to make clear
   arcane Greek research in Latin verse,
   chiefly because words must often be freshly coined
   since our tongue is deficient and the subject new.
   But your great merit and the pleasure I hope for
   of your friendship encourage me to face
   any effort, to work late in the still of night,
   asking myself what words, what kind of poem
   I can employ to shed light upon your thoughts,
   so you may see obscure subjects completely clarified.

   Of course the struggle to find the right words is part of the artistic *tour de force*. A quarter of a century later Cicero in his philosophical dialogues will still have to invent Latin equivalents for Greek philosophical terms. But Cicero writes in a medium (Latin prose of the 40s) in which the efficient expression of abstract thought is within the grasp of the practised writer, even if Cicero cannot manage the easy, simple grace that Seneca will bring to the discussion of philosophical thought in the 50s and 60s of the first century AD. For Lucretius words and syntax are still something to be mastered. A passage like the following shows him at his best, fully capable of clear exposition of complicated material, the line of argument constantly enlivened by the flash of the poetic imagination (2. 308–32):

Thus, there is nothing here to be wondered at
since all the atoms are in motion and yet
the totality seems totally at rest,
save in so far as the structure itself moves.
For the nature of atoms lies far below
the threshold of our perception; and since the atoms
themselves are invisible, so must their motion be also.
This must follow since the things we can see cannot often
be perceived to move because of their distance from us.
Often woolly sheep, as they crop the lush pastures
on a hillside, edge slowly in whatever direction
the grass glistening with fresh dew invites,
while lambs, their bellies full, play or butt guilelessly:
yet all this is not seen clearly by us because of distance
and the whole mass seems stationary on the green hillside.
Then too when great legions double to deploy across
a plain in the course of some military exercise,
a flash of arms rises to heaven and the whole earth
around is resplendent with brass, and beneath the army's feet
the ground trembles and their cries rebound
from the hills to the stars on high;
the cavalry circle, then make a sudden charge
right across the quivering plain.
And yet, from a position high on the hills,
all on the plain seems at rest, a stationary blaze of light.

But this clarity of exposition is secured only by a conscious effort of a characteristically Roman intellect. Comparison with the didactic prose of Cato a century earlier is instructive; a gulf separates Lucretius from Seneca, the urbane cosmopolitan of the first century AD.

Poetically, Lucretius is the last of the old Romans. He is closer to Ennius (weighty, sober, rising without strain to a slow-moving eloquence) than to Virgil or Ovid. He is of course Virgil's great master. But so long as a literary tradition is still developing, reaching out towards its ultimate excellence, style is a matter where it is a poor pupil who cannot outdo his master. What puts Lucretius in the front rank, apart from the sheer magnitude of his achievement, is the extraordinarily vivid, wide-ranging, deeply sensitive but utterly serious spontaneity of his poetic imagination.

IV   VIRGIL ON FARMING

The *Georgics* tells the reader how to run the typical small farm of Virgil's day. Book 1 tells him how to raise crops and how to cultivate a weather

133

eye. Book 2 tells him how to grow trees, and produce those friends of the small Mediterranean farmer today as in antiquity—the olive and the vine: from the one he gets his oil, from the other his wine. Book 3 tells him how to rear cattle: oxen to pull his plough and his carts, horses to ride (and for sale), sheep for their wool, goats for milk and cheese. (Animals were not reared to provide meat. They did, of course, as an occasional treat, after the sacrifice of an animal to a god, for example. But the Roman farmer ate little meat.) Book 4 tells him how to keep bees, the source of honey, which took the place of sugar in the ancient world. The tone is practical, not theoretical. Together, the four books contain a summary of the routine of the farmer's life. For the ancient farmer did not specialize; his farm was a self-sufficient economic unit. Virgil does not use such terms; he does not have to. His audience are familiar with the small farm as a kind of state in miniature, producing the basic needs of those who work it, providing a surplus for the owner to use as barter for the things he cannot produce.

About the details of the farmer's life Virgil is as scrupulously detailed and systematic as Lucretius is about the structure of the universe. Where he is wrong or talks nonsense, it is because the information is fanciful rather than inaccurate, and it is fanciful because Virgil has surrendered to traditional beliefs (about weather signs, about the spontaneous generation of bees from the decaying carcass of an ox), rather than to his own poetic fancy. Systematic presentation of detailed information is as much the keynote of the *Georgics* as it is of *On the Universe*.

At the same time it is plain that the poem was not written to cater to an audience which was primarily, or even seriously, interested in the acquisition of detailed information about the routine of farming life. Like *On the Universe*, perhaps even more plainly, the *Georgics* is a poem, not a treatise in verse. Two important differences between Virgil's poem and Lucretius' are easily pointed to, however. One is a matter of subject, the other, a matter of the poet's purpose.

To take the matter of subject first. Where Lucretius appeals to the intellectual pleasure which is aroused when we attempt to follow a complicated abstract theory, Virgil appeals to sentiment rather than to the intellect. Where Lucretius deals with the reality behind what ordinarily passes for the 'real world', and only occasionally enters that world (if with great poetic sensitivity) in order to establish its relation to the true reality behind it, Virgil's subject is what for most people is first and foremost the 'real world', the world of nature: the world which, if it was not quite the familiar everyday world his audience had around them (he is not writing for farmers but for town-dwellers), was never far distant, physically or emotionally, from the reading public of Augustan

Rome; a world with which the most sophisticated town-dweller had ancestral, easily evoked associations and some kind of personal familiarity. Many, like Horace, owned their own country retreat, a place to retire to from the frustrations of the city where they could feel themselves in harmony with an older, more wholesome way of life.

Frustrations, not despair: Rome in the years preceding and immediately following the battle of Actium (the *Georgics* belongs, probably, to the period 36–29 BC) was not the corrupt city, torn apart by mob violence, of a generation earlier, from which Lucretius turned in revulsion. In the second half of the 30s, a new system was beginning to emerge, and even when all could see that a final confrontation with Antony was inevitable, it remained possible to feel that Rome, or rather Italy, had recovered strength enough to survive; the *Georgics* reflects that mood of hope; hope not so much perhaps in the regeneration of the political system at Rome as in the vitality of Italy as one country, uniting against the renegade Antony and his foreign queen, and built on solid, ancient foundations. The poem represents a movement away from the escapism of Virgil's *Eclogues* (see Chapter 4) to something more like positive engagement with contemporary reality; it is a first step in the direction of the more complete commitment of the *Aeneid*.

This brings us to the nature of Virgil's moral purpose. For obviously if it can be said, without gross simplification, that Lucretius' purpose is to convert his readers to the Epicurean way of life, it is hardly Virgil's purpose to make his audience farmers. Yet the poem is not wholly innocent of a moral intention.

Talk of subject and purpose must not make us lose sight, however, of the fact that the *Georgics* had, first and foremost, like *On the Universe*, to work as a poem. Virgil wrote for an audience who were willing to be charmed by the stylish, urbane presentation of the rustic and the recondite; the fantasy, for example (based on traditional lore and keen, sympathetic, imaginative observation, with obvious political overtones), of the republic of the bees (*Georgics* 4. 149–69; Dryden's version of what he called 'the best Poem of the best Poet'):

> Describe we next the nature of the bees,
> Bestowed by Jove for secret services,
> When, by the tinkling sound of timbrels led,
> The king of heaven in Cretan caves they fed.
> Of all the race of animals, alone
> The bees have common cities of their own,
> And common sons; beneath one law they live,
> And with one common stock their traffic drive.

Each has a certain home, a several stall:
All is the state's; the state provides for all.
Mindful of coming cold, they share the pain,
And hoard, for winter's use, the summer's gain.
Some o'er the public magazines preside;
And some are sent new forage to provide:
These drudge in fields abroad; and those at home
Lay deep foundations for the laboured comb,
With dew, narcissus leaves, and clammy gum.
To pitch the waxen flooring some contrive;
Some nurse the future nation of the hive;
Sweet honey some condense; some purge the grout;
The rest, in cells apart, the liquid nectar shut:
All, with united force, combine to drive
The lazy drones from the laborious hive:
With envy stung, they view each other's deeds:
With diligence the fragrant work proceeds.
[Translation: Dryden]

It was an audience willing to have their eye for a fine cow developed by an obvious connoisseur of cows who is at the same time a poet (*Georgics* 3. 51–9):

> Optima torvae
> forma bovis cui turpe caput, cui plurima cervix
> et crurum tenus a mento palearia pendent;
> tum longo nullus lateri modus; omnia magna,
> pes etiam; et camuris hirtae sub cornibus aures.
> nec mihi displiceat maculis insignis et albo
> aut iuga detractans interdumque aspera cornu
> et faciem tauro propior quaeque ardua tota
> et gradiens ima verrit vestigia cauda.

> The mother-cow must wear a lowering look,
> Sour-headed, strongly necked, to bear the yoke.
> Her double dewlap from her chin descends,
> And at her thighs the ponderous burden ends.
> Long are her sides and large; her limbs are great;
> Rough are her ears, and broad her horny feet.
> Her colour shining black, but flecked with white;
> She tosses from the yoke; provokes the fight:
> She rises in her gait, is free from fears,
> And in her face a bull's resemblance bears:

> Her ample forehead with a star is crowned,
> And with her length of tail she sweeps the ground.
>
> [Translation: Dryden]

It was equally an audience who were willing to extend their interest to the exposition of technical detail: the different timbers that go into the construction of a plough, for example (*Georgics* 1. 169–75):

> Continuo in silvis magna vi flexa domatur
> in burim et curvi formam accipit ulmus aratri;
> huic a stirpe pedes temo protentus in octo,
> binae aures, duplici aptantur dentalia dorso.
> caeditur et tilia ante iguo levis altaque fagus
> stivaque, quae currus a tergo torqueat imos,
> et suspensa focis explorat robora fumus

> Young elms, with early force, in copses bow,
> Fit for the figure of the crooked plough.
> Of eight feet long a fastened beam prepare
> On either side the head, produce an ear;
> And sink a socket for the shining share.
> Of beech the plough-tail, and the bending yoke,
> Or softer linden hardened in the smoke.
>
> [Translation: Dryden]

But it was an audience who expected that interest to be sustained by the kind of graphic, sharply focused imagery which creates the illusion of clarity, rather than the objective clarity didacticism proper requires: no ancient reader would have found it easy to construct a plough, if he had never made or seen a plough, from Virgil's description; but then none of Virgil's readers would have wanted to.

An audience like this can be invited to surrender to an agreeably sentimental picture of the shepherd's life (*Georgics* 3. 322–38):

> But, when the western winds with vital power
> Call forth the tender grass and budding flower,
> Then, at the last, produce in open air
> Both flocks, and send them to their summer fare.
> Before the sun while Hesperus appears,
> First let them sip from herbs the pearly tears
> Of morning dews, and after break their fast
> On greensward ground—a cool and grateful state.
> But, when the day's fourth hour has drawn the dews,
> And the sun's sultry heat their thirst renews;
> When creaking grasshoppers on shrubs complain,

137

Then lead them to their watering-troughs again.
In summer's heat, some bending valley find,
Closed from the sun, but open to the wind;
Or seek some ancient oak, whose arms extend
In ample breadth, thy cattle to defend,
Or solitary grove, or gloomy glade,
To shield them with its venerable shade.
Once more to watering lead; and feed again
When the low sun is sinking to the main,
When rising Cynthia sheds her silver dews,
And the cool evening-breeze the meads renews,
When linnets fill the woods with tuneful sound,
And hollow shores the halcyon's voice rebound.

[Translation: Dryden]

We are close here to the idealized countryside of the *Eclogues*; the descriptions of scene are lush, almost idyllic, the first and last lines warmly evocative. But the mode remains expository (the simple routine of the shepherd's day is traced through from early spring morning to evening) and didactic (precept follows precept with exemplary regularity, different times of day and tasks appropriate to them are precisely indicated).

Finally (and here we see the beginnings of a moral purpose) it is an audience who accept that the farmer's life is harsh and laborious but are still willing to be persuaded that there is something wholesome, something morally right, about the tough, almost crippling routine of the Italian countryside (as opposed to the decadence and false ease of city life, though the opposition is never explicitly drawn by Virgil); an audience who can see none the less, if not the 'dignity of labour' (a concept unknown to the ancient world—it dates from the nineteenth century), at any rate the poetry of labour (*Georgics* 1. 121–46):

The sire of gods and men, with hard decrees,
Forbids our plenty to be bought with ease,
And wills that mortal men, inured to toil,
Should exercise with pains the grudging soil;
Himself invented first the shining share;
And whetted human industry by care;
Himself did handicrafts and arts ordain,
Nor suffered sloth to rust his active reign.
Ere this, no peasant vexed the peaceful ground,
Which only turfs and greens for altars found:
No fences parted fields, nor marks nor bounds

Distinguished acres of litigious grounds;
But all was common, and the fruitful earth
Was free to give her unexacted birth.
Jove added venom to the viper's broad,
And swelled, with raging storms, the peaceful flood;
Commissioned hungry wolves to infest the fold,
And shook from oaken leaves the liquid gold;
Removed from human reach the cheerful fire,
And from the rivers bade the wine retire;
That studious need might useful arts explore;
From furrowed fields to reap the foodful store,
And force the veins of clashing flints to expire
The lurking seeds of their celestial fire.
Then first on seas the hollowed alder swam;
Then sailors quartered heaven, and found a name
For every fixed and every wandering star—
The Pleiads, Hyads, and the Northern Car.
Then toils for beasts, and lime for birds, were found,
And deep-mouthed dogs did forest walks surround;
And casting-nets were spread in shallow brooks,
Drags in the deep, and baits were hung on hooks.
Then saws were toothed, and sounding axes made;
(For wedges first did yielding wood invade;)
And various arts in order did succeed,
(What cannot endless labour, urged by need?)

[Translation: Dryden]

Here is Virgil's answer to Lucretius' attempt to reconcile two distinct traditions: the first tradition is of the idyllic picture of the hard life of primitive man, filled with echoes of the Golden Age (Lucretius 5. 925–57):

But this race of men living in the fields was much harder,
as was to be expected, for a hard earth had brought it forth. . . .
And for many cycles of the sun in its rolling course
through the heavens they lived their lives wandering like beasts.
No tough pilot was there of the curving plough,
nor did they know how to till fields with iron,
or how to plant new trees in the ground, how to cut
old branches from grown trees with a pruning hook.
Such things as sun and rain had given, the earth had on its own
produced, these they were content to accept as gifts.
Mostly, they nourished their bodies on acorns;
the arbutus berries which now in winter-time

one sees ripen to a bright red hue,
the earth bore larger then and in great numbers. . . .
Nor did they know yet how to treat things with fire, or the use
of skins, how to clothe their bodies with the spoils
of hunting, but lived in glades and hillside caves
and forests, protecting their shaggy frames at need
in thickets from howling wind and driving rain.

A newer tradition accepts the rightness of progress and the advance of
civilization, which for Lucretius is the result of a softening of human
nature and the surrender of hard, brute individualism to the softer ethos
of the social contract (Lucretius 5. 1014–27):

> tum genus humanum primum mollescere coepit.
> ignis enim curavit ut alsia corpora frigus
> non ita iam possent caeli sub tegmine ferre,
> et Venus imminuit viris puerique parentum
> blanditiis facile ingenium fregere superbum.
> tum et amicitiem coeperunt iungere aventes
> finitimi inter se nec laedere nec violari,
> et pueros commendarunt muliebreque saeclum,
> vocibus et gestu cum balbe significarent
> imbecillorum esse aequum miserier omnis.
> nec tamen omnimodis poterat concordia gigni,
> sed bona magnaque pars servabat foedera caste;
> aut genus humanum iam tum foret omne peremptum
> nec potuisset adhuc perducere saecla propago.

> Then first the human race began to get softer.
> Fire had seen to it that bodies sensitive now to chill
> could not endure the cold with no shelter save the sky.
> Love made them weaker, children had no trouble
> in coaxing stubborn parents to relent.
> Soon they were all eagerness to make friends
> neighbour with neighbour, anxious neither to offer nor to
> suffer harm, appealing for respect of children and of womenfolk
> with voice and gesture, stumbling to signify in words
> the common obligation to pity those without defence.
> Agreement about all things was beyond them to produce,
> but a good many did keep honestly to their word.
> Else had the human race been forthwith wiped out,
> nor could propagation have extended through the ages to this day.

Virgil's explanation of the curse of labour (*improbus labor*) is apt to seem a poor explanation alongside Lucretius' uncompromising rationalism. But the curse is no more than a device that permits Virgil to appeal to a belief deep-seated in us all and the primary motivation of our struggle for existence, our belief in man's redemption, or self-fulfilment, by labour. Here is Virgil's concept of the Italian farmer's unremitting struggle against a hostile environment (*Georgics* 1. 197–203):

> Yet is not the success for years assured
> Though chosen is the seed, and fully cured,
> Unless the peasant, with his annual pain,
> Renews his choice, and culls the largest grain.
> Thus all below, whether by Nature's curse,
> Or Fate's decree, degenerate still to worse.
> So the boat's brawny crew the current stem,
> And, slow advancing, struggle with the stream:
> But if they slack their hands, or cease to strive,
> Then down the flood with headlong haste they drive.
>
> [Translation: Dryden]

Set this against the almost casual optimism with which Lucretius represents the progress of civilization (to which he is committed by his argument) as a natural and inevitable phenomenon. Virgil's grimmer, more realistic picture looks at first like pessimism. But it is not the simplistic rhetorical pessimism to which Horace once surrendered in lines (they come from the last of the Roman Odes) that paint, as proof of the degeneration of the present day, a sentimental picture of the good old days when Rome's strength lay in her army of tough sons of the farm (*Odes* 3. 6. 33–48):

> Not from parents such as these were sprung
> the men who stained the sea with Punic blood,
> overthrew Pyrrhus, beat back Antiochus
> and grim Hannibal:
>
> they were virile soldier-farmers' sons,
> taught to till the fields
> with Sabellian hoe and to fetch
> the cut fire logs
>
> at their stern mother's bidding, when the Sun-god
> stretched the shadows of the hills and took
> the yokes from the tired oxen as his chariot sped away,
> leaving the welcome evening hour.

What has ruinous time not diminished?
Our parents, not their parents' match,
produced our more corrupt generation, soon to bear
sons and daughters more degenerate still.

Virgil's picture is an attempt to come to terms with a hard world in which there is still room for hope. He neither glorifies an unreal past, nor extols military glory. The simple, hard life of the farmer is not a thing of the past; it is the element of continuity in a world in which wars are fought and forgotten, even the war of Roman against Roman which now dominates men's minds (*Georgics* 1. 489–514):

> Ye home-born deities, of mortal birth!
> Thou father Romulus, and mother Earth,
> Goddess unmoved! whose guardian arms extend
> O'er Tuscan Tiber's course, and Roman towers defend;
> With youthful Caesar your joint powers engage,
> Nor hinder him to save the sinking age.
> O! let the blood, already spilt, atone
> For the past crimes of cursed Laomedon!
> Heaven wants thee there; and long the gods, we know,
> Have grudged thee, Caesar, to the world below,
> Where fraud and rapine right and wrong confound,
> Where impious arms from every part resound,
> And monstrous crimes in every shape are crowned.
> The peaceful peasant to the wars is pressed;
> The fields lie fallow in inglorious rest;
> The plain no pasture to the flock affords;
> The crooked scythes are straightened into swords:
> And there Euphrates her soft offspring arms,
> And here the Rhine rebellows with alarms;
> The neighbouring cities range on several sides;
> Perfidious Mars long-plighted leagues divides,
> And o'er the wasted world in triumph rides.
> So four fierce coursers, starting to the race,
> Scour through the plain, and lengthen every pace;
> Nor reins, nor curbs, nor threatening cries, they fear,
> But force along the trembling charioteer.

> [Translation: Dryden]

V OVID ON LOVE

With Ovid the formal identity weakens. The *Art of Love* is not written in hexameters (the traditional metre for a didactic poem), but—like Ovid's

Fasti—in elegiac couplets. The primary assertion of the text remains: the *Art of Love* demands to be taken as a didactic poem. In fact, however, all serious didactic function disappears, and with it any easily recognizable moral purpose.

In the Augustan Age prose finally establishes itself as the proper medium for instruction; its claim is not seriously contested by learned *tours de force* such as Manilius' *On the Stars*. Poetry continues to exercise its moral function and indeed extends it in the hands of the two greatest poets of the age, Virgil and Horace. But when Horace moralizes in the *Satires* and *Epistles,* he does so in a new off-the-cuff fashion, asserting no moral authority save that which can reasonably be claimed by a sensible, thoughtful observer of the human comedy. In the *Odes* he abandons more and more even this explicit moralizing stance in favour of an extension, by subtle suggestion, of his readers' imaginative sensibility. After Horace, the moral function passes into the unsubtle hands of such acknowledged castigators of human weakness and folly as Persius and Juvenal, and satire becomes what it was for French and English writers of the seventeenth and eighteenth centuries.

One can say that Ovid's *Art of Love*, like Lucretius' *On the Universe* and Virgil's *Georgics,* provides detailed instruction on the subject Ovid has chosen to treat. But it is not so much a particular kind of information which characterizes the didactic mode in Ovid's hands and justifies the application of the term 'didactic' to the *Art of Love* as a particular tone: the businesslike, down-to-earth tone of a man who has information to impart of practical concern.

The *Art of Love* is a mockery of a form that has outgrown its humble beginnings, and a mockery of a society that can almost take seriously a poem which purports to instruct the smart young man about town in the technique of seducing every pretty girl he meets. The Latin word *ars* in this context denotes a craft or a profession, and then, by an easy extension, the body of knowledge (usually empirical knowledge: rules of thumb, tricks that have been found to work) handed down from the old hand at the trade to the young apprentice. (Thus Horace's *Ars Poetica,* though the title is probably not Horace's, is a series of practical hints about how to write certain kinds of poetry.) The *Art of Love* is a parody, in short, of a sub-species of didactic verse, the treatise filled with practical hints.

It is this practical, matter-of-fact approach (what every lover needs to know) to a subject where that approach is felt to be wittily inappropriate which constitutes the irony of Ovid's handbook. The *Art of Love* has no claim to a place among the erotica of the western world; only once or twice does Ovid go beyond the limits of what might safely be read in adult mixed company as witty entertainment. His subject is seduction, not sex: the technique of conquest in a highly civilized society where conquest was a game to be played with style, according to well-recognized, unwritten rules, not an expression of, or a concession to, lust. The fun lies in codifying, with witty explicitness and appropriate literary examples, the unwritten rules.

The young apprentice for whom Ovid's handbook is intended is not the future Don Juan, the exceptional profligate of exceptional powers and exceptional tastes, but the man about town in Augustan Rome. It is part of the fun to pretend that womanizing is his normal pursuit. The notion is not Ovid's invention, any more than the notion of representing the lover as just another kind of artisan. Horace plays with the conceit in a famous ode in which the retiring lover is likened to a soldier about to take his discharge who, like any artisan on retirement, dedicates the tools of his trade to the appropriate patron goddess—in this case, Venus (*Odes* 3. 26. 1–8):

> I've always been fit for female service,
> done my time, been mentioned in despatches,
> now I shall hang battle gear and lyre
> upon this wall
>
> that guards the left flank of Venus
> of the sea. Set down here the flaming torches,
> here the pince-bars and bows we lovers use
> in front-door assault.

Ovid imitated Horace's poem in a short poem of his own (*Amores* 1. 9, *Militat omnis amans et habet sua castra Cupido*, 'Every lover's a soldier, a campaigner for Cupid'). The *Art of Love* takes the idea several steps further: like so much of Ovid, the poem is a brilliant *reductio ad absurdum*.

It is hardly surprising if the result is more than once a transposition to the didactic mode of themes also treated in the *Amores*. And it can be interesting on such occasions to compare Ovid's use of the same data in different styles and contexts. In Book 1 of the *Art of Love* (1. 375–98) he issues a warning against an affair with your mistress's maid: the unscrupulous girl is likely to blackmail you. In *Amores* 2. 7 and 2. 8 we find Ovid practising what he had preached against, and forestalling blackmail by threatening to tell all (literally all!) himself if the maid does not continue to co-operate. In another passage in the *Art of Love* he tells the apprentice lover how to press his attentions upon a pretty girl seated next to him at the chariot races in the Circus Maximus (*Art of Love* 1. 135–62):

Furthermore, don't overlook the meetings when horses are running;
  In the crowds at the track opportunity waits.
There is no need for a code of finger-signals or nodding.
  Sit as close as you like; no one will stop you at all.
In fact, you will have to sit close—that's one of the rules,
    at a race track.
  Whether she likes it or not, contact is part of the game.
Try to find something in common, to open the conversation;
  Don't care too much what you say, just so that every one hears.
Ask her, 'Whose colors are those?'—that's good for an
    opening gambit.
  Put your own bet down, fast, on whatever she plays.
Then, when the gods come along in procession, ivory, golden,
  Outcheer every young man, shouting for Venus, the queen.
Often it happens that dust may fall on the blouse of the lady.
  If such dust should fall, carefully brush it away.
Even if there's no dust, brush off whatever there isn't.
  Any excuse will do: why do you think you have hands?
If her cloak hangs low, and the ground is getting it dirty,
  Gather it up with care, lift it a little, so!
Maybe, by way of reward, and not without her indulgence,
  You'll be able to see ankle or possibly knee.
Then look around and glare at the fellow who's sitting behind you,
  Don't let him crowd his knees into her delicate spine.
Girls, as everyone knows, adore these little attentions:
  Getting the cushion just right, that's in itself quite an art;
Yes, and it takes a technique in making a fan of your program
  Or in fixing a stool under the feet of a girl.

[Translation: Humphries]

The elegiac version is a witty dramatic monologue in the third book of the *Amores* in which we listen as Ovid adroitly insinuates himself upon the girl, brooking no rebuff, gaily confident of success (*Amores* 3. 2. 19–46):

> 'It's no use edging away. The line brings us together—
> that's the advantage of the seating here.
>
> You on the right, sir—please be careful.
> Your elbow's hurting the lady.
>
> And you in the row behind—sit up, sir!
> Your knees are digging into her back.

My dear, your dress is trailing on the ground.
Lift it up—or there you are, I've done it for you.

What mean material to hide those legs!
Yes, the more one looks the meaner it seems.

Legs like Atalanta,
Milanion's dream of bliss.

A painter's model for Diana
running wilder than the beasts.

My blood was on fire before. What happens now?
You're fuelling a furnace, flooding the Red Sea.

I'm sure that lightweight dress is hiding
still more delightful revelations.

But what about a breath of air while we wait?
This programme will do as a fan.

Is it really as hot as I feel? Or merely my imagination
fired by your sultry presence?

Just then a speck of dust fell on your white dress.
Forgive me—out, damned spot!

But here's the procession. Everybody hush.
Give them a hand. The golden procession's here.

First comes Victory, wings outstretched.
Goddess, grant me victory in love!'

[Translation: Lee]

Nor does Ovid confine his instruction to men about town. After two
books on how to get your girl, he sportingly added a third for girls about
town on how to get your man. Once again the instruction is practical and
down to earth; but the standard set is high, as the following reading list of
popular authors (the girl about town must be, or appear, well-read) will
show (*Art of Love* 3. 329–46):

Read some poets, too, Callimachus, and the Coan,
   All that Anacreon wrote, rollicking drinking-songs.

146

Study Sappho—what girl could set more alluring example?—
  Read Menander, whose plots tell of the wiles of the slave.
You should be able, I hope, to read some lines of Propertius,
  Poet of our own time, Gallus, Tibullus as well.
Quote from *The Golden Fleece,* that masterpiece written by Varro,
  Don't forget Arms and the Man; Virgil's our greatest and best.
Possibly works of my own may not be considered unworthy,
  Nor will the Lethean stream carry my writings away.
Someone will say: 'Be sure to read the songs of our master,
  Ovid, whose elegant art teaches the lore of the heart.
You have three books of the *Loves,* and that is plenty to choose
    from,
  Speaking them soft and low, lines that all lovers should know.
Or, with a practiced voice, read something from one of the Letters:
  That was a form of his own; others have left it untried.'

[Translation: Humphries]

But before we identify Ovid as a forerunner of women's liberation and
praise him for his enlightened views on the place of women in society, it is
as well to read a few lines in which Ovid's truer opinions can be felt to
pierce the benevolence and the mockery (*Art of Love* 3. 251–80;
297–310):

I am not running my school for Semele's sake, nor for Leda's.
  Nor for the girl the white bull carried far over the sea,
Neither for Helen's sake, whom Menelaus demanded,
  Paris wanted to keep, each of them wise in his way.
I teach the rank and file, the pretty ones, also the homely;
  Don't suppose that the good ever outnumber the worse.
Beautiful girls require no help from art, no instruction;
  They have their natural gifts, talents more potent than art.
When the seas are calm, the captain is carefree, unworried;
  When they rise in their wrath, then he appeals to his crew.
Still, the face is rare that has no sign of a blemish;
  Faults of the face or physique call for attempts at disguise.
If you are short, sit down, lest, standing, you seem to be sitting,
  Little as you may be, stretch out full length on your couch.
Even here, if you fear some critic might notice your stature,
  See that a cover is thrown, hide yourself under a spread.
If you're the lanky type, wear somewhat billowy garments,
  Loosely let the robe fall from the shoulders down.
If you're inclined to be pale, wear stripes of scarlet or crimson,
  If you're inclined to be dark, white is an absolute must.

147

Let an ugly foot hide in a snow-covered sandal;
    If your ankles are thick, don't be unlacing your shoes.
Do your collarbones show? Then wear a clasp at each shoulder.
    Have you a bust too flat? Bandages ought to fix that.
If your fingers are fat, or your fingernails brittle and ugly,
    Watch what you do when you talk; don't wave your hands in the air.
Eat a lozenge or two, if you think your breath is offensive,
    If you have something to say, speak from some distance away.
If a tooth is too black, or too large, or the least bit uneven,
    Pay no attention to jokes; laughter might give you away. . . .
Pay close heed to all this, because it is, all of it, useful:
    Posture's important, and poise; walk with a womanly step.
When you go out for the air, remember that people are watching,
    People, men you don't know; you can attract or repel.
Some overdo it, of course, affectedly mincing or swaying,
    Letting the wind blow their clothes, placing their sandals
        just so,
Others go striding along like the sunburnt wife of a farmer,
    Waddle, or take huge strides, jumping a puddle, it seems.
Look! As in everything else, the golden mean is the answer:
    Neither too short nor too long, neither too country nor town.
Keep your snowy arms (if your arms are snowy) uncovered,
    Visible from the left; walk with your shoulders bare.
This is a pleasure to see, and every time that I see it,
    Where the shoulder is bare, I'd put a kiss if I could.

                        [Translation: Humphries]

CHAPTER 4

The Poet as Himself

I   PERSONAL POETRY

Lucretius and Catullus were both the products of an age when the thinking individual began to feel that his emotional and intellectual life meant more to him than the state, if only because the state, the *Res Publica,* had ceased suddenly to mean much to anybody. Both were first-class poets. Both took poetry very seriously. Between them they gave Roman poetry an emotional integrity and a concern with the world around them that made their poetry feel fresh and exciting to themselves, and to readers ever since. Where they differ is in the manner in which they allowed a consciousness of their own individuality to express itself in their poetry. In Lucretius the personal note is muted and the tone kept strictly professional. Catullus' poetry is almost wholly the expression of the poet's personality.

The applicability of the term 'personal poetry' to the poetry of Catullus or Horace or Propertius is obvious. Something more is meant than that these are poets who write about themselves. For Horace, Catullus, even Propertius do not always write only about themselves. Their personality comes, however, into all they write; it is an important, relevant, constituent element of their poetry. We hear, as it were, *the poet's speaking voice,* speaking for himself as an individual—not in the voice of a man delivering a lecture, or telling a story as a professional entertainer. However involved we become in what he has to say, we are conscious of the personality of the man who is talking.

Unlike 'personal poetry', the term 'public poetry' is not in common use. It can serve, however, as an apt description of a kind of writing that is common enough; and the two terms facilitate a useful distinction between fundamentally different kinds of ancient poetry. It is the kind of distinction we make every day between cars and trucks. Nobody confuses a car with a truck; everybody knows they are used for different purposes. It wouldn't occur to anybody to argue that cars and trucks have so much in

149

common, it really isn't possible to tell one from the other. What keeps them apart is their different function in society. It is the same with 'personal poetry' and 'public poetry'.

Thus, personal poetry has this in common, for example, with public poetry that it frequently expresses, not merely moral concern, but an attitude of moral authority. But it is a personal authority, recognized by the reader as the opinion of an individual and accepted by him only in so far as he regards the speaker, on other grounds, as someone whose opinions he can take seriously. It is not the impersonal authority of the poet as teacher.

The distinction is very much that between the leading article or editorial in a newspaper and an article in the same paper by a well-known columnist: 'well-known' in the sense that his readers feel they know him from reading his column. The leading article states the views of the paper; but it speaks with the voice of a man who takes it for granted that he is only saying what all sensible people think, or will agree with, whether that is in fact the case (and often it isn't) or not. The columnist speaks for himself; or to be more precise, he speaks in the tone of voice of a man who is speaking for himself: often indeed about himself, but often too about the events of the day as he sees them, or as they involve him. His object is to create the illusion of an informality that breaks through the formal constraints which speaking for the paper impose.

The leading article is a sophisticated version of a behaviour pattern characteristic of primitive societies and surviving in certain paraliterary contexts and (in one or two specialized forms of literature) in our own society. In older societies the moment you spoke on behalf of the community, you felt the need to speak as a different person; you were in fact depersonalized by a sense of what the occasion demanded. All who have experience of sitting on committees are familiar with the phenomenon: men who are in their normal private lives literate human beings endowed with a normal sense of humour feel, when they speak in a committee, an impulse to fall into the special, humourless, illiterate jargon that people use on such occasions in obedience to an acquired instinct that virtually forces the individual to subordinate his own personality to the public occasion.

The full-scale leading article is a dying form, confined to what we call the highbrow papers; the popular papers retain no more than a simplified, truncated version. On radio and television the role of the editorial writer is discharged by the commentator, who is, like the columnist, a practitioner of personal literature, if often of a rather boring kind. In most serious forms of literature (novels, poems, biographies) the personal mode—that way of talking which creates the illusion of the writer's speaking voice—has become the normal thing. More and more, where the printed word is concerned, the public persona is something one expects to find only in textbooks and government reports: its grandest representative is the article in an encyclopaedia.

In an age which cultivates the individual personality, when queens and prime ministers have to be on their guard to be just themselves in public, to be only oneself seems perhaps to behave naturally. It is easy to forget that in most forms of ancient literature and public life (and indeed in public life until recent times, if never quite as much in poetry in modern times as in the ancient world) the public persona was obligatory. The typical ancient poet was a craftsman. No doubt his readers would want to know who he was; but they would not expect him to speak to them in his own person in what he wrote. To do so would have been as serious a breach of professional etiquette as if the writer of an article in a respectable modern encyclopaedia were to start talking to us like a newspaper columnist. The exceptions occur when the poet is off duty (just being himself, as we say), or when the sense of community has, in one way or another, been destroyed: at such times the individual voice begins to be heard, in politics and in literature. We hear it in the old Greek lyric and iambic poets; we hear it in Roman personal poetry of the last half century BC.

The distinction between the public and the personal modes seems to have been underpinned almost from the beginning by formal distinctions. The most obvious is length: an epic poem, a didactic poem, are major structures; one expects them to obey their own internal, impersonal logic. A personal poem is short; it follows a train of thought which reflects the speaker and the occasion. Metre also comes into the matter, at least to begin with; for at Rome the original, specialized functions of the different metres are not preserved. Roman personal poetry has a mixed origin. Its most obvious link is with Greek lyric poetry: within the limits imposed by the awareness of himself as an individual which it was possible for a poet to possess in sixth- and fifth-century Greece, lyric poetry assumed from the outset a personal note; compare the impersonal stance of the chorus in Greek tragedy, or that of Pindar. But Roman personal poetry also owes much to Greek elegiac and iambic poetry; it represents as well, in the case of satire (or in that of Horace's *Epistles*), a new, deliberately casual use of the oldest of the public forms, the dactylic hexameter.

The emergence of Roman personal poetry around 60 BC is a symptom of the breaking loose of the individual from the constraints of what had been till then a tightly structured society. By 60 BC the state had ceased to command either the allegiance or the respect of the individual. Those who claim new freedoms abandon old loyalties. When the state breaks down, people say openly what before they had said only in private.

To make poetry out of this new mood of self-awareness wasn't something anybody might have done. Even if one had the ability, or felt one had, it was hardly an assault to be planned in cold blood upon accepted notions about what literature was. What happens is that one discovers afterwards that the poems one had written for fun, for one's friends, for one's private satisfaction, are good enough to be published, good enough to last. Though one hadn't thought of them as literature, one realizes afterwards that they can stand comparison with what passes for literature when literature is at a low ebb. The provocation lies not in the act of writing, but in the act of publishing. But once it has been done successfully, publication can be comtemplated from the outset by others. A fundamental change of attitude then results: a man will sit down to write personal poetry for publication, as men had sat down to write an epic or a tragedy. A new kind of poetry has come into existence.

Personal poetry cannot be manufactured, however, as one might manufacture a historical epic or a play, simply because one is, so to speak, in the business. There is involved a kind of reversal of priorities. The personal poet cannot say to himself, as a public poet can, 'I am going to write a poem or a play', and then look for a suitable story in which to become artistically involved (a normal enough procedure for the craftsman poet): the situation which provoked the poem comes first, unsought and unbidden. Here lies the problem of the personal poet. So long as there is an emotional crisis to cope with, something in the world around him which has exasperated him or intrigued him, so that he feels he wants to give that experience permanent form in verse, things are all right: the impulse to express is there and he can concentrate on the poetic statement of his feelings. The problem which came to confront the Roman personal poets was how to preserve that urgently personal note which justified the precise, disciplined statement of serious verse when everything the poet could think of to write about had been said. The area within which the Roman personal poets operate is a limited one; they seem inhibited, out of excessive respect for tradition, or by associating too much with one another (living and writing as members of an exclusive coterie), from extending that area. The old eternal problems—love, hate, death—are only capable of fresh exploration so long as there is an expansion of sensibility or technique. The Augustan poets tended to confine themselves to these, and, even within this limited area, to concentrate on perfection of technique instead of using the new form as a stimulant to perception and understanding in an ever-widening (because consciously extended) field of personal experience.

152

The term 'Roman personal poetry' as used in this chapter covers two phases which are historically distinct, and might indeed be regarded as remote from one another if the second were not a conscious revival of the first. The first phase is spread over a space of some seventy-five years (60 BC to the death of Ovid in AD 17) and comprises the three generations of poets from Catullus to Ovid. It is the richest period in Roman poetry, and one of the richest in the history of world literature. Personal poetry is represented by the verse of Catullus and Horace, the *Eclogues* of Virgil, the verse of Tibullus and Propertius (both of whom wrote only personal poetry), and about one third of the verse of that most productive of Roman poets, Ovid (whom we have met already as a writer of narrative and didactic poetry). To these are to be added the *Catalepton* collection attributed to Virgil (fifteen short poems in various metres), such waifs and strays as the *Priapea* (a collection of eighty-five poems including a few attributed to Virgil, Tibullus and Ovid, the remainder composed, probably, under Augustus), and the pitifully meagre fragments of such poets as Calvus and Cinna.

The second phase begins with the *Epigrams* of Martial about AD 60, over forty years after the death of Ovid. Martial's writing life (he died about AD 104) only just overlaps that of Juvenal, whose *Satires* belong to the thirty years of the reigns of Trajan and Hadrian (AD 98–128).

II   CATULLUS

The poetry of Catullus seems so fresh, so direct, so unliterary, it is easy to forget that verse like this can be written only in a society where the use of language has reached a high level of efficient, conscious, sophisticated art. Political decay is not in itself a sufficient stimulus; personal poetry is only possible where individuals can feel competent to engage in the struggle to express themselves as individuals.

That Roman society in the time of Julius Caesar had reached a quite unusually high level of cultivated articulateness hardly needs arguing. That it was a society in which individuals were learning to express themselves as individuals is another matter. This is something about which the traditional forms of literature can provide little information. As it happens, however, the evidence which might easily have been lacking is provided by the survival of the voluminous correspondence of Cicero. The collection comprises not only hundreds of letters written by Cicero himself, but also large numbers of letters to Cicero from friends and acquaintances. The formal letters to and from political associates tell us little about the ability of Cicero and his contemporaries to express in words what went on in their private thoughts. It is the intimate, personal letters which enable us to form a fairly adequate impression of the ordinary, everyday, informal written Latin of an educated Roman in the time of Catullus. They constitute a standard of comparison for the Latin of Catullus' poems: in both the object aimed at is the same; the illusion sought is that the reader should seem to catch the speaking voice of the writer.

To the literary historian of Roman poetry in the Classical period it is plain that by the time Catullus began writing the high style of tragedy and epic and the plain style closer to conversation of comedy were both spent forces. The great practitioners belong to the previous century, or earlier; the need to innovate has not been met; nothing worth reading will be written in these styles until they are brought to life again, as Virgil brought epic to life, or Seneca tragedy, by deliberately reaching back into the past to revive a dead or decadent style in order to transform it.

A contemporary (Cicero, say, or Caesar—or a young poet of the late 60s) would naturally have looked at the matter rather differently. He would have felt, if he had a feeling for literature, that these styles had been worked out. But the great writers of the past would have been alive for him in a way that it is easy for us to forget. The literary historian likes to relegate each writer to his proper period, the period to which, as we say, that writer belongs. But the works of the great writers do not die with them. What they wrote lives on in the minds of those who come afterwards. The young poet's imagination is fired by the great works of the past. From them he learns what it is to be a writer. However much he wants to do something different, it would be unnatural for him to shut his mind to what the literature of the past can offer. To want to say something for himself without modelling himself to some extent upon those writers who had discovered how to tell a story, how to frame a line of verse, how to express an idea, would be as impossible as it would be absurd.

Hence Lucretius, the decision once taken to write in verse, adopts the traditional high style: it was the obvious style to choose. Catullus, when he turns to a style of writing that is consciously literary—in Poem 64, for example—will do the same, though more guardedly, never quite abandoning a note of conscious, distancing irony. But in his short poems, the decision once taken to renounce the grand manner, Catullus had to build on something closer to the way men actually spoke. That meant denying himself not merely the acknowledged rhetoric of the grand manner, but also the richly connotative diction of traditional serious poetry; the diction we find in Lucretius when the poetic imagination takes over from logical exposition, the style which reaches its perfection in Latin in Virgil's *Aeneid*: words which will not let themselves be pinned down to a simple statement, because they are too richly allusive, or evoke the kind of complex imagery which it is impossible to visualize sharply, or ever to exhaust of significance. Catullus' poems are written in the language of comedy rather than the language of tragedy or epic, for comedy purports to be about real life and the real speech of men while indulging a fantasy of its own. The model for the short poems of Catullus, as for the letters of Cicero, is what their contemporary Julius Caesar (himself a careful stylist) called, in a famous epigram, the 'pure talk' (*purus sermo*—'pure' in the sense of purified, freed from the dross of disjointed, unedited speech). We may call it the language of conversation improved upon.

The differences are more a matter of structure than of style. For if comedy or the kind of Latin we find in Cicero's letters provides a style, it does not provide a form. Even when they pretend to be letters, the poems display the characteristic architectural features of well-constructed poems. A poem must possess an internal unity which a letter need not possess. The layout of the argument may follow the linear logic of prose (as is the case, more often than not, in Catullus' elegiac verse, Poems 65–116). But it is just as likely to follow a more emotional poetic logic: the poem revolves around its theme, exploring the theme imaginatively, and returns at the end to the point from which it set out (so the last line of a Catullan poem not infrequently repeats the opening line). A poem has moreover a rhythmical and a metrical structure in addition to its syntactical and logical structure. The illusion of the poet's speaking voice is therefore a double illusion: behind these seemingly so fresh, so direct, so unliterary poems of Catullus, there lie not only the complicated rules of expression of a highly cultivated society (a letter of Cicero and a poem of Catullus are demonstrations of that quality which the Romans called *urbanitas*); there lie also the conventions and the achievements of a complex tradition of writing in verse.

But if, structurally speaking, these short poems are poems and work pretty much according to our notion of how poems should work, the common description of them as 'lyrics' is misleading. Though saturated in Greek literature, Catullus clearly avoided the traditional forms of Greek lyric poetry. Except in two or three special cases which might almost be described as parodies of Greek lyric form (though with a serious objective), it probably did not occur to him to take lyric forms as his models: they were too literary, too pretentious, for his purpose. Though it permitted simple, direct statement, the lyric tradition precluded the dry, sharp vivacity, the irony—the 'urbanity', in short—at which he aimed. Today, the term 'lyric' is used to describe almost any short personal poem. But in so far as the essence of lyric is song and the simple emotional incitement, the limpid line of sense, which go with song, these poems are

155

not lyrics.

The tradition in which Catullus writes is represented by a variety of slighter forms which hitherto had hardly belonged to literature at all, but to what has been called in this book 'paraliterature'.

One was that compact verse form, normally in elegiac couplets, which the Greeks called 'epigram'. Its original social function was to organize factual statement and make it worthy of being cut upon stone, in order to put a person or event on record for posterity. Long after epigrams ceased to be actual inscriptions, they continued to retain that limpid structural finality which we still call 'lapidary'. Though practising poets wrote commemorative epigrams (one naturally turned to a professional for a first-class job) and continued to write literary versions of epigrams throughout antiquity (Cicero's client Archias, if it is the same Archias, is credited with forty-one epigrams in the Greek Anthology), among the Romans an epigram seems to have become more the sort of thing a gentleman could turn his hand to in a moment of relaxation. Cicero speaks with approval of some epigrams of Atticus; they had apparently good words to say of Cicero, and he regarded them as compensating to some extent for missing out on a full-scale poem in the high style from one of the professionals. Cicero himself is credited by Pliny with tossing off the occasional epigram. We are left with the impression it was a common accomplishment, even if the successful handling of the form was not within the capabilities of all.

Characteristic of epigram was that it dealt with the realities of the world around you rather than the world of literature and the poetic imagination. When it was not purely functional, its object was to put a matter of fact, or an intellectual insight, well. The hallmark of a good epigram was its wit; there was no place for the poetic imagination in a form which kept statement under tight intellectual and syntactical control.

There are signs that the elegiac epigram is a form which is more purely Roman, owing less to Greek influences, than the other forms of personal poetry—less in particular than Augustan elegy. But perhaps we should be nearer the mark in saying that Roman epigram seems to have been (like the forms used by Lucilius) a form in which a consciously poetic, literary style could be dispensed with; a form in short in which it was not necessary to write in the style of a professional poet. One could, if one chose, attempt an epigram in the best Greek manner: take this epigram of Lutatius Catullus, for example, which dates from the generation before Catullus:

> Aufugit mi animus; credo, ut solet, ad Theotimum
> devenit. sic est, perfugium illud habet. . .

156

> My heart has run away. Once more, I think to Theotimus
> it has fled. Yes, it has taken refuge there. . .

It is an adaptation, wholly Hellenistic in spirit, of an epigram of Callimachus. But an epigram could also be the real thing, a poem actually written to be placed upon a grave. And the real thing was apt to have a different ring, such as this couplet written some time in the first century BC for the grave of a young woman:

> Ut rosa amoena homini est quom primo tempore floret,
>   quei me viderunt, seic ego amoena fui.

> Just as a rose seems beautiful to a man when first it flowers,
> so I was beautiful for those who saw me.

This simple dignity is found already in the well-known epitaph for Claudia which dates from the previous century:

> Hospes, quod deico, paullum est, asta ac pellege:
> heic est sepulcrum haud pulcrum pulcrai feminae.

> Stranger, what I say is short: stand and read.
> Here is the unlovely grave of a lovely woman.

This time, however, the epitaph, which runs into eight lines, is written in crude iambics.

Epigram is only one of a number of different minor verse forms (called *versiculi* by the Romans) which lay on the border between literature and paraliterature. Some are very much what we call 'occasional verse'. Others had what we might call a more practical social function. There existed, for example, a tradition of personal invective in verse, ridiculing an enemy or a political opponent. It was as much the function of paraliterature to attack the living as to commemorate the famous and the dead.

Such forms too had Greek antecedents. They were written in iambic and trochaic verse forms in the manner of the Greek poet Archilochus, and in 'limping iambic' trimeters (also called 'scazons') traditionally associated with the name of the Greek poet Hipponax, who was noted for the violence of his invective. The evidence for the development of these forms at Rome is scanty. One would like to know for certain, for example, that the eleven-syllable, partly iambic, partly trochaic line so much favoured by Catullus and called by him *hendecasyllabus* belongs, like the limping iambic, among the forms used by Roman writers of abusive or derisive *versiculi*. It is, however, a reasonable conjecture that this is the tradition in which Catullus writes in Poems 1–60 (forty of the sixty are in hendecasyllabics), while in Poems 69–116 he follows the epigrammatic tradition of writing in elegiac couplets. The break with his predecessor Laevius is clear and is confirmed by the fragments of Laevius which survive. Though he called them 'fun-poems about love' (*Erotopaegnia*), Laevius' poems are consciously poetic, intended as literature, so that their style is accordingly a consciously poetic style. Catullus wrenches us back into the real world. His scraps of verse—his 'stuff' as he called it (*nugae*) with deliberate casualness when he introduced it to the public (Poem 1)—openly proclaim their allegiance to the traditions of paraliterature.

Within the smart set with which Catullus became intimately associated there must have been many who could turn an epigram in verse, or toss off a short, witty lampoon. Some of them were avid readers of poetry. They knew their Callimachus and could appreciate a clever Latin translation of a clever Greek original, such as Catullus' translation of Callimachus' *Lock of Berenice* (Poem 66). They were attracted by the Callimachean ideal of a way of writing in which irony and precision of craftsmanship replaced loosely structured grandiloquence; several of them attempted to write poetry that matched up to that ideal (Catullus' *Attis*, Poem 63; his *Marriage of Peleus and Thetis*, Poem 64; the *Zmyrna* of his friend Helvius Cinna, see Poem 95); if a serious poem with real poetic pretensions was what you wanted, they were able, in technical skill and virtuosity, to beat the professionals hands down. For them, writing a poem was something as technically complicated as writing a string quartet in eighteenth-century Vienna: a work of art rather than an expression of the artist's personality. But they were also men who knew their Sappho, their Alcaeus, and their Archilochus. They were aware that the voice of the individual had once been heard in poetry, before it was overshadowed by the great public form of the drama and relegated to the status of a private amusement, to emerge again into literature only in that curiously stereotyped, depersonalized personal poetry upon which bookish scholar-poets of the Hellenistic age, living as they did in a cultural vacuum, found it amusing to expend their talent. It must have been exhilarating for Catullus and his friends when they hit, as it were by accident, upon the idea of turning their technical competence, their literary sophistication and the zest that came from feeling themselves youthful rebels against an ageing, corrupt society to the forms of paraliterature—and making of them forms in which the voice of the individual spoke out about the world around him with a new, urbanely casual eloquence.

If their verse was naughtier often than traditional ideas about what could be said in literature permitted, the answer was that they were not

writing literature. For the arch innuendo of the stilted tradition of
Hellenistic epigram they substituted elegantly structured, blunt words.
Many of the scraps of verse they wrote dealt with topics which were
hardly edifying; but in a society which appreciated wit and prided itself on
broadmindedness, such devastating sallies were hard to resist; it became
possible even to publish these short, clever, emotionally true, often
daring, often ruthlessly cruel, genuinely personal poems, and demand
that they be taken seriously as 'stuff' worth publishing. One could feel
one had gone back to Archilochus and made a fresh start.

When they are seen against this background—on the one hand, a new,
intense experimentation with serious poetic form in such poems as
Catullus' *Attis* and his *Marriage of Peleus and Thetis* and, on the other, a
conscious remodelling of the traditions of paraliterature—the Lesbia
poems emerge in a truer light. We begin to see that the Lesbia poems
aren't lyrics either. Apart from two conscious imitations (Poems 11 and
51), they owe no more to the love poetry of Sappho (Alcaeus, it seems,
wrote little love poetry) than Sappho's confident self-assurance in
exploring the theme of her own passionate feelings.

In tone, the Lesbia poems in the first part of the Catullan collection
belong, along with the rest of Poems 1–60, to the iambic mode. The note
of irony varies. It can take the form of urbane mockery, often shading off
into self-mockery, the tone of voice of the civilized man who consciously
understates while things go well (Poem 5):

> Let us live, my Lesbia, and let us love.
> If old men murmur protest, given to a stricter view,
> let us not give a damn for all their mutterings!
> The sun can go on quitting the bed he sank in;
> but we, when our brief day's light is done,
> must sleep through a night that will never end.
> Give me a thousand kisses. Then a hundred.
> Another thousand then. Then a second hundred.
> Then a further thousand. Then a hundred.
> Then when we've accumulated many thousands—
> let's muddle all the totals, so's we shan't know,
> nor will any nasty, nosy person be able to be jealous
> when he knows there's been heavy transacting in kisses.

Catullus adopts the same tone when he forces himself to pretend that a
mistress lost, or as good as lost, is a matter of small moment (Poem 8.
1–11):

> Don't be a fool, my poor Catullus, you must stop it,
> and count as lost what you see is lost.

There was a time when the bright sun shone for you:
the girl was leader and you her ready companion,
and you loved her then as none will be loved.
Then there were done those many merry things,
things you wanted, and she was ready enough.
There is no doubt the bright sun shone for you.
But now it's No she says. Say No too, control yourself.
Don't chase a girl that runs away. Don't live dejected,
but with hardened heart, face it out. Be firm. . . .

But Catullus can also adopt a tone of open, aggressive, militant irony (backed up by the fantasy and extravagance in attack which are characteristic of invective) when betrayal really hurts, or contempt for his rivals cannot, or in Catullus' view should not, be held in check (Poem 37. 1–8; 11–16):

Leaping house and you, the clientèle—
ninth pillar from the felt-crapped brothers—
do you fancy only you have all it takes,
only you the right, to fuck all the girls there are,
and do you fancy all others stinking oafs?
Just because you sit, a hundred in a stupid row
(or two hundred, then), do you fancy I won't
dare bugger all two hundred in one go?. . .
The girl who has deserted my embrace,
loved by me as none will be loved,
for whose sake I have many battles fought,
now sits with you. Her, you fine gentlemen love—
the lot of you; and what's more to be ashamed about,
all you small-time back-street lechers too. . . .

In the third part of the collection (Poems 69–116) the Lesbia poems are written in the drier, more intellectual tradition of epigram. They display the same passionate, firmly restrained logical structure as the rest of Catullus' epigrams, endowed with a new eloquence because it has been turned to a new purpose (Poem 70):

The woman who is mine wants to marry none, she says,
more than me—not if Jove himself were suitor,
she says; but for what woman says to eager lover
the wind is aptest record, and fast-flowing water.

But the primary allegiance throughout is to the tradition of paraliterature. The starting point is a conscious surrender to an illusion: a

160

proclamation, passionate but elegantly urbane, of Catullus' affair with another man's wife, in which an ironical display of verbal wit (one aspect of what the Romans called *doctrina*) adds a veneer of urbanity that never conceals altogether the intense feeling which lies just below the surface (7. 1–8):

> You ask me, Lesbia, how many kissings
> it will take to make me really satisfied.
> As many as the sands of Libya's desert
> that lies round Cyrene where the silphium grows,
> stretching between the oracle of sweltering Jove
> and the holy tomb of Battus long ago departed.
> Or as many as the stars that in night's quiet
> look down on us mortals stealing love.

Quickly, things start to go wrong: the affair so coolly embarked upon is almost as coolly shaken off when Lesbia loses interest; he will not 'chase a girl that runs away'. Then, unexpectedly, the affair is resumed—and, it seems, on a new note of seriousness (107. 1–4):

> Si quicquam cupido optantique obtigit umquam
>   insperanti, hoc est gratum animo proprie:
> quare hoc est gratum, nobis quoque, carius auro
>   quod te restituis, Lesbia, mi cupido. . . .

> Whenever a man gets something he wants, desires, but
> doesn't hope for, he feels truly grateful for it.
> And so I too am grateful, it is more to me than gold,
> that you restore yourself to me who wanted you. . . .

The resumed affair degenerates into an infatuation which Catullus explores and re-explores in short, compact elegiac poems, using the discipline imposed by the epigrammatic form to maintain tight intellectual control upon the emotional stresses within himself while he struggles for the simplest, most perfect formulation of a complex state of mind (Poem 85):

> I hate and I love: you ask perhaps the reason?
> I don't know. But I feel it happen and I go through hell.

The final dismissal comes in lines which are not an epigram but a poem 24 lines long in Sapphic stanzas, a public dismissal, written after it was all over, and a bitterly ironic echo of the version of Sappho he had once sent Lesbia as a hidden confession of his love. Unable to face her and break with her openly, he asks two friends to take 'a few plain words' to his mistress (11. 17–24):

Tell her to live with her lovers and be good riddance,
those three hundred lechers that share the embraces
of one who loves no man truly but time and again
drains all men dry;

tell her not to count on my love as till now
she could, for by her fault it lies like a flower
snapped off at the meadow's edge, while
the plough passes on.

Whether Catullus is writing about himself, about the world around him or about the world of legend and romance, the note of irony is never wholly absent. Sometimes the irony is bitterly sardonic: the poet's anger, or contempt, threatens to break the bonds which hold it in check. At other times (in some of the happier of the love poems, or in some of the more light-hearted of what are perhaps best called the poems of social comment) the irony is muted almost to the level of whimsy. At other times again it serves to place the poet at a distance from his narrative, warning us (as constantly in the *Attis* and the *Marriage of Peleus and Thetis*) that full commitment to the story told is being withheld: Catullus neither wholly identifies himself, nor wants us to identify ourselves, with the legendary situation.

But despite this note of irony we can see Catullus exploring new ways of expressing things in verse that are emotionally important to him—not playing, as the writers of the Greek Anthology had played (and as Laevius seems to have played), at writing verse whose primary justification was what Ezra Pound once called 'the dance of the intellect' along the line of sense. What above all makes the poetry of Catullus personal poetry is that the things talked about matter (in very different ways—one of the most striking things about the Catullan collection is its diversity) to the man who talks about them.

III   THE 'AVANT-GARDE' POETS AND THEIR SUCCESSORS

The Catullan collection makes it clear that their author belonged to a group of smart young men keenly interested in poetry. We can identify a few of them and some fragments of what they wrote survive. They are not poets as that term had been understood at Rome—professional writers working for their living and protected by a patron—but brilliant amateurs. Not just the sort of amateur who could turn the occasional competent epigram, but the kind whose enthusiastic devotion to the detail of technique and the zest which accompanies that devotion can sometimes revitalize an artistic tradition when conservatism (the besetting sin of all professionals) has allowed inspiration to be lost and the familiar techniques to become threadbare. As proof of their technical virtuosity, the 'new poets' devoted themselves to the production of that complex masterpiece in miniature to which modern scholars have given the name 'epyllion'. We hear of several such 'mini-epics'. There were no doubt several poets who could rival Catullus at putting a line together, at pruning and shaping a legend till it seemed to strut in verses out of the past. Without this intense interest in craftsmanship it is not likely that Roman personal poetry would ever have come to anything of importance.

It is usually supposed that Cicero had the group in mind when, on his way home from Cilicia (he had been governor there) at the end of 50 BC, he wrote to Atticus to announce his safe arrival at Brundisium, tossing off, in the exhilaration of the moment, a spondaic hexameter in the best Catullan style:

Flavit ab Epiro lenissimus Onchesmites.

Ever so gently from Epirus wafted Onchesmites [name of a wind].

He added the remark, 'You can sell that one to any of the avant-garde you like as your own'. The remark has a playful tone: the Greek word *neoteroi* which Cicero uses, as well as denoting the younger generation, has overtones of political revolution. Had Cicero been reading 'the avant-garde poets' in Cilicia? Perhaps his words are one more sign of that spirit of benevolent indulgence towards the young which he had flaunted since his successful defence a few years before of Caelius Rufus (a young man about town who had been accused of swindling the widow of a consul, with whom he had had a notorious affair, and then attempting to poison her). A few years later the tone seems less sympathetic: after quoting some lines of Ennius with warm approval, Cicero remarks that Ennius 'is looked down upon by those declaimers of Euphorion' (*ab his cantoribus Euphorionis contemnitur*). As in the previous passage, we are left with the impression that Cicero is thinking of hexameter verse in the high style (Euphorion was a Hellenistic poet, a notorious practitioner of the 'learned' style). Whether he realized the extent of the revolution Catullus and his friends had brought about in the field of personal poetry there is no way of telling.

The fragments of Licinius Calvus, Helvius Cinna, Furius Bibaculus and the rest are too scanty to permit any critical judgment. Propertius seems disposed to take Calvus seriously as a love poet, to be ranked alongside

Catullus. He perhaps made some contribution to the development of Latin elegy. The implicit judgment of antiquity places him among the minor talents, an orator with a flair for verse. We are told by Suetonius that he lampooned Julius Caesar. Two fragments of his invective poems survive (one on Caesar, one on Pompey). Like Catullus, he seems to have written wedding hymns, and at least one epyllion, an *Io* (we have six unconnected lines). With the others the story is similar. Their importance is that they carry the new poetry into the 40s and give ground for supposing that it existed as an active force when Virgil came to Rome and Horace returned there after his adventures on the field of battle at Philippi, fifteen years or so after the death of Catullus.

From Catullus to Ovid the line of development of the short personal poem is relatively easy to trace. We start with a style which is consciously non-poetic according to the conventional notions of the time of what poetry was. To the modern reader it is clearer if we call the style 'non-literary', provided we remember that the Romans had no equivalent for what we mean by literature. Because the poet is speaking in his own person, expressing his feelings on matters about which he feels intensely, there is no place for the grand manner of the impersonal artist, whose subject is the non-contemporary, unreal world, the public world of epic and tragedy. Poetry so understood stands in the way of honest, direct expression. In its place Catullus adopts the language of conversation improved upon. We overhear, as it were, the poet's speaking voice as he addresses his mistress, a friend, an enemy, or himself. Catullus, we may say, is a highly competent writer of occasional verse who had the makings of a poet of genius. Above all, he possessed the spontaneity of feeling without which well-constructed verse, however brilliant, remains no more than well-constructed verse. Even the poems on slighter themes are torn from their original ephemeral, trivial context by the intensity of the emotions expressed. But they show too the skill which enabled a young man possessed of an unusual talent and a highly developed technical competence to pin those emotions down with simple, direct precision. It was only afterwards (as he tells us in the first poem of the collection) that he was persuaded that what he had written could claim to be regarded as poetry; and towards the end of his short life, it seems, he published his poems, or began publishing them, those at any rate which he chose to represent what he had done, leaving them more or less as he had first written them. Though not written for publication, or even with the thought that they were poetry at all, they were good enough to be published, good enough to be taken seriously as poetry. A frontier had been crossed, as it were, unintentionally.

It is the sort of accident that can happen only once in a literary tradition. The poets who come after know what they are doing; they know the possibilities of the new style; they are poets, or would-be poets, from the outset. The Roman personal poets of the generation after Catullus are thus committed to the preservation of an illusion. They pretend to be writing occasional verse: a letter to a mistress or a friend. In fact they are writing poetry to be published; publication enters into their thoughts from the start. To preserve the illusion they keep the poet's speaking voice. But the voice is an increasingly mannered voice.

Horace is the only poet who can successfully maintain the illusion. Though the style of the *Odes* is complex, remote from anything you could call natural conversation, Horace manages to make it suggest none the less the conversational voice of the poet. Because the voice with which Horace speaks in the *Odes* resembles one common voice of lyric poetry in our own day, we are apt to underestimate the startling originality of Horace's achievement. It is a graver voice than that of Catullus, the voice of a man who views life from a moral standpoint; he expects his audience to take the trouble to ponder over what he means, and relies on his audience not to miss the undercurrent of irony which is hardly ever absent. There are no successors to the Horace of the *Odes*, none at any rate worth worrying about. A century after his death Quintilian could observe that Horace was 'just about the only Roman lyric poet worth reading' (*lyricorum fere solus legi dignus*).

The three elegists Propertius, Tibullus and Ovid stand also in the direct line of descent from Catullus, but differ from Horace in form (they confine themselves to the elegiac couplet) and in their strict adherence to the Catullan hypothesis of passionate love. They ask us to take seriously that a man can allow love to crowd out all else in life, that love can last. To the usual ancient view of the matter, such notions were contrary to common sense. Propertius comes closest to success with a distinctive, highly mannered, intellectual form of poetry. The fiction is maintained that the reader is listening to the poet's speaking voice, but Propertius has not Horace's dramatic skill; he cannot half-persuade us for the duration of the poem that we are listening to the actual speaking voice of the poet. Tibullus attempts to bolster up competent but essentially mediocre verse in the Catullan tradition by combining that tradition with a tradition of pastoral love poetry. Ovid, like Propertius, sticks to town love. His contribution to personal poetry, like his contribution to narrative and didactic poetry, amounts to an elegant debunking of an established form that has got out of touch with social function. The debunking was a success, so much so it really became impossible for anybody to write love elegy after Ovid.

The spectacular development from Catullus to Ovid never wholly suppresses the paraliterary tradition of occasional verse out of which it grew. Among the poems traditionally attributed to Virgil are some fifteen short poems (230 lines) which make up the collection usually called *Catalepton*. All but one are in metres used by Catullus (pure iambics, limping iambics, elegiac couplets). One (*Catalepton* 10) is in fact a close parody of Catullus' famous 'Yacht' poem, and there are obvious Catullan echoes in others. They form a very mixed bag: some obscure, one obscene. How many, if any, are genuine examples of Virgil's juvenilia is uncertain; how they came to form a collection is not known. Their interest is as specimens of paraliterature in the generation following Catullus, the sort of thing upon which Horace's *Epodes* represent a first attempt at refinement. No doubt a good deal of such verse was written during the Augustan Age. We can point to the collection which has come down to us under the title *Priapea* (eighty-five poems, mostly hendeca-syllabics and elegiacs, mostly obscene), and to the poems of Maecenas (three bits of poems and some isolated lines survive). We hear of others.

The tradition continues into the following century. We find such scraps of verse, mixed up with parodies of the grand manner, in the *Satyricon* of Petronius. Indeed, in the Postclassical period the short personal poem falls back into the hands of dilettanti, versifiers who have really nothing to say, however much they like to think of themselves as continuing a distinguished tradition. With Pliny, writing *versiculi* and reciting them to his friends becomes a sterile affectation (for an example see *Epistles* 7. 9). A century earlier it had been a living institution of social life; the *versiculi* of Catullus and his friends had often been violently abusive, even libellous, bordering on the outrageous. Changed circumstances left no place for verse in the Archilochean tradition; that sort of thing was not any more tolerated by a new, much more repressive social order.

Even a dabbler in paraliterature like Cicero (given pride of place by Pliny in an impressive list of famous men of the past who had written occasional verse) had been able to feel he was responding, in his modest way, to the intellectual ferment of his day. Pliny prides himself on the naughtiness of his verses (they were, he said, *'severos parum'*), but one suspects it was a very milk-and-water indecency. Statius in his prose-prefaces to a collection of short poems (mainly in hexameters) which he called *Silvae* ('undressed timber') actually boasts of hasty composition. Pieces such as his lines on a friend's dead parrot were 'dashed off', he says, 'like epigrams'. Comparison of the poem (*Silvae* 2.4—incidentally, it is 37 lines long) with Ovid's lines on Corinna's parrot (*Amores* 2. 6), or with Catullus' lines on Lesbia's dead sparrow, is instructive. What Statius' lines lack is not so much formal elegance as intellectual strength and all intensity or refinement of feeling: as Quintilian remarks about those who affect the 'undressed' style, 'the words and the metre are tidied up, but the original triviality of hastily-strung-together content remains' (*manet in rebus temere congestis quae fuit levitas*). The only professional in the Postclassical period is Martial. He attempts a rehabilitation of the Catullan tradition of paraliterature on a massive scale that is as cold-blooded and as flagrantly indecent as it is clever. But it is a wholly artificial revival, unprompted by anything in contemporary cultural life, unless it is the pursuit of indecency for its own sake. His slick, clever, coldly obscene *Epigrams* represent a final reduction to triviality of the Catullan tradition.

IV   VIRGIL'S *Eclogues*

If a warning were needed against drawing the line of descent from Catullus to Ovid too clearly, it would be provided by Virgil's *Eclogues*. They point to an upsurge of pastoral poetry of some importance in the generation following Catullus. Again we have names, but—apart from the *Eclogues*—little else.

The *Eclogues* (ten poems, average length about 80 lines, all in hexameters) are not to everybody's taste. They are not for the reader who expects poetry to tell a story, or present an argument, or pinpoint a moral situation. Yet they are something more than 'imitations' of Theocritus. As well as the stylized realism of a rustic world in which shepherds contend in song and protest at length their unrequited loves—a world nearer to buffoonery (the love lament of Corydon in *Eclogue* 2, the argument between the rival singers with which *Eclogue* 3 begins) than to idealism—the *Eclogues* express eloquently but discreetly the primaeval innocence with which Lucretius invests pastoral song in the fifth book of *On the Universe*.

At the same time the real contemporary world is never far distant. It looms on the horizon of *Eclogues* 1 and 9; elsewhere a name, an allusion, evokes for a moment the contemporary political scene. The *Eclogues*, in short, are also personal poetry. Admittedly, the personal element is hard to disengage. One is never sure which of Virgil's characters we are expected to unmask as real persons. It is one component of that curious tantalizing property of the poems to which nearly every reader responds, one which has ensured their continuing popularity, if not their comprehension. We feel it should be possible to regard the collection as the poet's way of coping with some kind of personal problem, environmental or artistic. The difficulty is, the problem has been coped with more by evading it, more by a retreat into literature, than by confronting it. There is a sense in which the *Eclogues* must be described as escapist poetry, a way out of the intolerable reality of Rome in the dark, anguished years which followed the break-up of the unholy alliance between Caesar's heirs; an escape from reality into art, into a curiously unreal form of realism upon which the cruder realities of the world from which the poet has attempted to escape keep impinging.

The order of composition of the poems is hard to determine. We have to allow for a difference between dramatic date and actual date of composition. In the form in which the poems were published, however, the plan seems clear. *Eclogues* 1 and 9 form a frame, an outer context of contemporary events which threaten to destroy the simple, idyllic peace of the pastoral world. *Eclogue* 1 is followed by two poems which retreat into the dream world of pastoral, where the only conflicts are those of unrequited love and rival singers. Three quite different poems (*Eclogues* 4–6) occupy the centre of the collection. In *Eclogues* 7 and 8 we return to the world of *Eclogues* 2 and 3. *Eclogue* 10 is a kind of epilogue.

Eclogue 1, while an introductory poem, a dialogue between two inhabitants of the pastoral world, is perhaps to be read also as Virgil's farewell to pastoral poetry. Tityrus has recently been freed and, along with others, confirmed in his position as shepherd or tenant-farmer on the land he has long lived on as a slave. Meliboeus has been evicted and faces the prospect of emigration and making life anew in a distant land. It was doubtless a common experience in the years following Philippi for one tenant-farmer to lose his land through confiscation (the land was needed for army veterans), while another escaped confiscation through luck or influence. Indeed, if we may believe Servius, Virgil himself lost the farm which had belonged to his father, and was then reconfirmed in possession of it through the intervention of one of the land commissioners, the amateur poet Asinius Pollio. Which is not to say that Virgil is Tityrus, any more than that he is Meliboeus. If Virgil is anybody in the poems, it seems he must be the singer Menalcas. But he has a special personal insight into the tragedy which overshadowed the lives of these simple folk; their experience is in a sense his experience. The poem is a symbol of the disintegration of the world of Virgil's boyhood, a symbolic statement of how contemporary reality has broken in upon the dream world of pastoral. When Virgil revised the poem for publication as the opening poem of a collection, he perhaps intended it also (along with *Eclogue* 9) as a symbolic statement that this kind of poetry was no longer possible, or no longer possible for him. Like Meliboeus, he can perhaps envy Tityrus his tranquil property remote from a mad world (*Eclogue* 1. 46–52):

Lucky old man, your farm will stay yours, then.
Big enough for you too, even if bare rock everywhere

and swamp reeds encroach on the pastures.
You won't have strange fodder upsetting your pregnant ewes,
or sickness spreading from a neighbour's flocks.
Lucky old man! Here, amid streams you know
and holy springs, you will rest in cool shade.

But for him that life lies in the past. The dream world of the *Eclogues* will
be followed by the emotional commitment to the realities of Italian rural
life (its harsh, exacting routine as much as its beauty) of the *Georgics*.

Eclogue 2 begins the retreat into the serene world of pastoral. The
poem is a very arch literary pastiche with echoes of Theocritus' Poly-
phemus and the high-style tragic lament (compare Ariadne's in Catullus'
Marriage of Peleus and Thetis), a challenge to look at the humble reality
of country life through the rose-tinted spectacles of pastoral and to extend
an elegant literary tradition to the lowly (or at any rate non-tragic) theme
of homosexual passion. It is part of the delicate irony of the *Eclogues*
that Corydon should be quite insensitive to the natural beauty which he
describes in such detail. But though pastiche, the poem is also graceful,
charming, sophisticated poetry.

Eclogue 3, a singing contest between two shepherds, represents a
further retreat into a vanishing world. *Eclogue* 4 has 'a somewhat loftier
theme' (*paulo maiora canamus*) and looks into the future, not the past.
Virgil's theme is the coming of an age of peace and plenty: the transformation of the world is at hand and will be accomplished in the lifetime of
an unnamed infant child in whose honour the poem is written. *Eclogue* 4
is the best known of all the *Eclogues,* having been supposed in the Middle
Ages to predict the birth of Jesus Christ. The theme is not, however, one
that is seriously explored, and the climax does not bear, and is surely not
intended to bear, serious examination. Comparison with the tough
realistic picture in the *Georgics* of a world in which man must fight against
a hostile environment shows up this Golden Age fantasy with conventional pastoral trappings for what it is. The occasion of *Eclogue* 4 isn't one
that permits dwelling on the brutal realities of life. They can be allowed to
do no more than threaten the dream world from outside. There is no
place for them within the fantasy.

The extravagance of *Eclogue* 4 has to be taken in the context of the
extravagance of *Eclogue* 5 and of *Eclogue* 6. The subject of *Eclogue* 5 is
the death and apotheosis of the shepherd Daphnis. It has long been
supposed that this charming and beautiful poem is an allegory of the
death of Julius Caesar, already accorded divine honours before his death.
Virgil perhaps also intends us to see in Daphnis a friend and patron of
poets: that the poems are a pastoral transposition of the activities of a

169

circle of poets around Julius Caesar, in which contemporaries might identify or suspect the identities of the main characters, does not seem wholly fanciful. *Eclogue* 6 is a version of the legend recounted by Ovid in *Metamorphoses* of Silenus, an amiable, elderly, drunken associate of Dionysus who was captured by King Midas and bound with flowers, and then hospitably treated; in return Midas was given the touch of gold. In Virgil's poem Silenus is captured and bound by two youngsters with the assistance of a girl. In return for his release he sings the trio a song recounting the creation of the world, and then a series of myths, and, mixed with these, the tale of how the poet Gallus came to write a poem in the manner of Hesiod. The narrative is charming and much of the rest pleasant verse, but what we are to make of it all is far from clear.

Eclogue 7 brings us back to the more familiar world of pastoral. Daphnis is still alive and he invites Meliboeus to witness the great contest between Corydon (the singer of *Eclogue* 2) and the shepherd Thyrsis, described as a 'rising poet' (*crescentem poetam*), whom we meet only here. *Eclogue* 8, like *Eclogue* 2, is about unrequited love.

Eclogue 9 brings us back out of the dream world into the unwelcome realities of the land confiscations which followed Octavian's victory at Philippi. Lycidas is surprised to learn that Moeris has been dispossessed; he had heard that Menalcas had saved the land of all the shepherds in these parts. So people said, replies Moeris; but in the end they had to give in to superior force. This leads the pair to recalling favourite passages from Menalcas' poems, as they go on their way, and the poem ends in a mood of gentle, bucolic melancholy with some of the most beautiful lines in the collection (*Eclogue* 9. 57–64):

> Et nunc omne tibi stratum silet aequor, et omnes,
> aspice, ventosi ceciderunt murmuris aurae.
> hinc adeo media est nobis via; namque sepulcrum
> incipit apparere Bianoris, hic ubi densas
> agricolae stringunt frondes, hic, Moeri, canamus;
> hic haedos depone, tamen veniemus in urbem.
> aut si nox pluviam ne colligat ante veremur,
> cantantes licet usque (minus via laedet) eamus.

> And now, the whole sea is calm, and, look!
> the gentle breeze has dropped, not a murmur left.
> We're half-way on our road now, you can just see
> Bianor's grave ahead. Here where the farmers
> are thinning out the leaves, here's the place for a song.
> Put down your kids, we'll get to town all right.

Or if you're afraid night will bring on a shower,
we can sing as we walk, it'll make the journey lighter.

Eclogue 10 (described as a poem for the soldier-poet Cornelius Gallus
and his mistress Lycoris, formerly the mistress of Mark Antony) breaks
the tight formal pattern. Virgil calls his poem an *'extremus labor'*, a final
excursion, perhaps, into pastoral poetry after his collection was
complete, or a poem added for a second edition. Gallus is an intruder
from the outside world. He is discovered, pining away with unrequited
love, in a pastoral setting. He expresses his regret that he has not adopted
the pastoral life himself instead of becoming a soldier; he would have
been happier, and his mistress would not have deserted him. Virgil
perhaps felt the subject called for a poem more to Gallus' taste than his
own, a learned poem for a learned poet. At any rate, if in *Eclogues* 1–9
the focus often seems deliberately left unsharp (no doubt to warn the
reader against excessive curiosity about details), *Eclogue* 10 is difficult to
the point of obscurity. While the model remains Theocritus, the manner
is more that of Callimachus and Euphorion.

V HORACE'S *Odes* AND *Epodes*

If Catullus represents the adolescence of Roman personal poetry, with
Horace personal poetry reaches full maturity. Yet Horace was not, either
in the eyes of his contemporaries or in the verdict of history, the leading
poet of the Augustan Age: that title belongs beyond question to Virgil.
But in a period comparable only in antiquity to the age of Pericles in its
acceptance of full-time devotion to the making of poetry as an honoured
profession, Horace stands out as the poet who claimed and won a new
role for poets in society. During the last decade of his life he occupied a
position of authority as the leading spokesman for literature, the man
who could publish an open letter to the Emperor on the state of poetry
(*Epistles* 2. 1) and speak his mind with the easy familiarity of one who
knows it is his right to do so.

Yet Horace had never written an epic, and had indeed proclaimed his
incompetence to write one; he had never attempted a tragedy or comedy,
though he was willing to tell others how the job should be done. His claim
to fame, his *monumentum aere perennius,* rested on a kind of poetry of
which he was, to all intents and purposes, the sole Roman practitioner. A
generation before, Cicero had found it hard to take lyric poetry (that is to
say, Greek lyric poetry) seriously: he felt it was not worth a busy man's

time. Horace showed his contemporaries what could be done with lyric: in his hands it became a kind of poetry which established him as one of the greatest and most original poets of all time. He was also, in the sense in which we have come to understand the term, the first man of letters in the western world.

Horace had learnt as a young student in Athens in the late 40s to regard poets as important people. It was a city where a young man might learn to think seriously, if not deeply, about the problems of moral philosophy and to be idealistic about liberty and personal independence. We should not be surprised if this son of a freed slave, swept away by the enthusiasm with which the Athenians received the murderers of Caesar, joined the army of Brutus in a mood of youthful rebellion against dictatorship.

His military career was a fiasco; but when he returned to Rome under the terms of the generous amnesty which followed the victory of Caesar's heirs at Philippi (42 BC), it was as a young man in his late twenties who had felt the intoxication of a way of life in which ideas counted, and who had come to think of himself, half-humorously, as a successor of the soldier-poets of ancient Greece. Like them, he was to write about wine, women and song, and put personal independence before material success. When youthful enthusiasm had matured into a wry detachment, Horace's true individuality as a poet emerged: the man who had moulded himself on others became himself.

Horace was introduced by Virgil to Maecenas, and Maecenas became his patron and friend. Professional poets at Rome had always had patrons. It was an aspect of the traditional link between the man of influence and his clients which formed the basis of so many relationships in Roman society. A habit of thought existed ready made; a niche stood waiting to receive the poet, like any other craftsman. If Catullus and his friends fall outside this pattern it is because they are amateurs. Horace and Virgil accept the traditional role. But in the Augustan Age things were not quite the same as in Republican times: to be a member of the circle of Maecenas meant accepting something closer to state patronage than the patronage of an individual. At the same time Horace and Virgil claim, and receive, a new independence from their patron. They come to assume in the Roman social scale a position more akin to the status which distinguished Greek philosophers who had made their home in Rome had been accorded for a century or more by their Roman protectors. They are respected and protected, not as entertainers, or as men whose eloquence was politically useful, not in short as craftsmen, but as thinking individuals with a serious claim on men's opinions.

Horace takes up personal poetry where Catullus left off. A generation after Catullus it had become normal for a poet to bring himself into his poetry, as Virgil does (though not openly) in the *Eclogues*. Horace will do so openly in all his poetry, as will Propertius, Tibullus and Ovid in their varying ways. But since he is not, like Catullus, a brilliant amateur, he does not allow himself to be committed to the anti-establishment *persona* which the elegists in their closer adherence to the Catullan tradition of passionate love accept. Horace's first objective is respectability: a highly individual respectability, to be sure, but one that was beyond question.

He approached the matter in characteristically Roman fashion. To be accepted as a professional writer, one had to have a recognized tradition (which meant normally a Greek tradition) behind one. Thus, where Catullus (certain of the long poems apart) had aimed at freshness by a kind of writing that was assertively non-literary, Horace in the poetry he took seriously (apart, that is to say, from the *Satires* and *Epistles*) adopted from the outset a style of writing which was assertively literary. Where Catullus had done no more than take over and make his own a style which could be loosely described as Archilochean or iambic, Horace attempted already in the *Epodes* a conscious full-scale transposition of Archilochus. In the *Odes* he set his sights progressively higher and higher: first, the Hellenistic successors of Sappho and Alcaeus, then the great masters of the lyric form themselves.

A mixture of diffidence and independence (to read between the lines of what he tells us about the beginnings of his poetic career) led him first to a more modest rehabilitation. His model was Lucilius, the originator of the form which the Romans called *satura* and which we call 'satire'. (See Section X.) At the same time he began writing in a style very close to the short poems of Catullus or the *Catalepton* collection.

After ten years of experiment he published about 30 BC a small book of seventeen poems, many quite short; sixteen are in alternating shorter and longer lines (usually iambic combinations), a form not used by Catullus. Horace seems to have called the collection *Iambi*; we know it as the *Epodes*. The earliest are hardly to be taken very seriously; what we may take to be the last to be written are very respectable poems.

Horace had the good sense to reject the role of *epigonos,* the man who merely imitates; he wanted to be something more than a successor of Catullus. His object is to win acceptance as a poet. If, like Catullus, he rejects outworn native traditions, the rejection is more carefully planned. Like the first Roman poets of the third and second centuries BC, he sets out to make something new of a way of writing which had proved successful in the hands of a Greek poet in a different time, language and culture. His acknowledged models are Archilochus and Hipponax, the recognized creators of the iambic form.

Six of the seventeen poems are none the less very self-conscious exercises full of echoes of Catullus. *Epode* 3 is a mock-serious denunciation of garlic addressed to his patron Maecenas. *Epode* 4 attacks an upstart *tribunus militum* very much in the manner of Catullus 52 (if a little unconvincingly on the lips of a man who on his own admission had himself been mocked as an upstart *tribunus militum*); *Epode* 6 (in which allegiance to the tradition of Archilochus and Hipponax is specifically claimed) threatens an unknown enemy; *Epode* 10 is a mock bon-voyage poem. *Epodes* 8 and 12 are detailed and revolting attacks on an ageing nymphomaniac with literary pretensions in the best tradition of invective, but disgusting in a way that Catullus' attacks on Ipsitilla (Poem 32) or Aemilianus (Poem 97) are not.

Epode 1, which introduces the collection, also contains obvious echoes of Catullus 11: Maecenas is represented (rather unrealistically) as braving the dangers of Actium while Horace stays at home in safety. The style, however, is very un-Catullan: there is a kind of breathlessness about this strangely wooden poem, as though Horace were trying too hard to free himself from conventional rhetoric structure and already moving towards the compact, sinewy style of the *Odes*. When, some twenty years later, he wrote in *The Art of Poetry* 'by struggling for brevity I become obscure' (*brevis esse laboro, obscurus fio*) he was giving advice, not making a personal confession: perhaps all the same he had his own early struggle for brevity in mind.

In the remainder the influence of Catullus is less apparent. The two long *Epodes* 5 and 17 are to some extent modelled on Theocritus' *Pharmaceutria*. But *Epode* 5 is a vivid and original poem, a dramatic study in horror and low-life realism; *Epode* 17 is a long, ironical recantation, very unlike Catullus 36 (of which Horace later made a very self-assured ironical imitation in *Odes* 1. 16). *Epode* 2 claims allegiance to pastoral: it reads as a long, conventional encomium of rural life which would pass (in a different metre) for good Tibullan pastiche until the game is given away in the concluding lines: the speaker, we discover, is not Horace but the moneylender Alfius. Perhaps the Roman ear would have detected Horace's detachment from the facile sentimentality of lines 1–66. *Epode* 9 is a rather forced song of triumph for the victory at Actium. *Epodes* 7 and 16 are impassioned addresses to the Roman people, denouncing the folly of the civil war.

Epode 11 is the first of three poems which break fresh ground: Horace is in love, but it is the love-sickness of a strictly orthodox Epicurean, weak enough to surrender to infatuation, strong enough to face the fact that love does not last. It will remain the characteristic Horatian stance in the matter of love; a cool implicit rejection of the Catullan tradition of passion ironically surrendered to and then desperately struggled against as the poet's ideal recedes; an explicit rejection of the elegiac cult of love as the most important thing in life and the Propertian ideal of a passionate attachment that holds poet-lover and his mistress together until they are parted by death. This epode is an agreeable poem, but the data are conventional and Hellenistic (Horace confesses a weakness for boys as much as girls).

Epode 15 is a pleasantly ironical but at the same time genuinely poetical dismissal of a faithless mistress (Horace's way of handling the situation of Catullus 8 and 76). *Epode* 13 is a dramatic monologue in the tradition of Anacreon and Greek sympotic poetry, in which a speaker at a party invites his companions to put aside cares for the morrow and concentrate on the drinking. Though slight (it cannot compare as moral statement with Odes such as 1. 11, in which, with exquisite restraint, Horace communicates his considered philosophy of life), *Epode* 13 comes nearest to the more familiar, mature Horace of the *Odes*. The opening appeal to nature symbolism (compare *Odes* 1. 9, or the spring odes 1. 4 and 4. 7), the exploitation of myth in the concluding lines (compare *Odes* 1. 7) and the emergence of a characteristically Horatian melancholy are all signs that Horace is finding his poetic feet. In *Epode* 14 Horace offers his excuses to Maecenas for his inability to complete the book. The reason, he says, is that he is in love. Reading between the lines, one suspects Horace regrets the crude realism of *Epodes* 8 and 12 and would like to make a fresh start. He has, in short, outgrown the form.

The interest of the collection is that it shows Horace trying to find out what he can do with personal poetry once he is no longer writing occasional verse but verse that has detached itself from a particular occasion. For it is plain that the invective is not motivated, as in Catullus, by genuine enmity or grievance; nor are the epodes about love motivated by the poet's passionate involvement with a real mistress, as Catullus' love poetry is motivated by his affair with Lesbia.

The *Odes* will show that Horace has learnt to eliminate gauche gestures at humour, the mark of a speaker who is not at ease with his audience. Having experimented both in the *Epodes* and the *Satires* with low-life realism, he will reject it from his serious poetry. There is realism in the *Odes*; but, though the blows hit hard and true (for example, in *Odes* 4. 13), they are aimed with a new, cool detachment. Horace's experiments with political themes in the *Epodes* were rather more successful and he will come back to these (for example, *Odes* 1. 14 or 2. 1) but here too he will exercise an admirable restraint; Horace is not a politically committed poet and most of his life he will have the good sense not to pretend he is. In the *Epodes* he learnt to abandon the facile emotional incitement of the grand manner in favour of a more sinewy, less simply rhetorical style, if one that was as yet over-complicated syntactically. An important turning point had been reached. In moving away from occasional verse, Horace might have seen the function of personal poetry as merely providing light entertainment. He decided instead to set himself a more serious objective.

Horace's *Odes* represent a determined and successful break with the Catullan tradition. They have been compared to Bach's *Well-tempered Clavier*; like the Preludes and Fugues, these 103 short poems represent one of the triumphs of western intellect. If that makes them sound rather monumental, this is how Horace intended them: the lyric form asserts a claim to seriousness of intent well beyond that of Archilochean epode.

Their history in modern times has been curious. The *Odes* have never recovered from the Romantic revolt at the end of the eighteenth century. But that revolt was more a revolt against an educational tradition (it was the way he had been taught Horace at Harrow—'to comprehend, but never love thy verse'—that made Byron hate Horace) and a worn-out literary tradition that made the simpler, cruder manner of German lyric seem preferable to the mannered, polished obliqueness of the English Augustans. Now that we have escaped from Romanticism and are almost ideally conditioned by our best modern poetry to appreciate Horace, we have forgotten what he is like; those who make and talk about poetry are too ignorant to appreciate the real Horace behind the Romantic distortion.

For the formal perfection is only one side of the *Odes*. They are a demonstration that Sappho and Alcaeus (poets almost as remote in time as Archilochus, but surrounded with a halo of respect not accorded to Archilochus) can be revived and Romanized; that poetry which is neither didactic nor ostensibly serious in tone can be the expression of a serious attitude to life. Horace's Epicurean and Lucretian detachment is as different from Catullus' openly passionate involvement as it is from the feigned, or counterfeit, involvement which rather too obviously takes the place of the real thing in the *Epodes*.

When he gathered his poems for publication Catullus allowed some at any rate of the scraps of verse on trivial and obscene themes through which he had discovered and developed his talent to stand alongside those other scraps in which his genius found full expression: scraps hardly different from the rest in form or language, but none the less poems which demand to be taken seriously because in them things that are emotionally important to the poet find increasingly precise expression. To lump all together with apparent nonchalance was part of the characteristic bravado of a young man who has discovered his talent practically by accident.

Horace pretended he had done the same in the *Epodes*. There is the same element of bravado, a little more calculated no doubt, as in the Catullan collection. But in the *Odes* there is no place for the trivial and the crude. *Odes* 1. 25 is a cruel poem. So too is *Odes* 4. 13:

> The gods have answered my entreaty, Lyce,
> amply answered! You're old, and yet
> you want to look a beauty still,
> you flirt and drink unblushingly,
>
> in shaky, tipsy song importune love's
> unreceptive ear. . . .

But one need only compare these poems with *Epodes* 8 and 12 to see how completely Horace has discarded the Archilochean tradition. It is a mistake to regard them as personal attacks: their cruelty comes from their truth to the human condition; it is a cruelty to be complained of only by those who expect poetry to be sentimental about the realities of life.

The social circumstances are also different. The *Odes* show not only an evolving understanding of what poetry can do: but an evolving understanding of what poetry is for. They are the work of an established poet supported by a patron whose patronage is the symbol of support at the highest political level; what Horace writes is considered worthy of support as art, as an expression of the civilized Roman intellect. With the exception of the Roman Odes (3. 1–6) they are not laureate odes, not at any rate until the fourth book (published something like ten years later than Books 1–3, after the balance between poet and patron had begun to shift, to the disadvantage of poetry).

The forms are in the main those with which the names of Sappho and Alcaeus had always been linked, and forms with which the name had come to be linked of the Hellenistic poet Asclepiades, though these too were based on forms used by Sappho and Alcaeus. Horace's formal model is above all Alcaeus: of the 103 odes, more than one-third are written in Alcaic stanzas. But plainly, if they were to achieve the ends Horace wanted, his *Odes* could resemble their acknowledged models in little more than form. No doubt he saw in Alcaeus, the socially involved soldier-poet, an idealized version of himself, a personality that fitted his own sufficiently for him to feel he could endow this intensification of himself with the speaking voice of a Roman in the time of Augustus. But if he did see himself that way, it was only after a good deal of experiment. And fused with this Alcaic Horace is the Horace of the *Satires* and *Epistles,* if more elusive and more urbanely reticent.

Take a famous poem (*Odes* 1. 9. 1–8):

Look at all the snow: Mount Soracte stiff, sheer,
shining white; trees struggling with the load,
scarce able to cope; streams that a piercing, freezing
grip has pulled up short.

Melt the cold away, pile logs
upon the fire and with more liberal hand
decant, Thaliarchus, the two-lugged jar
of strong Sabine wine. . . .

In both metre and sense the two first stanzas follow a surviving poem of
Alcaeus closely enough to establish a link in the mind of a well-read
contemporary reader between Alcaeus' poem and the poem he had
before him. It is an important aspect of what we may call the element of
artifice in the. *Odes*. To some the *Odes* have seemed little more than a
mosaic of themes from Greek poetry. In fact, the object of the echoes is to
establish a tension between the associations with Greek poetry touched
off by Horace's words and the contemporary real world that is being
talked about in those words. Interwoven with the element of artifice is a
contrasting element in the poet's speaking voice, which is non-Sapphic,
non-Alcaic and non-Greek. We may call it the element of irony.

The ironic stance which Horace adopts in the *Odes* has often been
remarked on. It has usually been assumed it was merely the personality of
Horace himself showing through, so to speak, not very opportunely in
what was supposed to be lyric poetry; an indication of poetic inadequacy;
proof, if we liked, that Horace was a charming fellow, but not really able
to do more than rise occasionally', as Quintilian said (*nam et insurgit
aliquando*), to the lofty heights of poetry. This is to misjudge Horace: his
object is to establish a further calculated tension in which the tradition of
Greek lyric poetry and the Catullan tradition of paraliterature are held in
balance.

In an attempt to arouse his reader's responsiveness, to make it clear
that the *Odes* were not just literature, Horace worked out a style which is
common enough in modern poetry, but had not existed till he created it.
It depends essentially on a subdued flippancy of tone, an ironical
understating lightness that would not have seemed compatible with
poetry until Catullus proved it could be more effective than a vague
rhetorical sublimity (which is apt to dull our responsiveness, instead of
sharpening it). This flippancy of tone is strengthened in Horace by a
degree of artifice that goes a good deal beyond the Catullan style of
conversation improved upon: there is a terse complexity of statement, in
which the reader keeps catching echoes, but in a different key, so to
speak, from poetry of the past.

Horatian satire, like the *nugae* of Catullus, could permit itself no more than an occasional trace of oratorical or poetical grandiloquence: in general the style aimed at was that of 'the sophisticated citizen' (the *urbanus*), the man who 'can hold eloquence in check'. It had not yet occurred to Horace that this is a possible style for serious poetry: he still equated poetry with the grand manner. The *Odes* are a challenge to the reader to admit that Catullan *urbanitas*, the style of conversation improved upon, can be made the medium of a new kind of poetry. The result is one of those effective combinations of realism and non-realism which seem to be the basis of true art, in literature as in painting or sculpture. The speaking voice is also the voice of poetry. An illusion of conversational immediacy involves the reader in an apparently everyday situation (*Odes* 1. 5. 1–5):

> What slip of a boy amid a profusion of roses,
> scent-drenched, gleaming, importunes you, Pyrrha,
> in this attractive grotto? For whom do you
> bind back your blonde hair
>
> all chic simplicity? . . .

Or somebody is told to do something, or not to do something (*Odes* 1. 11. 1–3):

> Stop enquiring, Leuconoe, what end the gods have fixed for you,
> what end for me—it's unpermitted knowledge; stop your
> meddling with Babylonian cyphers. . . .

Then, after a more complicated central section, the ode ends perhaps (as this ode does) with a further instruction:

> Carpe diem, quam minimum credula postero.
>
> Snatch the day, trusting as little as you can in tomorrow.

The rapier-like precision of the speaking voice compels a second and a third reading, while a coolly chiselled final image (for example, *Odes* 1. 5 or 2. 14), or a concluding retreat into myth (for example, *Odes* 1. 8 or 3. 20), ensures that the situation from real life is presented in a way that excludes facile, one-sided judgment.

The *Odes*, like the *Satires* and the *Epistles*, are the work of a conscious moralist. Horace's use of the lyric form for the expression of moral attitudes was almost without precedent and created difficulties. The problem was to find a way of writing acceptable as a creative development of the traditional rhetoric of lyric. A form which was in origin spontaneous and almost morally neutral (the political poems of Alcaeus are hardly the work of a moralist) had to be adapted and expanded until it could express the complex attitudes and moral insights of a sophisticated, analytic mind. Where the insight was intuitive (a quick perception of the inner significance of a human situation), one Horace might have had considerable difficulty in expressing in prose with any acceptable completeness and economy, the communication of that insight in essentially visual terms can be tremendously effective; where the insight had to be backed up by argument, success often eluded him.

Consider the odes about love: the Pyrrha ode (1. 5), for example, the Sybaris ode (1. 8), the ode to Neobule (3. 12). Or take the Soracte ode (1. 9) or the code to Postumus (2. 14), in which the moral perspective is wider. Horace speaks as the observer of life as he sees it. But he is at pains to make clear that the view expressed is a personal, emotionally involved view. To emphasize his involvement and to eliminate a didactic, preaching stance, he substitutes for the poet's speaking voice that of a character in a dramatic monologue. There is no attempt to persuade us, to commit us to a clear-cut moral judgment. Our minds are set working to form their own judgment, so that his object is achieved more economically and more memorably than the more explicit techniques of the hexameter essay would permit. The speaker's thoughts unwind, as it were, as he talks; the rhetorical structure is more often psychological than logical. The role of the addressee may be that of the person spoken to or it may be that of the person spoken about, as in the ode to the ageing Lyce (4.13). Often, we may be sure the addressee is not an actual person, but a convenient fiction, just as sometimes Horace allows himself to talk as men do talk in the setting he asks us to imagine, rather than as the poet expressing his personal opinions.

In these implicitly moralizing odes, no surrender of the ironic stance is necessary. But there are also odes where Horace attempts explicit moralizing, and here success tended to elude him. Let the reader consider such odes as 2. 2, 2. 15, 2. 16, 2. 18, 3. 16, 3. 24 and especially the Roman odes (3. 1–6). Here the moral insight is abstract, an argument sketched out to defend a way of life, not the intuitive appraisal of a situation. Horace's argument is one he could have expressed without difficulty in prose; the ideas are the product of a moralizing tradition which had learnt how to deal with such concepts in explicit, analytic terms. We need only turn to Cicero (most of whose moral treatises belong to the last years of Cicero's life, when Horace was already in his twenties) to see such ideas discussed with easy confidence. In these odes what Horace presents us with is too often logical argument thinly disguised as lyric. Explicit moralizing in the manner of the *Satires* and *Epistles* takes the place of that imaginative co-operation between poet and reader which recreates the vivacity and the immediacy of the original intuition. The worst failures seem sometimes to occur when Horace is trying hardest. Compare the first Roman ode (3. 1) with 2. 18, of which 3. 1 is a transposition into the grander rhetoric of a public occasion. The oracular tone, the openly satirical stance, sit uneasily upon Horace; the dismissal of the ostentatious lifestyle of the power-seeking *patronus* and the defence of Horace's own simpler way of life are more compactly organized and more convincing in 2. 18; the flash of sympathy for the tenant-farmer and his family dispossessed by the *nouveau-riche* owner gives 2. 18 a lyrical strength not achieved in 3. 1.

But if he is guilty sometimes of confusing the rhetoric of satire with the rhetoric of lyric, guilty even of a failure to see that explicit moral argument had become something better left to prose, Horace's poetic achievement is impressive. His pseudo-classicism represents a logical refinement of the new poetry of Catullus. The form is classical. And yet the poet's speaking voice, despite constant echoes of past poetry, is recognizable as the living voice of a Roman of the Augustan Age. The attitudes expressed are those of a man who has come to terms with the realities of life around him. Horace's *Odes* are a formally perfect transposition of ancient Greek lyric into Latin verse; but the complex, coolly ironical personality they express is that of a succesor to Catullus.

VI   AUGUSTAN ELEGY

Propertius, Tibullus and Ovid are direct descendants of Catullus; each of the three has his own personality, but all write consciously in a tradition that goes back to Catullus and the other 'avant-garde' poets, especially Calvus. Propertius and Ovid openly acknowledge the debt, adding the name of Cornelius Gallus (the soldier-poet of *Eclogues* 6 and 10). Tibullus is more reticent; it is not his way to speak of other poets.

What they owe to Catullus is a theme (a passionate love affair with an irresistible but faithless mistress), a confidence in treating that theme as something so important it sets all else aside, a style based upon the illusion that we are listening to the poet's speaking voice, and a metre, the elegiac couplet. Augustan elegy quickly evolves its own characteristic form: a longish poem (20 to 40 lines in the case of Propertius and Ovid, 80 to 100 lines in the case of Tibullus) in which the poet pleads, argues, remonstrates with his mistress, or relates, in tones varying between triumph and despair, episodes and crises in a continuing affair. In Ovid the individual poems are set against a background of everyday life in

Rome, and this is the background which is usually to be presumed in Propertius; in Tibullus the setting is occasionally a small farm near Rome.

Only two of the poems in elegiacs of Catullus are comparable in length to the typical Augustan elegy, and there is nothing like the same concentration on a single theme. If the poetry of Gallus had survived, the line of formal development would probably have been easier to trace. As it is, we have, over a space of two generations (roughly 30 BC to AD 17), three poets of stature all writing within the constraints of a quite rigid form: a single metre (the pentameter more inflexible than the hexameter, the rules even more rigid in Ovid than in Propertius and Tibullus), a narrow range of variations on a single theme, a set of conventions which seem to emerge fully developed from nowhere. It is hardly surprising if the similarities between the work of the three main elegists are such that, given a passage of 20 lines or so, the modern reader might sometimes be hard put to decide which of the three was the author. It is a little like the development of the string quartet from Haydn and Mozart to Beethoven, though the comparison flatters Augustan love elegy. For despite the similarities, the total oeuvre of each has its distinctive contribution to make to the working out of a tradition which comes to an end with the death of the third.

VII   PROPERTIUS

Propertius outlived Tibullus by some years; in many ways his later poetry foreshadows not only the *Amores* of Ovid, but also the *Art of Love* and the *Fasti*. Yet it is Propertius who represents most plainly the line of descent from Catullus. The theme of both is hopeless infatuation with a mistress who can never adequately return the poet's passionate love; the sensitivity of his reaction to the affair always outstrips hers. There are important differences, however. When we read Catullus, we find it easy to believe it all happened; Propertius arouses no such conviction, nor does he really seem to want to. He offers us an approach to his theme which is best described as 'ironic reversal'. Catullus came to hate a mistress who was utterly promiscuous, who never paid more than lip-service to his ideal of a permanent relationship based on true affection; his only hope is to tear himself free; it is for this he prays. Propertius has come to hate a permanent liaison with a mistress who *is* faithful; he cannot stand the loss of liberty which results from the demands she makes on him; his only hope is to tear himself free—but he does not want that either.

The opening elegy of the collection strikes this ironic, paradoxical note (Propertius 1. 1. 1–8):

> Cynthia fixed me with her eyes and I was her luckless prisoner,
> I who had never been bowled over by a woman before.
> Then she made me avert that coolly appraising look of mine,
> and Cupid planted both feet on top of my head,
> until he taught me to hate girls who are straight,
> the scoundrel, and made my life utter confusion.
> This madness has been going on for a whole year
> and all the time I've had to have the gods against me.

The modern reader may suppose at first, as he attempts to make sense of these intriguing, angry-sounding lines, that Propertius has been, like some mediaeval troubadour, the hapless victim for a twelvemonth of an aloof mistress who spurns every advance. A moment's thought suffices to suggest this is an improbable reading of a Roman poem; and that reaction is confirmed (if confirmation were needed) when we learn in a later poem that Propertius, like Catullus (and, presumably, any normal young Roman), made first acquaintance with love at an early age (Propertius 3. 15. 3–6):

> As soon as I'd put boyish toga and shame aside,
> and was free to make acquaintance with the path of love,
> it was Lycinna who initiated me, who conspired with me
> those first nights, and she did it without charge.

What has reduced Propertius to despair in the elegy which opens the collection is that Cynthia has a will of her own, and is not to be tamed into accepting a liaison on the terms her lover took for granted; the Cynthia poems are a tale of the reluctant, rueful, angry loss of male domination by a lover accustomed to have things his own way (Propertius 1. 1. 25–36):

> But you, friends, who call me back too late
> when I've already fallen, seek help for a heart disordered.
> I'll face the cauterer's knife, his searing fire,
> if only I'm free to speak as anger prompts.
> Take me to the ends of earth, across the seas,
> to places where no woman can keep track of me.
> You can remain to whom the god lends ready ear,
> and may you stay paired off in an affair that's safe.
> The Venus I serve imposes nights of frustration,
> not for a moment does my passion relent.
> Avoid, I urge, misfortune like this. Let each stick
> to the girl he's got: don't go experimenting in love.

His only comfort is in recourse to paradox, a constant process of ironic reversal of the accepted and the commonplace. In a later elegy we see the irony directed not at his mistress (to whom Propertius is faithful in his way, clinging, as it were, despite himself to an ideal that proves at times unendurable), but at conventional views of mortality and the values they reflect (Propertius 2. 11):

> Others can write of you, or you can remain unknown.
> Let him praise who places seed in sterile ground.
> All your gifts, believe me, along with you, on a single bed,
> The black day of death which is the end will carry off.
> The indifferent traveller as he passes by your bones
> will not say, 'This dust was once a clever girl.'

The others are those who will write (or not, as it chances) of Cynthia when she and her poet-lover are dead. Praise then will be a waste of time. Death means the end of all that matters; let Cynthia set no store by a flattering inscription on her grave; the wayfarer (conventionally addressed in inscriptions on tombs) won't even trouble to read what is written. The poem is a striking, bitter, compact reversal of the conventional Roman intellectual's belief that to live on in the thoughts of others was a form of immortality worth striving for, applied to a case which fits—the beautiful woman in love with a poet able to celebrate her beauty while she lives.

In the elegies which follow the opening elegy Propertius sets out to give fresh colour and variety to the hypothesis. Denied the analysis of passionate feeling which makes Catullus so exciting, Propertius is reduced to contrived themes: visits, separations, quarrels, explanations to friends. Some are brilliantly handled, for example, 1. 3: a sensitive fantasy (imitated by Goethe in a well-known poem) relating Propertius' return to his mistress after a party, full of drunken remorse. But such narrative *tours de force* are rare (4. 7 is another). Propertius prefers argument to narrative, and the modern reader is inclined to complain that too little happens.

The explanation is perhaps that Propertius found the argumentative structure of Catullus' elegiac epigrams more congenial, or easier to handle. The case is argued each time at greater length than in Catullus, but there is a forward thrust in the argument very different from the characteristic Ovidian technique of theme and variation. Propertius' object is to convey an exhilarated state of mind more than to carry conviction, but the need to convince us of his passionate involvement is respected; whereas Ovid's object is to arouse our admiration by the fluent, outrageous presentation of his chosen persona, the reluctant, irresistible lover.

Book 2 is a year or so later, apparently, than Book 1 (published around

28 BC). We gather from the long opening elegy to Maecenas that in the interval the young poet with bitter memories of the Perusine War (see 1. 21 and 1. 22) had been accepted into the circle of Maecenas. But despite protestations of eagerness to raise his voice in praise of the new régime, Propertius is slow to reform his ways: Book 2 like Book 1 sings the praises of his mistress Cynthia, a little more enthusiastically even. She is Propertius' constant inspiration for his poetry: beautiful, accomplished, a second Helen. The Catullan anguish is still formally present (for example, 2. 3. 5–8), but Propertius can toy with the idea that, when death comes to him, Cynthia will be there, faithful to the last, weeping at his graveside (Propertius 2. 13b. 1–20):

> And so when one day death shuts my eyes for me,
> here's the procedure for my funeral service.
> No procession, please, no long line of ancestral busts,
> no lamentation of flute idly bemoaning my fate.
> Let no ivory funeral couch be decked for me;
> let there be no bier worthy of an Attalus for my corpse,
> no row of incense-laden dishes: what I want
> is a common man's unpretentious funeral.
> It will be procession enough if three books accompany me.
> I'll take *them* to Persephone as my greatest gift.
> You are to follow behind, beating bare breast,
> calling my name untiringly,
> placing last kisses on my chill lips
> as the box filled with Syrian scent is handed over.
> Then, when the fire beneath has reduced me to ashes.
> let a small urn receive what remains of me,
> let a bay-tree be placed above my tiny grave
> to shade the place where the pyre was quenched.
> And I want this couplet: 'He who lies here repulsive dust,
> was once the slave of a single love.'

Propertius' terms for acceptance of membership of the circle of Maecenas are the same as Horace's: freedom to go his own way as a poet. But where Horace is the spectator of life, Propertius has as yet only one theme.

Already in Book 2, however, the theme has become a little threadbare. The fact is that passionate, idealizing love had been intellectually discredited. Lucretius made great sport of the folly of lovers in his famous dismissal of the subject in Book 4 of *On the Universe*. More recently, Horace had made himself, in a bluntly-worded satire (1.2), the sardonic exponent of the Epicurean view of love as a passing madness about a matter which to sane men was of little importance; in the *Odes* he quietly ridicules the fuss made about love by the writers of elegy. It is fairly plain that the intellectual climate was becoming unfavourable for love poetry in the passionate manner of Book 1. One sign of Propertius' adjustment to the changed climate is the increasingly ironic treatment of love in a handful of elegies in Book 2. We are still asked to assume that the poet is passionately in love. But the fact has become little more than an initial presupposition upon which is constructed the elegant exploration of an intellectual conceit. For example, he explores urbanely the old superstition that the lover is exempt from the ordinary perils of life because he is destined to die of love (Propertius 2. 27. 11–16):

> Only the lover knows when he'll die and how meet
> death, fearing neither war nor stormy northerly.
> Even on reedy Styx, seated at the rower's bench,
> gazing at the gloomy canvas of the bark of Hell,
> let him catch a breath of summons from his mistress,
> and he will make the journey back no law allows.

Horace's version of the same conceit ends on an equally extravagant note (*Odes* 1. 22. 21–4):

> Pone sub curru nimium propinqui
> solis, in terra domibus negata:
> dulce ridentem Lalagen amabo,
>   dulce loquentem.

> Place me beneath the chariot of the too close
> sun in the land where none may make his home:
> I shall love my Lalage, whose smile is sweet,
> whose voice is sweet.

But the Horatian irony is more whimsical; it avoids the characteristic Propertian note of intellectual challenge. In both poems, however, the line of descent from Catullus is clear, though different paths have brought both a long way from the simple, hard-hitting directness of the poetry of conversation improved upon.

Cynthia's appearances in Book 3 are more perfunctory: the verse is often elegant (for example, 3. 10, on his mistress's birthday), but one feels Propertius' heart is not in it, and the book ends with a pair of elegies (3. 24 and 25) in which he attempts a final, contemptuous dismissal of the woman whose slave he had been for five years. Already he is starting to think of himself as a Roman Callimachus, a storyteller as much as a love poet; he is impatient to expand his range of themes and to perfect a new, distinctive style.

186

The outstanding quality of the elegiac epigrams of Catullus is precision, the disciplined use of language to hammer away at an idea until it has been lucidly and compactly presented in all its complexity. The chief quality of Propertius' style already in the earlier books is an allusive imprecision. We can still fancy we are listening to the poet's speaking voice. This is still personal poetry. But Propertius' way of talking is more mannered, more precious, more consciously poetic. In Book 4 a style which has never been easy becomes exceptionally difficult, and at the same time a tradition which had begun in paraliterature becomes unashamedly literary. The difficulty of Book 4 is the by-product of a technique of allusiveness rather than an objective directly aimed at. Too much of the time one needs to know the story to decode the information conveyed. To a reader with no knowledge of the story to guide him, the words can mean so many different things, he is hard put to attach meaning to them at all.

All allusive poetry, of course, demands knowledge of the story. What is distinctive—distinctive in Latin poetry, for behind Propertius' new manner lie the aetiological elegies of Callimachus—is that the code, instead of touching off the right responses, draws attention to itself; ingenuity and quickwittedness are demanded of the reader, and also erudition. Propertius is often compared with Ezra Pound (as a result of Pound's impressionist translations of him), but the nearest equivalent to the elegies of Book 4 in English is probably the cold-bloodedly cerebral verse of William Empson. The words are in no sense the natural Latin for the idea. Often the allusion escapes the modern reader, for, though the subject of an elegy (Penelope, Hercules and Cacus) may be familiar, recondite details are sought out and hinted at; not infrequently, these are so obscure, we are disqualified altogether from participating in the game the poet proposes.

VIII   THE TIBULLAN COLLECTION

From Catullus to Horace, to Propertius, to Ovid, the development is clear: the four represent a tradition of love poetry which is both urban and urbane. Tibullus is the odd man out. His allegiance to that tradition is perfunctory. What makes his verse worth reading is his introduction into the tradition of urban love of themes from pastoral; what makes it at any rate interesting and unlike that of the others is the prominence given to homosexual, or rather ambisexual, love. He shows a true peasant's feeling for the Italian countryside; which is not to say, of course, that

Tibullus is a peasant, or that he writes like one. His verse is elegant, the product of a well-stocked literary mind. What makes it something more than that is the hint it contains of a sensibility struggling to break free from the convention of love elegy that city life is the be-all and end-all of existence.

Tibullus' output is slender, the sixteen poems of Books 1 and 2, plus a handful in Book 3 of doubtful authenticity. His claim to be recognized as a love poet rests on four elegies in his first book. They seem, if not to tell a continuous story, to be built at any rate round a reconstructable hypothesis: Tibullus has a mistress who is a married woman; he hopes she will leave her husband to come and live with him in the country, where he has a family estate, once large, but now comparatively humble; the project never comes to anything, however, because Delia deserts him for a richer lover. Elegy 1.1 proclaims Tibullus' decision to renounce the pursuit of material gain and service abroad in favour of life with his mistress; in 1. 2 he is reduced to despair because the husband, his suspicions aroused, has put a close watch on his wife; in 1. 5 we learn that the dream of rural bliss, to which Tibullus has clung during his mistress's illness, has been shattered: she has betrayed him. In 1. 6 the infidelity of 1. 5 is over and forgotten; but things are once more not going well, for Tibullus suspects he has a rival and urges Delia's husband to keep more careful watch on her (1. 6 is thus a counterpoise to 1. 2).

The story is a conventional one, and probably we should not take it very seriously: much of it (Tibullus' urgent advice to the husband to keep his wife out of temptation, for example) reads like bland, somewhat undistinguished Ovid. Tibullus seems not to have made up his mind whether he wants to be a passionate lover like Propertius, or a delicately witty parodist of conventional themes. The wit is not sustained, however, and the mood it invites clashes with the charming, sentimental daydreaming of 1. 1 and 1. 5.

Mixed up with the Delia elegies are three elegies (1. 4, 1. 8 and 1. 9) in which Tibullus reveals his affection for the young man he calls Marathus, while expressing at the same time his interest in Marathus' own first steps in heterosexual love. Despite the tone of unassuming frankness, the decision seems easier here that the predominant element is meant to be wit, not true confession. One is left, however, with the suspicion that Tibullus merely writes elegy because elegy is fashionable, not as a result of any impulse to self-expression, and is therefore willing to cater for all tastes. As for the rest, in 1. 3 Tibullus has attempted to follow his patron Messalla Corvinus to the East, but has been left behind in Corfu because of illness; 1. 7 is in honour of Messalla's birthday. The concluding elegy is an eloquent expression of Tibullus' disenchantment with military life.

He is about to be dragged off to the wars, and his views on the wrongness of war are not, therefore, disinterested. All the same he is able to make the joys of peace and country life (where the only wars are those over which Venus presides) sound convincing.

Book 2 begins with a full-scale description of a rustic festival, the sort of thing Tibullus does well (he is better at description of scene than at argument). A birthday poem for a young married friend Cornutus follows. Then come four elegies in which Tibullus returns to love elegy with a fresh mistress. The Nemesis elegies are inferior to the Delia elegies, the work of a second-rate practitioner in a minor genre: personal love poetry has become a shallow pretence.

Even when he has little to say Tibullus is a graceful stylist, more conventionally poetic than Propertius and certainly less verbally witty than Ovid. His structural technique resembles Ovid's, but is more crudely accumulative: well-turned couplet follows well-turned couplet until the idea has been exhausted. He lacks not only Propertius' ability to build up an argument, but also Ovid's ingenuity in stringing out the variations on a theme; the individual couplets are graceful, but the gracefulness cloys because the poems lack a clearly thought-out structure and therefore any positive onward thrust, any real vitality.

The third book of the Tibullan collection is generally assumed to be the work of other members of the circle of Tibullus' patron, Messalla. In some ways they are like a breath of fresh air. The unknown Lygdamus of the first six elegies is something of a mystery, and his relationship to the Neaera to whom they are addressed is obscure. Lygdamus can maintain a clear, logical line of sense, but his poems have many of the awkwardnesses of the amateur or the semi-professional. He has nothing like Tibullus' skill in getting a couplet just right. His style is cliché-ridden and occasionally disfigured by maudlin prolixity. And yet the poems are surprisingly simple and effective. For all their faults they leave the impression of a genuine sensibility, if one that is neither very deep nor very original. A formal panegyric of Messalla in hexameters, included in the collection by some editor, separates the Lygdamus elegies from five elegies (3. 8–12) which purport to be an exchange of letters between Messalla's ward Sulpicia and her lover Cerinthus. Some have suggested they are in fact by Tibullus. Whatever view one takes of them, they are somewhat unsatisfactory poems, as are 3. 19 and 3. 20 (a four-line epigram), also ascribed sometimes to Tibullus. Very different are the six short elegies 3. 13–18 (40 lines in all), the work, apparently, of Sulpicia herself. In these striking, hard-hitting trifles, the line of statement is neither direct nor spontaneous; the syntax is compressed, almost tortured, occasionally obscure. Take the first and longest (3. 13):

Tandem venit amor, qualem texisse pudori
  quam nudasse alicui sit mihi fama magis.
Exorata meis illum Cytherea Camenis
  adtulit in nostrum deposuitque sinum.
Exsoluit promissa Venus: mea gaudia narret
  dicetur si quis non habuisse sua.
Non ego signatis quicquam mandare tabellis,
  ne legat id nemo quam meus ante, velim:
sed pecasse iuvat, voltus componere famae
  taedet; cum digno digna fuisse ferar.

At last a love has come such that I would have it said
I was more ashamed of concealing than uncovering it.
In answer to my verses the goddess of love has
brought him to my arms and placed him there.
Venus has kept her promise. Let any tell stories of my joy
of whom it shall be said he had no joy of his to tell.
It is not my wish to confide in sealed tablets
lest another read my words before the man I love.
I'm glad I yielded. To compose a face for fame leaves me
indifferent: let them say each was worthy of the other.

It is the style of a writer who is not expert enough in the use of words to say
what she wants to say without sacrifice of clarity. For all that, these short
poems are the real gems of the Tibullan collection. Though Sulpicia was
not the only Roman woman to write verse (Ovid praises the verse of his
step-daughter Perilla, for example, in *Tristia* 3. 7), this is the only time we
hear the voice of a woman, and it is the voice, not of a Lesbia or a Cynthia,
but of a respectable Roman girl who has given herself to the man she loves
and wants to proclaim her feelings for all who care to read.

IX   OVID'S *Amores*

The members of the circle of Messalla bring us back to amateur poetry.
The great wave of morally committed poetry which found its highest
expression in Horace and Virgil is over; they will have no successors. Nor,
it seems, will Sulpicia's simple, gauche, sincere lines inspire others to
think of poetry as what it had been for Catullus: the precise, forceful
expression of passionate feeling. Propertius' fourth book shows the blind
alley into which poets wandered instead in the pursuit of poetic seriousness. Respect for Callimachus and other Hellenistic poets (for example,

Euphorion) seems to have made them neglectful of any audience other than the hermetic audience of their fellow-initiates.

Preciousness is a fault to which nearly all Roman writers after Plautus were prone. Catullus tries this kind of writing in its extreme form only once (Poem 66, a translation of Callimachus), but he toys with it in *The Marriage of Peleus and Thetis,* and does more than toy with it in the mythical sections of that tantalizing poem, Poem 68. Virgil throughout his writing life found preciousness hard to resist. In the pursuit of perfection of form Horace was prepared to sacrifice even a pretence of lyric spontaneity. True, if one is writing for a limited, sophisticated audience, preoccupation with form is not always a bad thing: it can lead to the extraordinarily penetrating concision of Tacitus' *Annals,* or it can lead to the fatuous preciosity of Pliny's *Letters.* But a tendency to go too far is a symptom of the precarious status of the writer as a serious artist in Roman society. Periods of confident growth alternate with periods of crisis. There are signs of such a crisis in the decade following Virgil's death in 19 BC: the *Aeneid* seems to have fallen, if not upon deaf ears (for the poem was much praised), upon uncomprehending ears, indifferent to what Virgil was trying to do. Horace seems to have been annoyed at the reception accorded the *Odes.* Perhaps Propertius felt that to write for anybody other than his fellow-poets was a waste of time.

If he thought that, Ovid proved him wrong. But it meant a drastic break with the whole trend of Roman poetry since Catullus, if not indeed since Plautus. Ovid abandons the pursuit of seriousness. He does not allow himself to be obsessed with beating Greek poets at their own game. He offers his readers instead a mixture of lucid, readily appreciated wit and frank sensuality which no Roman writer since Plautus had thought fit to offer in such palatable form. The recipe in the *Amores* is the same as it was to be in *The Art of Love.* Like Propertius and Tibullus, Ovid is the poet-lover for whom all that matters is love. But in Ovid's pursuit of love, the roles are reversed: instead of being the hapless victim of a cruel mistress, Ovid is the triumphant seducer, the professional Don Juan, the self-proclaimed devoted admirer of every pretty girl he meets, who enjoys every moment of love's sweet hell. Elegiac poetry ceases to be passionate confession and becomes fun; cleverness and wit take the place of feeling. It neatly solves, not only the artistic problem (how to revivify a worn-out tradition), but also the problem of the social status of the elegiac poet.

For the *Amores* are more than *seductio ad absurdum.* Like the *Metamorphoses,* like *The Art of Love,* they are the expression of an exquisitely sure taste in which a brilliant sense of fun is perfectly matched with verbal wit and effortless command over form with just the right hint of social criticism. The Catullan precision has been recovered, the Propertian allusive imprecision discarded; allusion is cut back to what the educated reader can be expected to cope with comfortably, his attention undistracted from the verbal fireworks. At his best Ovid writes the neatest Latin ever written, lines like those on the plight of the lover who has two mistresses (*Amores* 2. 10. 7–8):

> Pulchrior hac illa est, haec est quoque pulchrior illa,
>   et magis haec nobis et magis illa placet.

> The one is prettier than the other, the other prettier than she;
>   I prefer the one, the other I prefer.

Or take this couplet from the Ovidian original of Mozart's catalogue aria (*Amores* 2. 4. 39–40):

> Candida me capiet, capiet me flava puella,
>   est etiam in fusco grata colore venus.

> The blonde will ensnare me, so will the golden-haired;
>   the dusky girl also has her attraction.

Lines like these achieve a clarity of statement that Lucretius half a century earlier could attain only by sheer strength of intellect; they display a lightness of touch that those who think only of Cicero's speeches when they talk about Latin would deny Latin altogether. And in them Ovid manages apparently without effort complete perfection of rhythmical phrasing. Even when it results in wanton cleverness, this kind of brilliance is ideally suited to the kind of love poetry Ovid has chosen to write. Both in what he says and in the way he says it, he leaves the impression that he will stop at nothing (see, for example, *Amores* 1. 4. 47–8). We gasp at the nonchalant adroitness with which the words are put together, we gasp at the hair-raising implications of the *double-entendres,* and are left too breathless to protest. No doubt Ovid was not the man to take passionate love seriously. But what had been for Catullus, and for Propertius in his earlier work, a scandalous challenge to accepted ideas about morality had become a way of life for the audience for whom Ovid wrote: his audience was not an intellectual set, but the members of that large section of Roman society which lived in close contact with an imperial court increasingly notorious for its promiscuity.

You can still scandalize such an audience, and there were those who professed to be scandalized and the Emperor, it seems, was compelled to take their side. But there was no longer much point in a direct challenge to traditional morality: the old Roman morality had gone; Augustus' efforts to revive it created no more than a façade of conventional morality that concealed what people thought and did. Ovid makes no attempt to tear down that façade by direct attack. His tool is wit, not satire; he neatly disarms hypocrisy by a gaily maintained pretence that the way of life about which he sets himself up as an authority in *The Art of Love,* and of which he depicts himself in the *Amores* as the enthusiastic devotee, is really the ultimate expression of civilized behaviour, and therefore exempt from moral censure. Augustan Rome, Ovid implies (*The Art of Love,* 3. 113–28), has shaken off the shackles of the old crude, rustic morality; a new relationship between the sexes is one of its cultural achievements, not a proof of decadence. Of course the defence is advanced tongue-in-cheek, and so too is the picture Ovid paints of himself in the *Amores.* In this ironic parody of a society that puts the pursuit of love before all else a deftly-muted hint of social criticism is never far beneath the surface veneer of enthusiastic acceptance.

How clear the function of the *Amores* as social criticism was to Ovid when he began writing is hard to say. The version which has come down to us represents a drastically abbreviated text, in which the five books of the original edition have been reduced to three. The author's prefatory note sets the tone of the revised edition:

> Once five, now three slim volumes,
>   we are Naso's preference.
> Even if we give no pleasure
>   the pain will be two books less.
>
> [Translation: Lee]

We may be sure that Ovid revised as well as pruned, and that, as he worked over his poems, he started to see them in a new light: less as parody of love elegy, less as bogus true confessions, and more as an ironic comment on contemporary social attitudes. Like any true entertainer Ovid is a keen observer of the human comedy, but he is at the same time a scrupulous professional. His concept of his role as entertainer precludes satire (the satirist is an individualist who despises the professional entertainer's sharp sense of etiquette); but by appealing to their sense of fun and their sense of style, he can bring his audience a fair way none the less towards seeing the absurdities, the shallownesses, even the failures of humanity in contemporary society.

In the *Amores* Ovid recovered a new vitality and authenticity for the poet's speaking voice. The basis remains an illusion, if closer to the Catullan style of conversation improved upon than to the Horace of the *Odes.* No Roman could have talked in real life as Horace talks in his chosen persona, and no one would really have wanted to. No one, not

193

even Ovid, could have been as continuously witty and outrageous as Ovid in the *Amores*; but we may be sure that many would have liked to be—or fancied that in their more inspired moments they were.

We have met the style already in Ovid's *Art of Love* (the Latin even more limpid; the note of irony, the elegantly urbane debunking of a vicious society a little more sharply tuned) and in its more mature version in the *Metamorphoses*. It is distressing to turn from these to the verse Ovid wrote during the last decade of his life as an exile at Tomi: the five books of the *Tristia*, the four books of the *Letters from Pontus*. Ovid's faith in the new culture of the Augustan Age, of which his verse was so perfectly confident an expression, has been shattered. It is hard to feel any sympathy for his protestations that he is the victim of trumped-up charges. He is so long-winded. And he whines. The writing is never less than competent. Occasionally what he says about the Roman literary scene of his day is of interest: he knew Virgil, he tells us, by sight; he became a friend of Tibullus just before the latter's death; he heard Horace read his *Odes*, knew Propertius well. But all that was a quarter of a century and more ago. It was some consolation, no doubt, to feel he had been a worthy successor to poets such as these, however much poetic standards had slumped since. In one of his last poems (*Pont.* 4. 16) he reels off a list of poets of his own generation: most are to us mere names. Perhaps he was uneasily aware how much he had conceded (however brilliantly) to the degeneration of public taste. He must have been humiliated to have to protest now that his verse meant no harm. Yet, despite the shame of rejection, he wanted desperately to return. When we read Tacitus' brilliant, sardonic résumé of the reign of Augustus, it is worth remembering that, seen in another light, this is the witty, cultured imperial court for which Ovid pined in frustrated, lonely exile on the shores of the Black Sea.

X HORACE'S HEXAMETER ESSAYS

Horace's *Odes* are seriously, if unconventionally, poetic; the claim Horace makes to a place in literature is explicit. He is careful to maintain the personal illusion by giving prominent place to the more poetically promising of the themes for which Catullus had won a place in literature (love, social life, personal relationships). But the status of the *Odes* excludes stances, attitudes and ways of talking which are not compatible with serious poetry. For these, Horace developed a style in hexameter verse which he made the vehicle of something rather like the modern prose essay.

As Quintilian was to say, satire is wholly Roman (*satura quidem tota nostra est*). Its essence is the loose, unstructured talk of a man speaking off the cuff to his friends. The apparent absence of form is naturally as much an illusion as in comedy, not only because what is said is structured metrically (even if Horace's hexameters, like the metres of comedy, are more relaxed), but also because this is, as in Catullus, very much the language of conversation improved upon. It is a way of writing that began in the Preclassical period with Lucilius. Horace no doubt saw himself as filling, in the circle which Augustus' minister Maecenas gathered round himself in the years following Actium, a role similar to that Lucilius had occupied a century before in the circle of Scipio Aemilianus. Lucilius provided themes which could be handled afresh with a new dexterity, a personality (Lucilius is the first individualist in Roman literature) and a speaking voice which Horace found congenial. The voice is, of course, the voice of a Roman living in the thirties BC: this is the world which Horace evokes and whose foibles he attacks. When it comes to personalities, however, he is careful to concentrate on minor characters safely dead: there is nothing in the *Satires* comparable with Catullus' searing attacks on Caesar and Mamurra or those other representatives of the sick society of the fifties which Catullus castigated with such devastating frankness.

Horace rejects any suggestion that what he writes is to be considered poetry (*Satires* 1. 4. 39–44):

> In the first place I exclude myself from the list
> of those I'd call poets: it's not enough in my view
> just to turn out stuff that scans. As for someone who writes
> like me, more as people talk, you can't consider him a poet.
> A man needs genius, a mind a little like a god's and lips
> to frame high-sounding phrase to be worthy of that name.

But he has no patience with the rambling slovenliness of Lucilius. His generation has stricter standards. They are the standards of the 'avant-garde' poets of the previous generation; Horace says of Lucilius very much what Catullus said of Suffenus. He preserves the illusion of conversational spontaneity (the Latin title of the collection is *Sermones*, 'Conversations'). The more compact forms and stricter metres Catullus uses necessitate economy and make structural elegance a virtue to be perceived; Horace will go even further in this direction in the *Odes*. The style of the *Satires* stays closer to actual talk.

In the space of about a hundred lines, a topic from literature or a moral issue is discussed from an individual standpoint which is vigorously maintained. The tone is witty, the wit often pungent. The argument is marked by the kind of abrupt transitions that are characteristic of conversation, though closer scrutiny shows a planned structure, enlivened by moralizing anecdote and whimsical reminiscence. Of the ten satires of Book 1, two deal with literary criticism; four are sermons delivered from a practical, unintellectual standpoint (a kind of popular Epicureanism); four have a loose narrative form displaying that interest in character and situation which was to remain a feature of all of Horace's poetry. This last group includes two of the best known satires, 1. 5 (the 'Journey to Brundisium') and 1. 9 (the 'Encounter with the Bore'). The eight satires of the second book include a number of experiments with dramatic form and a good deal of that argument about rival ethical theories which fanned among the Romans of this period something akin to the heat of religious controversy. Horace belongs to the generation which was just reaching intellectual maturity at the time when Cicero's semi-popular treatises on philosophy (the *De Finibus,* the *De Officiis,* the *Tusculan Disputations*) were pouring from his pen. For us, largely because of their discursive, allusive form, the philosophical satires remain the only really dull section of all of Horace's work; 2. 6, a relaxed self-portrait drawn about 30 BC when Horace was about thirty-five, provides a welcome contrast.

In his mid-forties, with the first three books of the *Odes* behind him, Horace came back to the hexameter essay. Round about 20 BC he published a collection of what purport to be letters. The *Epistles* are of course no more real letters than the *Satires* are real conversations. The illusion of conversational spontaneity has been discarded in favour of a related illusion: instead of listening to the poet's speaking voice, we are invited to read his letters to personal friends.

The change permits distinct structural gains. Horace no longer has to appear to be talking off the cuff: though written with the candour one owes to a friend, the *Epistles* are carefully and elegantly written. Horace writes, moreover, with a new authority, as a known personality. The status of Horace in the *Satires* was that of a *scurra* who had been admitted to the close circle of Maecenas' friends because he was a witty conversationalist and showed some promise as a writer of verse. The Horace of the *Epistles* is a leading poet; in the concluding poem of his collection of *Odes* he was able with pride and confidence to use words that place poetry alongside the achievements of the highest in the land: *exegi monumentum aere perennius.* He has won a new independence in his relationship with his patron, and asserts that right in an open letter to Maecenas (*Epistles* 1.
7.1–13):

I said I would stay in the country no more than a week,
But, false to my word, I've made myself scarce all August.

Even so, if you want me to live safe and sound, Maecenas,
You will pardon me as much when I fear falling ill
As you do when I am in fact sick. This is the season
When the first figs and heavy heat elevate undertakers
And their black-robed attendants to positions of great importance,
The time when every father and mummy blanches
With fear for the children, when nerve-racking social functions
And minor details of business-going-on-as-usual
Bring on fevers, and bring out wills to be read.
But when winter whitens the Alban fields with snow,
Your bard will go down to the seaboard to care for himself,
And huddle up and read. He'll come back to you, dear friend
(By your leave), when the winds blow warm and the first swallow flies.

[Translation: Bovie]

The characteristic Horatian charm remains. He describes himself as 'a little baldish man, easy-going though quick-tempered, fond of the sun'. But he feels that his career as a serious lyric poet is over, and proposes to devote the rest of his life to thinking and writing about the problems of moral philosophy.

The charm and relaxed confidence of the twenty epistles of Book 1 are replaced in Book 2 by the sharper, almost querulous voice of a man who feels that the things he wanted out of life, and had got, are now beginning to elude him (*Epistles* 2. 2. 51–7):

Merciless poverty
Drove me to poetry. Now that I'm quite well fixed,
It would take a lot more than a shock infusion of hemlock
To cure me of thinking how much better off I am sleeping
Than writing. Our pleasures steal off, one by one, with the years,
Which have already snatched my zest for laughter and love,
For playing and feasting. And now they're trying to twist
The poems loose from my hand. What can I do?

[Translation: Bovie]

The book consists of three long open letters, all dealing more or less with literary criticism: 2.1 is a letter to Augustus on the state of poetry in Rome, a vigorous defence of contemporary writers; 2. 2 is a somewhat rambling discussion of Horace's reasons for abandoning lyric poetry; 2. 3, usually called the *Ars Poetica* is a practical survey of the history and theory of dramatic poetry, glancing occasionally at the lyric and epic, intensely personal in tone and valuable above all for the insights it permits into contemporary ideas about literature. There is much good sense and the essay is studded with aphorisms which have become part of the common coin of literary criticism; but the modern reader cannot help wishing Horace had taken the opportunity to add to his review in *Epistles* 1. 19 of his own achievements as a poet. Perhaps he felt a letter filled with practical hints, tossed off in a manner closer to that of the *Satires* than to the elegantly urbane manner of *Epistles* 1, was not the place for serious critical appraisal of his own work. Perhaps, disappointed at the reception of poems on which he had expended so much thought and effort, he was no longer so sure of his own success as when he wrote the *Exegi monumentum* ode ten years or more earlier.

XI   PERSIUS AND JUVENAL

In the Postclassical period the hexameter essay is represented by the six *Satires* of Persius and the sixteen *Satires* of Juvenal. About half a century separates the young Horace from Persius, who was a contemporary of Lucan, and that is about the period which separates Persius from Juvenal, who was a contemporary of Tacitus. The three wrote for very different audiences: Horace's *Satires* were written during the final decade of the Civil War, the years between the battle of Philippi (42 BC) and the final victory of Octavian at Actium (31 BC); Persius' audience is the flamboyant court of Nero; Juvenal's *Satires* are spread out over the thirty years of the reigns of Trajan and Hadrian (AD 98–128).

Persius may be described as a Horace who has turned Stoic and lost his sense of humour. He has much in common with Lucan and with Seneca, the Stoic philosopher and tragedian, but lacks their sense of style. In his version of the personal style the note of casualness is forced, the expression of thought often crabbed and obscure. History has taken its revenge. We are told that Lucan attended a reading of the satires and could not contain his admiration. Quintilian's 'his single book contains much real poetry' is nearer to damning with faint praise. In modern times he is almost forgotten.

Juvenal has been luckier. Though he is difficult too (probably the most difficult of the Roman poets who are still read), his compressed, allusive rhetoric is constantly enlivened by the short, biting, brilliant, memorable phrase. Take these lines from the tenth *Satire* (the original of Johnson's satire on 'The Vanity of Human Wishes') (Juvenal 10. 147–67):

> How are the mighty chang'd to dust! how small
> The urn that holds what once was Hannibal!
> Yet in these silent ashes dwelt a soul
> No fear could daunt, no limit could controul—

198

Not the wide space of Afric's fruitful reign,
From Nile's warm torrent to the Moorish main,
Stretching its vast interminable tracks
To other elephants, and other blacks.
Spain swells his empire, but he pants for more;
The steepy Pyrenees he rushes o'er—
In vain would Nature to the chief oppose
Her cloud-capt Alps, and everlasting snows;
Burst by his art, the solid mountain yields
A yawning passage to Italia's fields;
Italia's fields are his; but, thund'ring on,
Insatiate yet, he cries, 'We've nothing won!
'Till the detested gates we batter down,
'And sound our trumpets through the blazing town;
'Till I, myself, in mid Suburra, stand,
'And plant the Punic flag with conq'ring hand.'
Oh! what a picture would the chief have made, ⎫
The one-ey'd chief, when thus he proudly said, ⎬
On his triumphal elephant display'd! ⎭
Thy work, O Fame! thus gallantly begun,
How didst thou finish for thy favour'd son?
Swift Rout behind and skulking Terror wait
On his vain march—the glorious, and the great,
The godlike Hannibal, compell'd to fly
For shameful safety to a foreign sky,
Before a despot's tent, the cruel sport,
The wonder of an Asiatic court,
Bows his brave head with all a suppliant's fear,
Till the Bithynian deign to wake, and hear.
No hostile dart, no rocky fragment hurl'd,
Laid low this hot disturber of the world;
A little ring aveng'd the heaps of slain,
The streams of blood on Cannae's fatal plain.
Was it for this, infuriate chief, you crost
Each Alpine barrier of relentless frost;
Was it for this you triumph'd, to employ
The teaching pedant, and declaiming boy?

[Translation: Hodgson]

The whole character of satire has changed since Horace. Horace wrote satire, he tells us, because he felt he had no hope of competing with the leading writers in the established styles (Horace, *Satires* 1. 10. 36–49):

199

So, while Furius the Frenzied apocalyptically features
His epic account of the Gallic Wars and dismembers
The head of the Rhine in the process, or furiously mangles
Poor Memnon, his victim in the New Aethiopian Epic,
I just play along with these trivial pieces of mine,
Which will never be heard in the Official Workshop of Drama,
Where Tarpa can judge them, nor time and again on the stage.
Fundanius, you alone of the living can write
In your self-possessed way the crisp little lines that suit
The style of New Comedy: Watch the shrewd mistress—she
And Davus, the young man's slave-confidential-and-clerk,
Will fool the old father named Chremes. Pollio sings,
In his tragic trimeter rhythm, the sad death of kings.
Varius weaves the tough, strong fabric of epic
Better than anyone. Tenderly, playfully, Vergil
Has won the acclaim of the pastoral muses. But satire
Is mine: Varro Atacinus, and others, have tried it
In vain, while I have done better—though I still must yield
To Lucilius, who showed us the way. I'd never dare
To try to win from him the crown that clings to his brow
So gloriously.

[Translation: Bovie]

His ambition was the modest ambition of an amateur moralist anxious to sort out for himself the problems of right and wrong, wise and foolish, by observing the human comedy and then putting his understanding of it down in unpretentious verse. Juvenal writes in an age when the traditional forms of literature have decayed to the point where literature is a patent farce (Juvenal, *Satires* 1. 1–14):

Yet shall I hear yon croaking dolt rehearse,
Nor pay whole Theseids with a single verse?
Safely to me shall loud-tongued playwrights bawl,
And puling sonneteers, unpunish'd, drawl?
From hour to hour shall Telephus be read,
Or vast Orestes stun my wilder'd head,
O'er the Broad margin closely writ, and black
With floods of ink, and endless on the back?
Thy grotto, Mars! and Vulcan's rough abode,
Where Aetna labours with the hidden god;
These, and the roaring of the winds I know,
And the keen torments of the damn'd below;
Who the rich fleece from plunder'd Colchis brought,

How with uprooted oaks the Centaurs fought;
Well as my house I know such tales as these,
Sung all the day to Fronto's echoing trees—
The very statues tremble through the shades,
And the noise cracks the marble colonnades,
As o'er the dull, unvaried, trivial theme,
Or genuine bards, or genuine blockheads dream.

[Translation: Hodgson]

Petronius had made a similar complaint fifty years before, in the opening lines of his *Satyricon* about the fatuous, threadbare themes the professors of rhetoric taught their pupils. Now the disease has infected the whole of literature. So-called poets are pouring out so-called poems in the old grand manner, but their trite, turgid epics and tragedies are uniformly absurd. No less absurd is the social scene at Rome. Petronius had turned to fantasy. Juvenal rounds on his contemporaries and rails at them for their depraved surrender to every form of vice.

It is Juvenal who gives the word satire its modern meaning. In a society that is so sick, how can any writer, he asks, however mediocre his talent, *not* write satire? Juvenal poses, as it were, as the amoral moralist: he is not motivated by true moral concern; he is just unable to restrain himself. The disclaimer is of course an example of Juvenal's sardonic rhetoric, which seeks out the pettiest, most discreditable motive. Moral concern is too pure a motive; anyway, the world has had enough of so-called philosophers, as it has had enough of so-called poets. Plain, blazing indignation, he would have us believe, is the only honest reaction left.

For all that, Juvenal's passionately rhetorical verse is aggressively moralistic, if prone to lump the petty foibles of mankind along with the symptoms of a deeper depravity in a single sweeping gesture of dismissal. Yet his verse possesses a seriousness and a memorable precision of expression that guarantee it a kind of status. Neither as social criticism nor as literature do the *Satires* stand up to comparison with the much more deeply moralistic and much more compactly precise prose of Juvenal's contemporary, Tacitus. There is a depth of pessimism in Tacitus, a psychological acuity, a subtle employment of the traditional techniques of poetry which put Tacitus in the very front rank. Compare Juvenal, however, with the ordinary run of satirical journalism in our day, and one begins to understand why he has lasted so well.

CHAPTER 5

The Uses of Prose

I EVERYDAY PROSE: CATO

Roman prose has a long and distinguished history. But much of that history lies outside what can sensibly be called literature. Only in the Postclassical period does prose begin to supplant verse as the normal medium of literary expression. Throughout the Classical period the uses of prose remain almost wholly on the margin of literature; the only real exception, as we shall see, is history.

The earliest surviving Roman prose dates from the middle of the second century BC. The first complete work we possess is a handbook on farming by Cato the Censor (234–149 BC), often called 'the elder Cato' to distinguish him from Lucan's hero, Cato the Stoic. Cato was only a few years younger than Ennius; he was approaching fifty when Plautus died (traditional date, 184 BC) and approaching seventy when Terence began producing his comedies at Rome. It was a period of increasing enthusiasm for the culture, thought and literature of the Greek-speaking world of the eastern Mediterranean, with which Rome was coming for the first time into direct contact. As a forthright conservative, the staunch upholder of old Roman ideals (though he was not an aristocrat, but what the Romans called a *novus homo*), Cato was as outspoken in his opposition to Philhellenism as he was outspoken in his campaign for the ruthless destruction of Carthage: in Carthaginian military and economic power he saw a threat to Rome; in the cult of things Greek, a threat to the Roman way of life.

His prose (we have a few fragments of speeches as well as his treatise *On Agriculture*) is forceful, direct, not without rhetorical skill. What he says is always to the point; his command of words is sure; he has the characteristic Roman gift for pungent aphorism and more than a trace of sardonic wit. But what he writes is not literature. Cato was a practical man, or that was at any rate how he liked to think of himself. Almost as famous as the phrase *delenda est Carthago* ('I move that we destroy

Carthage') with which he was said to end all his speeches in the Senate, is the tag *rem tene, verba sequentur* ('get a hold of what you're talking about and the words will come'), a rejection of the tricks and graces of Greek oratory which were becoming fashionable at Rome. His reputation as a speaker was considerable.

When he extended his interests beyond the immediate concerns of public life, his style remained crisp and business-like. Take the opening sentences of his handbook on farming:

> It is true that to earn a living by trade might have its advantages, if it were not so risky; likewise moneylending, if it were equally respectable. Our ancestors took the view, and laid it down in their laws that a penalty of twice the amount should be imposed on a thief, and a penalty four times the amount on a usurer. From which one can judge how much worse a citizen they considered a moneylender than a thief. When they praised a good man, they praised him as 'a good farmer' and 'a good husbandman'. A man so praised was thought to receive the highest praise. As for the merchant, I consider him hardworking and devoted to profit; but, as I said above, his is a risky line and prone to disaster. On the other hand it is from farmers that our bravest men and our sturdiest soldiers spring. Farming is a thoroughly decent source of income and one that is exposed to the minimum of risk. It gets you into the least trouble with other people and those who are engaged in this pursuit are very seldom troublemakers.

Compare this decent, plain, unpretentious prose with the opening lines of Virgil's *Georgics*:

> Quid faciat laetas segetes, quo sidere terram
> vertere, Maecenas, ulmisque adiungere vitis
> conveniat, quae cura boum, qui cultus habendo
> sit pecori, apibus quanta experientia parcis,
> hinc canere incipiam. vos, o clarissima mundi
> lumina, labentem caelo quae ducitis annum;
> Liber et alma Ceres, vestro si munere tellus
> Chaoniam pingui glandem mutavit arista
> poculaque inventis Acheloia miscuit uvis;
> et vos, agrestum praesentia numina, Fauni,
> ferte simul Faunique pedem Dryadesque puellae;
> munera vestra cano.

What makes a plenteous harvest, when to turn
The fruitful soil, and when to sow the corn;
The care of sheep, of oxen, and of kine;
And how to raise on elms the teeming vine;
The birth and genius of the frugal bee,
I sing, Maecenas, and I sing to thee.
Ye deities! who fields and plains protect,
Who rule the seasons, and the year direct,
Bacchus and fostering Ceres, powers divine,
Who gave us corn for mast, for water, wine:
Ye Fauns, propitious to the rural swains,
Ye Nymphs that haunt the mountains and the plains,
Join in my work, and to my numbers bring
Your needful succour: for your gifts I sing.

[Translation: Dryden]

Virgil attempts an imaginative evocation of the beauty and the poetry of the Italian countryside, not concealing the harsh routine it imposes, but stressing its simple honesty. Cato, as he goes on to make clear, is concerned with practical advice to members of his own class who wish to invest their money in something more respectable (and less risky) than business:

When you are thinking of buying a farm, these are the points
to bear in mind. Don't be eager to buy. Don't spare your pains in
looking the place over—don't think it's enough to walk round
it once: each time you go, you'll like it more if it is a good place.
Observe how the neighbours keep their places up: if the district
is a good one, they should be well kept up. Go into it with your
eyes open, so that you can get out of it again. It should have a
good climate, not be subject to storms; the soil should be good,
so that the land is naturally fertile. If possible, it should be at
the foot of a hill, facing south. The area should be a healthy one,
there should be a good supply of labour, and a good water-
supply. It should be near a town where trade is brisk or else the
sea or a river navigable to ships or a good road with plenty of
traffic on it.

Neither Cato nor Virgil is concerned with giving advice to farmers. Virgil writes for readers who find the detail and the way in which it is presented fascinating; what he offers them is essentially a literary experience. Cato writes for readers who want to be sure they are making a good investment and want to understand enough about farming to satisfy themselves that their investment is being well managed. Writing for men of his own class, men who have arrived, he can permit himself an easy, relaxed intimacy with his readers, confident they will share his prejudices, aware that even in the matter of buying a farm there is a proper way for a gentleman to talk to his equals. But his object is strictly practical.

Roman prose writing is the direct outcome of the need and the opportunity provided by the daily routine of life for those who participated in public life in the Forum and the Senate to express their ideas effectively. It is hardly surprising, therefore, if the use of prose comes to be associated with practical objectives. Though prose and verse evolve alongside one another, each constantly influencing or reacting against the other, they are kept apart by social function. That function keeps changing as society itself changes, but almost to the end of the Republic the line of demarcation is clear. Verse is for entertainment and relaxation, for the cultivation of the mind; it serves as a civilizing force, or as an expression of one's own ideas and personality. Prose is for the practical things in life. As social life becomes less dominated by practical needs, the distinction becomes blurred: by the end of the Classical period there is an emerging sense of the possibilities of prose and the necessary limitations of verse.

II NEW USES FOR PROSE

In the last century BC Roman prose became something more than the workaday cousin of verse. By the end of the century, it had developed into a highly efficient instrument of persuasion and a reasonably efficient instrument of abstract thought. The ornate, complex artistry of Cicero's speeches is a remarkable instance of the interaction between social need and individual genius. The philosophical treatises on which Cicero spent the concluding years of his life show how a writer with a gift for words and a talent for argument can adapt the skills acquired in the Senate and the Forum to areas remote from the everyday, as part of a disciplined survey of the intellectual life of the Hellenistic world. To Cicero it was clear that the everyday and the more than everyday went hand in hand. The reading and reflection which belonged to his intellectual life (the pursuit he called *litterae*, which included, but was not confined to, what we should call literature) contributed a great deal to his professional competence as a speaker in the courts and in political life. The mastery over words, on the other hand, which he had won as an orator in a society which devoted almost unbelievably detailed attention to oratorical technique equipped him ideally, or so it seemed to Cicero, for the exposition of the problems of philosophy.

As verse and prose develop in the Classical period, the movement towards separate identities is clear. Partly this is a matter of structure: prose and verse acquire increasingly distinct principles of syntactical organization (something was said of this at the beginning of Chapter 2). But it is also a matter of function. And inevitably, as the writer of verse and the writer of prose make increasingly large areas of social and intellectual life their province, they learn from one another how to deal with the problems of expression which confront them. At the same time a kind of rivalry springs up between them.

In the courts and in politics there is, of course, no question of rivalry: lawyers and politicians had always spoken prose; there was never any question of their speaking verse. At most one can point to some interaction: as oratory becomes an art and plain speaking ceases to be enough, the orator borrows from the poet some of the tricks of the poet's trade. But he works out tricks of his own, and in his turn the epic poet or the dramatist, when he puts a speech on the lips of a character in his poem or play, learns to construct that speech according to the recognized principles of rhetoric; in the speeches in the *Aeneid*, for example, Virgil employs not only the figures, but also the syntax of prose rhetoric much more freely than in the narrative sections of his poem.

Rivalry begins when the prose writer takes over the function of teacher. Prose supersedes verse for most didactic purposes, leaving the poet-teacher to create a new role for himself. Here it is more a matter of developing separate identities than of learning from one another. Didactic verse moves over the border into literature, to become a kind of poetry in which the role of the poet as teacher is secondary. The writer of didactic prose, on the other hand, even when he moves out of the area of the practical and the everyday, does not allow himself to forget that his role is to instruct.

Lucretius' poem *On the Universe* and Cicero's discussions of the problems of philosophy have much in common as far as content is concerned. Where they differ is in the expectations the two arouse in their readers. The readers of Lucretius' poem expect a literary experience; their concern with the philosophical content of the poem is secondary; indeed, Lucretius' object in writing in verse is to overcome the resistance he expects in his readers to what he has to say. Cicero, writing a generation later, when Greek philosophers and talk about philosophy have become part of the everyday experience of an educated Roman, writes for readers motivated primarily by an interest in, or at any rate curiosity about, the different philosophical systems and the problems of conduct of which he sets out to give a lucid, readable account. One can hardly call that a practical concern. And Cicero, like Lucretius, sugars the bitter pill of philosophical argument: his treatises are modelled on the dialogues of Plato, though the dramatic illusion is only thinly sketched in. The difference is one of emphasis: Lucretius' object is to get his readers emotionally committed to a set of ideas without their realizing fully what is happening; like children, they are tricked into swallowing something which is good for them. The audience for which Cicero writes is one which is motivated by curiosity about philosophy; but since it is no more than an amateur interest, Cicero feels obliged to make the learning experience agreeable.

The expansion of prose leads, in short, to a natural tendency to restrict verse to those uses for which poetry is especially suitable. There are perhaps two of these. One is to say what cannot be said in prose because what is said is too emotionally charged or too complex; the other is to cope with things which cannot be spelled out plainly. The love poems of Catullus—and many of the hate poems of Catullus—are examples of writing that is emotionally charged beyond what is acceptable in prose; some of the *Odes* of Horace are examples of statement whose compact complexity is possible only in verse. For examples of things that are better not said in as many words one can point to those sections of the *Aeneid* where the poet's fiction expresses an implied challenge to contemporary attitudes and ideals. It isn't so much that poetry possesses some mysterious eloquence denied to prose, but rather that the two are held apart by a sense that different social functions prescribe different uses, so that it is almost bad manners to use one instead of the other. It is part of the etiquette of prose to be readily intelligible; poetry, because it is more compact and more intensely memorable and exciting, can demand a degree of concentration that permits techniques which transcend rational communication. Only the occasional writer of genius like Tacitus ignores etiquette and mixes the two.

The movement towards intensification and specialization of the role of poetry is one of the most exciting features of Roman literature. But there is another side of the picture. In the more traditional forms of verse, verse continues to be used simply because adherence to a traditional form is in itself a justification of the use of verse. Horace, for example, uses the loosely structured dactylic hexameter for his *Satires* in order to stake his claim to be recognized as a second Lucilius. Persius and Juvenal use the same form for the same reason, to emphasize their adherence to a recognized tradition.

This is natural enough, but there are dangers. One is that writers will go on using a form consecrated by tradition when they have absolutely nothing to say: technical competence in the conventions of the form is put at the service of material so threadbare as to be worthless. This does not happen with satire, but it keeps happening with epic. Another is that a writer who has something to say, overawed by the traditional prestige of verse, will fail to see that what he has to say would be better said in prose. It is not easy to keep abreast of change. Even as shrewd a writer as Horace is capable of such failures of vision. If, instead of the apparently casual style of the hexameter epistle with its elaborately contrived abrupt transitions, he had used prose for his *Art of Poetry*, his essay might not have been the obscure, confusing piece of writing that it is and might have deserved more to be compared with Aristotle's *Poetics*. In the Postclassical period the general slackening of creativity induces in the writer who is lacking in originality an increasing subservience to the prestige of verse. Pliny, for example, in a letter to his friend Caninius, writes him a careful, detailed account of the curious incident of the dolphin of Hippo with the suggestion that Caninius might care to work the account up into a poem: it is as though Pliny felt the subject had not been properly treated until it had been treated in verse.

Or take the case of historical writing. It was inevitable that prose history should eventually supplant historical epic. The justification which existed for Ennius no longer existed a hundred years later. Yet it took the Romans oddly long to realize that prose could simply do the job better. One would have thought that Livy's monumental work would have settled the matter, but it is another hundred years before prose history of the stature of Livy is written again at Rome. There was, however, no shortage of writers of historical epic. No doubt, the extraordinary persistence of epic in the first century AD is due to the prestige of Virgil's *Aeneid*. But it is due too to the sad fact that, with the exception of Lucan, the writers of epic in the first century AD were obsessed with form to the point that their interest in the content of what they wrote was minimal.

The evolution of imaginative fiction in prose was even more painfully slow: here there was not only the formal barrier to be broken down, there was also the rigid convention which restricted fiction to the traditional repertoire built up by Homer and the writers of Athenian tragedy. In the Postclassical period prose fiction is represented only by one wholly eccentric, iconoclastic work, Petronius' *Satyricon*.

III EVERYDAY PROSE IN THE CLASSICAL
PERIOD: CICERO

The classification of verse under three headings—the poet as storyteller, the poet as teacher and the poet as himself—can serve also for prose. Writing in prose does not rest, however, on the same easily discerned threefold tradition. The division into three types becomes no more than a convenient tool of analysis. There are no neat frontiers: the best one can say often is that a writer's work represents a mixture of two types in which one type preponderates. The order of historical development changes, moreover. Where prose is concerned, the appropriate order for discussion becomes: the prose-writer as teacher (didactic prose), the prose-writer as himself, and the prose-writer as storyteller; fiction is the last area to be surrendered to prose.

It is in the nature of things that didactic prose should come first. Prose writing begins with the presentation of practical information. Cato's handbook *On Agriculture* is an obvious case. As technology becomes more advanced, that function becomes more specialized: a good example is Vitruvius' textbook *On Architecture*. As social life becomes more complicated, there emerge writers who are less motivated by the wish to impart practical or useful information than by curiosity and a natural desire to pass on to others what they have found out. The diligent, persistent pursuit of information for its own sake is the basis of philosophy and of history, where it is guided by the desire to understand as well as the desire to know. The encyclopaedist is less discriminating; he is dominated by an active curiosity to find out; it seems only natural to him to record what he has found out, especially if the facts have not been recorded before, or are difficult of access. There is always an audience for such works. The passive acquisition of information is characteristic of the unsophisticated intelligence in all ages, whether it be the readers of that mine of piecemeal information, the *Natural History* of Pliny (the uncle of the letter-writer), Molière's *bourgeois gentilhomme,* to whom the smallest scraps of recondite information are a source of delight ('la belle chose que de savoir quelque chose'), or the readers of the *Reader's Digest.* We shall be concerned here only with those writers whose works have a claim to be regarded as literature.

Cicero began, as a writer of didactic prose, in a field where he could claim a special authority: the principles and practice of oratory. From these topics he moved in late middle life with a long experience of political life behind him to the composition of two more ambitious works loosely modelled on the two longest dialogues of Plato, the *Republic* and the *Laws.* In the last years of his life, he threw his energies into the active exposition of the problems of philosophy. We have to remember that Rome was by way of becoming the centre of the philosophical world; partly as a result of the rediscovery of the lost library of Aristotle, brought to Rome by Sulla, and the establishment of similar collections by wealthy Romans, leading Stoics and Epicureans were familiar figures.

Though he had always been interested in philosophy, Cicero made little claim to speak as an authority. Apart from two shorter dialogues *On Old Age* and *On Friendship*, which were more personal in character and where Cicero spoke more in the light of his own experience of life, his special competence was as an expositor of the views of others. His output was prodigious: it included four major works, the *De Finibus*, the *De Officiis*, the *De Natura Deorum* and the *Tusculan Disputations*. The following is typical of Cicero's more carefully worked-up manner (5. 12 *De Finibus*); the place is Athens, the date 79 BC:

> I had just been to a lecture by Antiochus. Marcus Piso was
> with me as usual; also present were my brother Quintus, Titus
> Pomponius and Lucius Cicero, whom I loved as a brother
> though he was really only a first cousin. We decided we would go
> for a walk in the afternoon, ending up in the Academy, mainly
> because at that time of day the place was quite empty of people.
> And so at the time appointed we met at Piso's lodgings. We spent
> the six stades from the Dipylon gate discussing various subjects.
> Then, when we reached the justly famous grounds of the
> Academy, we had the place to ourselves, as we had wanted.
> Whereupon Piso remarked, 'Tell me, is it something instinctive
> or an illusion of some kind? When we see places in which
> famous figures of the past are supposed to have spent their time,
> we are more affected than when we hear of their deeds or read
> something they wrote. For instance, I am affected in that way
> now. I think of Plato, who is supposed to have been the first to
> lecture here. His little garden over there doesn't just remind me
> of him: it actually makes me feel I see the man himself.'

The philosophical works were almost wholly written during the last year of the dictatorship of Julius Caesar and the short period of Cicero's brief return to public life following Caesar's assassination; this was the period of his increasingly reckless attacks upon Mark Antony which became known as the *Philippics*. It is an extraordinary accomplishment for a man in his sixties on the verge of despair and in increasing risk of his life. Mommsen's contemptuous dismissal of Cicero as a mere journalist is harsh. Mommsen meant of course a journalist in the nineteenth-century sense: a prolific writer with a rather showy style on subjects he imperfectly understood. It is true that Cicero has no head for philosophy. He lacks acuity of mind. He is wordy. Comparison with the dry, pointed, scalpel-like grace of Seneca is not to Cicero's advantage; comparison with his acknowledged model, Plato, is out of the question. But Cicero's philosophical works are more than journalism. They are the work of a man whose life has failed, who tries, while the world he struggled to preserve is crashing around him, to sort out his faith and find a reasoned base for optimism.

What is wrong to our ears is that Cicero writes as a man whose thinking has been too much corrupted by the rhetoric of public life. The syntactical structures are simpler, as is appropriate to expository prose. But he has not the patience to discuss things like a philosopher: in the pursuit of clarity his gifts as expositor are apt to get out of hand. When it is a matter of his personal convictions we feel he is saying what he would like us to believe, not what he believes. One misses the impressive simplicity and sincerity of Seneca's indifference in his *Letters to Lucilius*, not only to worldly goods but to life itself. That is of course unjust, a reaction of suspicion and alienation prompted by a way of writing more than by the substance of what is said. Cicero's devotion to the causes he believed in was at least as great as Seneca's; in the end he courted death by his open defiance of Antony, and his death at the hands of Antony's assassins was no less heroic than Seneca's contemptuous, theatrical enactment of Nero's instructions. But it is not wholly unjust. One feels the same with the prose writings of many politicians. It is almost as though they had lived too long in the public world to be wholly honest with anybody, even themselves.

Cicero's position in literature is not easily fixed. His role in the development of Latin prose is enormous. His influence upon a whole generation is not to be underrated. The philosophical treatises must have done much to stimulate that expansion of the moral consciousness which is evident in writers like Horace and Virgil when we compare them with the writers of the previous generation. Those who find Cicero's philosophical works hard to take seriously should consider the contribution of the *De Finibus* and the *De Officiis* (known affectionately as '*Tully's Ends*' and '*Tully's Offices*') to English moralist thinking in the seventeenth and eighteenth centuries and indeed to the whole formation of the English character from the Renaissance until recent times. To say of such works that in their day they did no more than provide a context for literature seems ungracious. But it is true. The claim to literary status implicit in Cicero's imitation of Plato is too casually sustained. In the first of his imitations, the *De Republica*, he took more trouble, it seems (only portions of the work remain), to integrate content and dramatic structure. The *De Finibus*, the *De Officiis*, the *De Natura Deorum* and the *Tusculan Disputations* are little more than textbooks, thinly disguised.

IV   POSTCLASSICAL DIDACTIC PROSE: SENECA

The generation after Cicero's was a generation of poets. Prose underwent a temporary eclipse. In the Postclassical period the pendulum swings the other way: there is a reversal in the roles of verse and prose. It starts with Livy, who began writing early in the reign of Augustus, and reaches its highest point with Tacitus over a century later.

The history of verse after the Augustan Age is a story of increasingly pathetic descent into bathos and fatuity. From the age of Nero onwards, both the writer who has something to say and the writer who wants to say what he has to say in a way that permits creativity will say it in prose. Until verse can find new forms and new emotions to express (which will not happen till the fourth century AD), the future is with prose. Naturally, not all the writers of the age of Nero and the second half of the century fully realize the change that has taken place. Even Juvenal, a writer of vigorous, independent talent, but a conservative in literary matters as well as in his social ideas, is content to flog a dead horse.

Not a great deal of really first-class prose is written. During most of the first century AD the political climate discouraged serious expression of one's thoughts. A writer who disregarded the dictates of prudence was likely to have his books burnt; and though, as Tacitus drily points out, this tended to ensure their popularity, for 'repression of genius increases its prestige' (*punitis ingeniis gliscit auctoritas*), the burning of books by imperial decree made writers think twice before committing anything that mattered to paper.

The circumstances encouraged didactic prose. The best-known names are those of the elder Pliny, the two Senecas and Quintilian. Pliny is an indefatigable collector of curious information; the 37 books of his *Natural History* are packed with facts about most things under the sun. The elder Seneca and Quintilian are professors of rhetoric. Seneca is remembered as the author of a textbook, a kind of annotated anthology made up of specimens of the style of over a hundred famous speakers on more than forty different subjects. Quintilian's *Institutio Oratoria* is a more ambitious textbook, a detailed programme for the education of the prospective lawyer, including a grounding in the humanities. The work was based on Quintilian's own experience over some twenty years as the head of a highly successful law school. Throughout the Postclassical period, though the importance of the courts declined, knowledge and practice of the law continued to be the acknowledged duty of every Roman of means and social standing. What we should call a legal education was really the only kind of advanced education available. Hence Quintilian's comprehensive treatment of the subject: his *Institutio* is more a programme for a liberal education than a textbook for budding lawyers. His pupil Pliny (nephew of the encyclopaedist) is a good specimen of the well-read, cultivated, conscientious, thoroughly conventional gentleman the school produced.

The younger Seneca is a more interesting figure and the only one of the four whose didactic prose has a serious claim to be regarded as literature. He had perhaps the most curious career of all Roman writers. Born in Spain, the son of the professor of rhetoric whom we call the elder Seneca, he established himself at Rome as a writer and philosopher of distinction, was appointed tutor to the future emperor Nero (then a boy of about thirteen), and became upon his pupil's accession his personal adviser and minister. The poet Lucan was his cousin, and for eight years, until his position became intolerable, he exercised a powerful and beneficial influence upon Nero; three years after his retirement he was accused of conspiring against Nero and forced to commit suicide.

In modern times his literary reputation rests more upon his verse than upon his prose. (For Seneca's tragedies, see Chapter 2.) But it is characteristic of the man and of the time that verse should be a kind of diversion, an experimental vehicle for a new kind of tragic experience, rather than the most concentrated expression of Seneca's thought. His surviving prose works—apart from one venture into prose satire, a skit with an absurd title (*Apocolocyntosis*, or 'Pumpkinification') on the deification of the Emperor Claudius—fall into two groups. The first group comprises his formal didactic prose: ten short dialogues on ethical themes, an 'Essay on Clemency' written for the edification of Nero, and a somewhat haphazard series of speculations on natural phenomena (*Quaestiones Naturales*). The second group consists of Seneca's most influential work upon the history of European thought and upon English and French prose style, the *Epistulae Morales*, a collection of 124 letters, some very long, addressed to his friend Lucilius. In these Seneca abandons the conventional didactic manner for the personal manner of Horace's hexameter essays.

The choice of the letter form is interesting. No doubt the voluminous correspondence of Cicero published after his death had something to do with it. But clearly the real model is Horace's *Epistles*, except that in place of verse Seneca opts for prose. To have done otherwise would have been an impossible affectation: in the eighty years since Horace published his *Epistles* prose had established itself as the normal vehicle of literary expression. Like the *Epistles*, Seneca's *Letters* are moral essays, not real letters (though Lucilius, like most of Horace's correspondents, is a real person, well known in public life). And like Horace, Seneca affects an informality and spontaneity appropriate to the epistolary form (*Letter* 75. 1–3):

I want my letters to be just like the way I'd talk to you if we were
sitting or walking together: not laboured, but easy. There is
nothing forced or artificial about them. I'd rather you could see
how I felt, instead of having me go on talking, if only that were
possible. Even if I were trying to make a point, I'd not stamp my
foot, or throw my hand around, or raise my voice. I'd leave that
sort of thing to those who speak in public, contenting myself
with having conveyed my meaning to you without dressing it
up in words—and not tossing words off with no reflection
either. This one thing I'd like to think I'd won your approval of,
that everything I say I really mean; and don't just mean it, but am
passionately committed to it.

But where Horace is a poet first and only an amateur philosopher,
Seneca thinks of himself as a professional philosopher, primarily a Stoic,
but with considerable sympathy for Epicureanism and able to speak with
authority upon the doctrines of all schools. Now that he has retired from
the turmoil of public affairs, his settled purpose is to devote what remains
of life to meditation upon the human condition in the light of his own
experience (and the quite exceptional opportunities it provided for
insight into men's characters), his convictions as a Stoic, and the ever-
present certainty of his own mortality. The *Letters* are a patient,
sometimes highly technical, explanation of the fundamental principles of
Stoicism and of rival philosophical theories, and an exhortation to a way
of life. They are in no sense systematic treatises, like the letters Epicurus
addressed to his disciples, but are aimed at producing the illusion of the
speaking voice of a highly cultivated man in earnest, relaxed conversation
with a friend. Seneca has a keen dramatic sense and can sketch in, vividly
and succinctly, the circumstances of a letter: the point he has reached on a
journey, the noises which assail his ears as he writes in his study at Rome.
But there is no gossip, none of the incidental comment on the current
social or political scene one would expect to find in ordinary letters. If
occasionally he sketches in a wider canvas, it is to express his detachment
from the incredible wealth and decadence of the contemporary world
(*Letter* 86. 1; 4–5):

I write these lines as I recline in the very house that belonged to
Scipio Africanus, having worshipped his departed spirit at the
altar which I take to be the place where the great man lies buried.
His soul, I am convinced, will have returned to heaven, whence it
came, not because he commanded great armies (so did
Cambyses, mad as he was—his madness, indeed, in no way

interfered with his success), but because of his outstanding
moderation and that sense of duty which I find more to be
admired when he left his country than when he defended it.
For the choice was: to have Scipio in Rome at all costs, or
to have a Rome that was free.

I have inspected the farmhouse, which is built of squared
stone, the wall that runs around the wood, and also the towers
erected on either side of the house as a protection for it, the well
(sufficient for an army) concealed among greenery and a group
of sheds, the tiny bathroom, an ill-lit place, as was the ancient
custom (our ancestors taking the view that the proper way to
take a hot bath was in the dark). I found it most agreeable to
reflect upon the way of life of Scipio, comparing it with our
own. It was in this humble abode that the 'Terror of the
Carthaginians', to whom Rome owes the fact that she has only
once been occupied by a foreign foe, used to perform his
ablutions after a hard day in the fields. For he kept himself fit
by work, tilling the earth with his own hands, as was the ancient
custom. He had this dingy roof over his head, this cheap pavement beneath his feet.

Seneca goes on to attack the mad, pointless extravagance of the
bathrooms equipped with every conceivable luxury and studded with
precious stones of his own day. If it sounds too much like conventional
moralizing, there are letters in which he expresses a less conventional
opinion (*Letter* 47. 11–13):

I am reluctant to get involved in a discussion of the whole subject
of the use of slaves, towards whom we display the utmost arrogance,
cruelty and contempt. The essence of my view is this: live on
the same terms with an inferior as you would have a superior live
with you. Every time you think of the power you have over a
slave, remember how much power your master has over you.
'But I have no master,' you say. You're young. Your turn will
come perhaps. Do you not remember the age Hecuba was when
she became a slave; or Croesus, or Darius' mother, or Plato, or
Diogenes? Live with your slave compassionately, on easy terms,
admit him to your conversation, your plans for the future,
your way of life generally. At this point the whole group of
those who pass for men of refinement will protest loudly,
'What could be more humiliating, or more degrading?' These
are the men I shall catch kissing the hands of other men's slaves.

The Uses of Prose

Critics have been harsh on Seneca. Quintilian allowed that, both as a man and as a writer, he had many qualities, but he was inclined to damn them with faint praise. He detested Seneca's style and deplored its popularity with the younger generation. In modern times it is the man rather than the stylist who is condemned.

No other Roman prose writer can combine in the same degree accurate, succinct statement of complex thought and simple, hard-hitting clarity of syntax; comparison with Ovid is inevitable and instructive. Cicero, like most Roman writers, has on command when it suits his purpose the art of simple, succinct narrative; when dealing with an idea, he prefers to let it ride triumphant on a wave of rhetoric. Virgil, confronted with hard sense, is extraordinarily skilful in exploiting the plangent, imprecise allusiveness of Latin words. Ovid and Seneca can cast a net of syntax around any idea they choose and hold it pinned down while they present each facet of it in turn for our attention. The difference is that we are not expected to take Ovid seriously: the posturing involved in this syntactical ingenuity is part of the Ovidian stance; he offers his readers a highly sophisticated entertainment; style is the vehicle of Ovid's special brand of wit. Seneca on the other hand expects to be taken seriously. His talk is of the right way for a man to conduct his life, or how a man should prepare his thoughts for the inevitability of death. When such subjects are being discussed, a style so slick, so clear that questions to which there can be no easy answer are made to sound simple and straightforward is apt to seem an offence against good taste. So too, of course, is Ciceronian rhetoric. But Seneca is supposed to be a philosopher, something more than an eloquent exponent of the ideas of others. Which brings us back from style to the man.

The personality which these highly personal moral essays express is not easy to come to terms with. No doubt we are less ready today to condemn Seneca out of hand than the Victorians were. They found the high-minded detachment of the letters hard to take from a man who had soiled his reputation beyond all forgiveness by his long association with Nero. The events of recent times have given us a more sympathetic understanding of the helplessness of the individual charged with advising a tyrant who is both mad and all-powerful. We have lost the taste for simple heroics. We are more sympathetic to the view that in such cases the true Stoic hero is not a Cato who allows blind, uncompromising opposition to that which he abhors to strip him of all power to control events, but the man who, like Seneca, stays on to do what he can to restrain the spread of evil; and then, when he sees he can do no more, retires, not in a blaze of heroics, but with his mind made up to go on living until life becomes intolerable (*Letter* 70. 13–15):

Thoughts like these are foolish: 'One person will say that my
conduct was not brave enough; another, that I was too rash; a
third, that there was a kind of death that would have shown
more courage.' You should tell yourself that you have in hand
something with which the talk of men has no concern! Your sole
aim should be to escape from Fortune's clutches as quickly as
possible; there will always be people who will think ill of what
you have done. You can find men who claim to be philosophers
and yet maintain one should not offer violence to one's own life,
and hold it wrong for a man to be the means of his own destruction: we should wait, they say, for the end which Nature has
decreed. A man who will say that does not see that he is barring
the path to freedom. The best thing that the eternal law ever laid
down was that it gave us one entrance to life, but many exits.
Am I to await the cruelty of disease, or of man, when I can depart
through the midst of torture, and shake off my troubles?

There are men with whom this is empty talk. It was not so with Seneca.
When the time came and the centurion arrived from Nero inviting Seneca
to take his own life, Seneca did not hesitate to practise what he had
preached. The story of his suicide is told at length by Tacitus and most of
the narrative is to Seneca's credit—no small compliment to Seneca from a
writer who does not dispense praise lavishly (*Annals* 15. 62):

Seneca, quite unmoved, asked for tablets on which to inscribe
his will, and, on the centurion's refusal, turned to his friends,
protesting that as he was forbidden to requite them, he bequeathed to them the only, but still the noblest possession yet
remaining to him, the pattern of his life, which if they
remembered, they would win a name for moral worth and
steadfast friendship. At the same time he called them back
from their tears to manly resolution, now with friendly talk,
and now with the sterner language of rebuke. 'Where,' he
asked again and again, 'are your maxims of philosophy, or the
preparation of so many years' study against evils to come? Who
knew not Nero's cruelty? After a mother's and a brother's
murder, nothing remains but to add the destruction of a guardian
and a tutor.'

[Translation: Church and Brodribb]

Suicide proves unexpectedly difficult, however; the simple, dignified act
of self-destruction eludes Seneca. First he cuts the veins in his arms; then
the veins in his legs; when that fails too, he resorts to poison; in the end,

his slaves suffocated him in a steam bath; his wife, who had attempted to commit suicide along with her husband, was saved. There is a theatrical quality in all this which Tacitus relishes. But the final act in the tragicomedy is less an indictment of Seneca than of the times in which he lived. Neither in death nor in life was there any opportunity left in the age of Nero for a man to play the role of Socrates. The continual need to stand apart from the depraved, the absurd and the horrible makes you in the end a character in the mad farce you despise and reject. The constant need to study your role and to interpret that role to others infects equally your thinking and the expression of your thoughts.

It is this studied, theatrical simplicity which gives Seneca's style a directness that attracts some and repels many. Its influence has been enormous. The style became the model for those who found the ample, flowing manner of Cicero and the cant of the public stance distasteful. To the seventeenth-century moralists (individualists like Bishop Hall and John Donne) the Senecan manner permitted a more honest, as well as a more vigorous, expression of their own personality. There was the added attraction that Senecan Stoicism came close to the teachings of Christianity—Christianity, that is, as it was preached in seventeenth-century England. Seneca was regarded as the great pagan divine. It was for such reasons that his prose became the model for the direct, non-periodic style, rather than the prose of Sallust or the younger Pliny.

A battle between Ciceronians and Senecans ensued. When Milton attacked Hall for making sentences 'by the statute, as if all above three inches long were confiscate', he was speaking as a Ciceronian deriding a Senecan. In the end the Senecans won. Modern English prose structure is closer to that of Seneca than it is to that of Cicero; the prose of Milton and Johnson (the two greatest English Ciceronians) sounds archaic to our ears compared with the prose of Dryden. Only in times of a resurgence of public attitudes (in late Victorian England, for example) does the Ciceronian manner feel congenial. We have all become Senecans without knowing it. In France the Senecan style is the basis of *la clarté française*. It is above all the voice of the individualist who finds it necessary to play a carefully studied part because his ideas are unpopular, or because the only tool that can penetrate the intellectual and moral torpor of his contemporaries is simple, sharp talk barbed with paradox. Among leading exponents of the Senecan manner are Francis Bacon, Voltaire and Bertrand Russell.

V HISTORICAL PROSE

Curiosity about the past, a desire to reconstruct the past, are among the commonest impulses of the reflecting mind. For some, knowledge of the past is a matter of knowing facts. For others it means ideas. For others again, the men and women in history are what matter.

The first is the crudest form of curiosity about the past. History is reduced for these people to a matter of describable events. Addressing themselves to the question, What happened? they are content to pin down *what?* in terms of *when?* and *where?*; *how?* is allowed to take precedence over *why?* because *how?* seems capable of reconstruction in its multitudinous particularity; *why?*, not being a matter of fact, is less straightforward. It is with such chroniclers of events that Roman historical prose emerges: the earliest known to us is Quintus Fabius Pictor, who is said to have been born around 250 BC, about the time when Roman literature (in verse) traditionally begins. He wrote in Greek, presumably because there was no other medium available to him: men had not yet learnt to express themselves in prose outside the limited contexts of religious ritual, law and the routine procedures of administration.

This is not what we mean by history. It is at best an undistinguished form of didacticism. What seems to us the next obvious step, to move on from a chronicle of events to something that we could call historical narrative, is delayed by the feeling that the proper form for telling a story was verse, not prose. Naevius and Ennius could give full scope to the pageantry of history because epic form provided the right conventions and the right audience.

During the next two centuries the development of prose is steady and impressive, even when we remember that, as always, the Romans had the Greeks to learn from. By the beginning of the Classical period, simple historical narrative had reached a very acceptable level of competence. There is, for example, the story told by Claudius Quadrigarius (quoted by Aulus Gellius 9.13. 7–19) of how in 361 BC Manlius Torquatus defeated a giant Gaul in single combat; it compares well with the more elaborately worked-up version of the same story in Livy (7. 9–10). Throughout the Classical and Postclassical periods there will continue to be writers who concern themselves with little more than the facts of what occurred. Their motives differ. Concentration on the facts can lend one's account a valuable, because deceptive, air of objectivity, as Caesar was quick to realize when he came to write his memoirs, first of the war in Gaul, and then of the civil war which broke out between him and his political opponents when he returned from Gaul at the head of his armies, determined not to relinquish the power he had won in the field. Suetonius, on the other hand, is consumed by a passion for facts: no Roman writer tells so bald a story in such a wealth of detail.

But as prose grew to maturity and historical epic lost much of its prestige, historians were quick to realize that, though facts cannot be dispensed with, to put together a coherent account involves more than telling a story: prose has a code of behaviour of its own, one that is distinct from the etiquette of verse; the mature prose writer feels the need to give a rational account of what occurred; he has, in short, not just to tell a story, but to make sense of the past.

The successful prose historian must have an awareness of history as a process and an understanding of history as something involving complex human beings whose motivation he can attempt to reconstruct and explain. Ideally, he should be motivated himself by a disinterested, compassionate curiosity that will enable him to see the human consequences of the historical process. At Rome, as a result of the didactic origins of prose and the feeling that the prose writer is a teacher as well as a storyteller, prose assumes a strongly moralistic tendency.

The moralizing takes various forms. At the opposite extreme from Suetonius is Tacitus. Tacitus is almost impatient of facts in his pursuit of a picture dominated by a single moral idea: how Rome fell victim to the exercise of absolute power. The history of the Julio-Claudian dynasty is for Tacitus a sick tragicomedy which he recasts for the moral instruction of his readers in a complex, soberly suggestive, almost poetic prose. Sallust and Livy stand at the opposite ends of a different scale. Sallust chooses the single, complex event from the comparatively recent past for reconstruction in detail; his approach is patient and analytical. Livy has the majestic sweep, the vision of history as a pageant, which places him in the tradition of Ennius and historical epic. His sentimental interest in story is backed up by a conscientious pursuit of fact, and also by a comprehensive, if uncritical and unpenetrating, understanding of the historical process that gives his story meaning. The tale he has to tell is of Rome's rise to greatness. But it is a past greatness, the greatness of the Republic. This idea is not pressed upon the reader, however; the facts are not relentlessly selected and adjusted, as Tacitus selects and adjusts them, lest there should be any mistaking the way they point.

VI   SALLUST, THE NOBLE OUTLAW AND THE NOBLE SAVAGE

Sallust was twenty years younger than Cicero. His two historical monographs belonged, as did Cicero's philosophical treatises, to the late forties. Like Cicero, Sallust had retired from public life; he was unable, he tells us, to endure the corruption of politics. We may suspect prudence entered into his decision; it was no time to stay in politics if you wanted to stay alive. Unlike Cicero, he survived the proscriptions.

Sallust's *Conspiracy of Catiline* was written while Cicero's murder was still fresh in men's minds. The last of the chief actors in the conspiracy was now dead: Catiline had been killed in the fighting which followed the exposure of his attempted coup; Cato had committed suicide after the defeat of Pompey at Pharsalus (48 BC); Caesar was assassinated in 44 BC; Cicero was murdered the following year. The time had come for a fresh look at the events of 63 BC.

It is a story with a modern ring. In a state where there exists great inequality of wealth, where the system is corrupt and the young see their only hope in revolution, a *coup d'état* is planned by an unscrupulous member of the establishment. He is backed by a few politicians and has at his command a large gang of toughs. Women prominent in public life are involved; the sympathies of a large following of intellectuals and pseudo-intellectuals are cynically exploited by a leader of undeniable personal charisma. The coup fails and the opportunity is seized by the right wing for a reversion to strong government and a ruthless stamping out of dissent.

It is the sort of story where there can be substantial agreement about the main facts and considerable variation in the way in which they are presented. The scenario just outlined is a reconstruction by modern historians. In Sallust's day the official version was that embodied in the published text of the four speeches which Cicero had delivered at the time. Naturally, the speeches do not present the whole story; their aim is to manipulate public opinion at a time of crisis, not to put the facts on record for posterity. Cicero himself painted a more conciliatory picture of Catiline half a dozen years later. Circumstances alter cases, as every lawyer knows: the storm had died down; his action in putting the conspirators to death had got Cicero into a deal of trouble; his client now was one of those young intellectuals who had found the charm of Catiline so hard to resist. Cicero was in the mood to be generous to a dead enemy (Cicero, *Pro Caelio* 12–14).

> As I think you remember, one could see signs of many excellent
> qualities in the man that had never fully developed. He
> numbered numerous rogues among his acquaintances, and yet
> he put on a show of being devoted to men of the highest prin-
> ciples. There was much about him that incited lust, but much
> also that aroused application and physical effort. Vices and
> passions burned in the man, but at the same time a zeal for the
> soldier's life. I don't think there ever was on this earth such an
> extraordinary mixture, one compounded of such contrary, such
> contradictory and mutually hostile impulses and desires. . . .

221

> There was a time when he almost deceived me. I took him for
> a patriotic citizen, anxious to associate himself with the best
> elements in our state, a firm and reliable friend. It wasn't until
> I had the evidence of his crimes before my eyes that I could
> believe them; it wasn't until I had caught him red-handed that
> I so much as suspected him.

But once again we are dealing with an astute mind manipulating facts that
cannot be got around till they appear in the best light. Cicero's motives
are clear: we know where we are.

Sallust is more of a puzzle. In 63 BC he was in his twenties. The young
intellectuals who supported Catiline were his contemporaries. But if he
felt any sneaking sympathy for them, he does not show it (*Catiline*
14; 16):

> It was the young above all whom he sought as associates. Their
> minds were still impressionable, they were of an age to be
> influenced, easily deceived by guile. According as the indi-
> vidual's youthful passion indicated, he procured women for
> some, bought others dogs and horses, spared in short no expense
> or disgrace to make them dependent on him. . . . He taught the
> young men he had ensnared as I have related a multitude of
> crimes. Some he used to bear false witness or forge seals to
> documents. He thought little of their credit or their fortunes or
> the dangers involved. Then when he had eroded their reputation
> and sense of shame, he set out to teach them greater crimes. If
> there was no pressing occasion for a criminal act, he plotted the
> ruin or the murder of the innocent equally as the deserving, per-
> petrating wanton evil and cruelty rather than have hands or
> minds get out of practice.

Sallust's object, apparently, is not to rebut the Ciceronian version, but to
transpose it into narrative form. Cicero had to select his facts for their
sensational or rhetorical effect, Sallust can embroider his account at
leisure. His Catiline is not the monster of Cicero's virulent attacks in the
Senate and before the people, but a carefully worked-up study in black
and white (*Catiline* 5):

> Lucius Catiline, a noble by birth, possessed great strength of
> mind and body, but an evil and corrupt nature. While still a
> young man he was attracted by civil war, murder, robbery, mob
> violence, and it was to these that he applied his talents as a
> grown man. He had a constitution able to an incredible degree to
> endure hunger, cold, lack of sleep; a mind that was daring,

subtle, adaptable, capable of any deceit or dissimulation. He was as ready to lay hands on another's possessions as he was free with his own. He burned with passions. He was an eloquent speaker, but too deficient in wisdom. His great, disordered mind constantly embraced projects that were extravagant, implausible, impossible.

What is surprising is that the historian's version differs so little from the politician's. Naturally, his is the fuller account; he quotes from the speeches of Cato and Caesar in the great debate in the Senate. There are minor discrepancies: either Sallust's memory was faulty, or he draws upon a different source. But little turns on the difference between one account and the other. One cannot help wondering why Sallust chose so familiar an episode from recent history if it was not to reject, or somehow substantially revise, the official version, either from his personal recollection or as the result of independent research.

It is true that the events of 63 BC are put in the context of a deep and pervasive corruption of society. The old standards of morality had gone; in their place all that remained were 'the two opposite but equally disastrous vices: love of luxury and love of money' (*divorsa inter se mala, luxuria atque avaritia*). There is a good deal of embroidery of that theme, both in the moralizing reflections with which the monograph opens and in some of the more colourful pen portraits with which the early pages are enlivened. Some have seen a political motive here: Sallust, they argue, is trying to get his own back, not so much on individuals (he is on the whole fair to individuals), as on a society and an epoch which had treated him badly.

No doubt there is more than a hint of embitterment in the words Sallust uses to explain his decision to abandon public life and take up writing (*Catiline* 4):

> Once my thoughts found peace after many hardships and
> dangers and the decision had been taken to put politics behind
> me for the remainder of my days, my intention was not to waste
> precious leisure in idleness and inactivity, any more than in
> farming and hunting (occupations fit for a slave). Returning
> instead to a study I had embarked upon but had been kept
> away from by misguided ambitions, I decided to write a com-
> prehensive history of the Roman people, concentrating on those
> episodes which seemed to me deserving of attention.

But it is well to remember that Sallust was attempting something that had not been done before in Latin. Sallust is Rome's first prose historian with a serious claim upon literature. Like all who tread fresh ground, he had to make decisions about things not decided upon before. They reflect the intellectual climate in which he lived, the temperament of the man and the traditions upon which he drew.

An historical epic in prose would have been contrary to the spirit of the times. The fashion was for short, intensely personal works. Did Sallust think in those terms? Probably not: the shaping force of literary tradition is not always consciously felt. The grand pageant of history may just not have appealed to Sallust. In any case, he decided to concentrate on the detailed study of selected episodes (*res gestas carptim perscribere*). His starting point was perhaps the biographical tradition, best known to us from the work of his contemporary Cornelius Nepos (the *Lives of Famous Men* seems to have been published a few years after the *Catiline*), eked out by fairly free and rather uncritical use of speeches made at the height of the affair by some of the major participants, or, more probably, invented for them in the tradition of ancient historians. To this minor genre Sallust brought a more personal approach, a deeper probing of men's motives; he was writing history for thinking men. But history as a serious study, not as an exercise in debunking. On fresh ground now, he must have felt, like Horace, the need for literary ancestors, to shape the persona he had assumed. Where Horace began by thinking of himself as an Archilochus or an Alcaeus, Sallust's models were Thucydides and Plato, the Plato especially of the famous seventh letter: honest, intelligent men who had withdrawn from political life, or had abandoned political life in disgust.

In Chapter 1 I warned the reader against over-facile explanation of a complex literary work. But explanation of this kind is of value in getting Sallust in clearer perspective. It helps us to understand why the *Catiline* took the shape it did. By comparison with Thucydides or Plato, Sallust's moral thinking is shallow. He is respectful of ideas, conscious of the obligation of the serious historian to do more than tell a story, but he thinks in moral clichés, his analysis is dominated by those stereotypes of Roman satirical writing from Horace to Juvenal, *avaritia* (love of money) and *luxuria* (love of luxury). His narrative structure is crude. He does not tell his story well.

He is more effective with people. He creates a Catiline who is arresting and memorable, even if the contrast between good and evil is overdrawn and unsubtle. (Tacitus' Sejanus in *Annals* 4. 1 is little better.) The contrasting portraits of Caesar and Cato which emerge from their speeches are competently contrived. He excels in the thumbnail sketch of the colourful minor character. Take, for example, his brilliant portrait of Sempronia (*Catiline* 25):

Among these was Sempronia. She had committed many crimes, often crimes that displayed the reckless daring of a man. Of good family, attractive, with a husband and children, she had little to complain of; knowledgeable about literature, both Greek and Latin, able to play the lyre and to dance more elegantly than is indispensable to a woman of virtue, she was in many ways cut out for a life of luxury. Respectability and chastity were ever least in her thoughts. It would be hard to decide whether she was more careless of money or of reputation. Her appetite for sex was such that she took the initiative with men more often than they with her. She had a long record of broken promises and unpaid debts, and had been party to murder. She was deeply involved in debauchery, desperately short of money, and yet she had a brain which was far from negligible: she could write poetry, raise a laugh, adapt her conversation so that it was modest, suggestive or quite shameless, while never failing to display considerable wit and even charm.

In *The War with Jugurtha* Sallust's study of the corruption of the Republic is carried back almost two generations further into the past: instead of the generation after Sulla, his setting now is the generation which saw the young Sulla rise to power as Marius' lieutenant. The narrative covers the years 118–105 BC. Like the *Catiline*, the *Jugurtha* has an oddly modern ring. It is the story of Rome's blundering attempts to bolster her commercial interests in Africa. The setting is Numidia (roughly, modern Tunisia). The old king was an ally of Rome; Jugurtha, his adopted son, had won his way to the throne by assassinating the rightful heir and then waging war against and killing the young king's brother. The first two years of the war are marked by the utter ineffectualness of the Roman commanders; they are succeeded by a competent but unimaginative commander of the old school, Metellus, who fares little better; one of his own men, Marius, is appointed over his head; with the aid of a junior officer, a clever, unscrupulous aristocrat called Sulla, Jugurtha is captured by a trick. In the concluding lines, he shares the stage with his two captors: Marius, the man of the people who will be six times consul; Sulla, the future dictator.

Sallust had been a provincial governor of Africa in the mid-40s and that perhaps suggested the subject to him. As he tells it, his story is a sardonic exposure of the criminal incompetence of the old Republic. But once again his interest is more in people than in politics. The *Jugurtha* carries a stage further an element which is already discernible in the *Catiline*: Sallust's sympathy for the anti-hero, the man who belongs to the

225

establishment but renounces its tarnished values. Where Catiline is the noble outlaw whose crimes are in part redeemed by his personal courage and his personal magnetism, Jugurtha is the noble savage. His contempt for the utter venality of those who set themselves up as the protectors of his country is a more telling condemnation of the system because it comes from the lips of a man who knew the Roman way of life from the inside: he had served as a subaltern in the Roman army in Spain, and had been disillusioned by his brother officers; Rome, they told him, was a city where only money talks. When the war begins he easily outwits the bungling Roman commanders. The only one who comes out of it at all well is Marius, the common soldier who proves himself the superior of the arrogant aristocrat Metellus. Jugurtha might have proved a match for Marius too, if he had not made the mistake of trusting the word of a Roman.

After the monographs on Catiline and Jugurtha Sallust began a systematic history of the post-Sullan era (78–67 BC). But this work (the *Histories*) has survived only in fragments. We must judge his achievement on the basis of what we have. All in all, it is a remarkable achievement. Many deride Sallust as a superficial imitator of Thucydides, but this is to do him less than justice. It is true that he strikes us as an amateurish historian: he has not the professional's patience with research, or even the professional's understanding of what research entails. He was no scholar. Like the poets who were his contemporaries he speaks in his own persona. He is the historian as himself. His object is to communicate his understanding of a complex historical event, to make us see the main actors in that event as he saw them. It is an intensely personal kind of history.

For that view of the historian's role Sallust evolved almost the perfect literary style. He avoids both the flamboyant rhetoric of Cicero's oratorical style and the easy fluency of Cicero's didactic manner in favour of a manner which is penetrating and concise, the voice of the true Roman conservative speaking to his fellows. One's first impression is of something closer to Cato than to Cicero, an artistic development of the old Roman fondness for terse aphorism. It is a strangely effective style and one that was much copied. Virgil's compressed, economical narrative manner (which is only one of Virgil's manners) owes more than is generally recognized to Sallust. More obvious is his influence upon the crisp, pointed style of Seneca, though Sallust lacks Seneca's easy grace. It was a style that continued to be much admired throughout the Post-classical period. Quintilian spoke of the 'immortal rapidity of Sallust' (*illam immortalem Sallusti velocitatem*). It made a deep impression upon Tacitus, who took the style of Sallust, indeed Sallust's whole manner of writing history, as the basis for his own savagely aphoristic exposure of the mad brutality of the Imperial court.

VII   LIVY'S PROSE EPIC

In the second half of the Augustan Age prose supplants verse as the normal form of literary expression. The most striking proof of the change that takes place is Livy's monumental *History of Rome from its Foundation*.

The task Livy set himself was the task Ennius had undertaken a century and a half earlier: to recount the history of Rome from its earliest beginnings to his own day. For Ennius, as for Naevius before him, the obvious medium had been verse. It wasn't that the thing could not be done in prose. Already in Ennius' day there were those who made it their business to go into the facts of what had happened in the past and put together the result of their researches in prose; old Cato devoted much of the last twenty years of his life to a rambling prose history which he called the *Origines*. Even in the last century BC a politician or a general might draft a set of *commentarii* ('memoirs'—a plain, factual account in prose of his achievements) with a view to having his account worked up into an historical epic by a professional: Caesar's *Commentarii* represent an artistic exploitation of this convention. Such works were, however, only the raw material for literature: if you wanted to fire men's imaginations about the past, you wrote an historical epic.

Livy is no mere chronicler of events. Like Ennius, he appeals to our historical imagination; the status as literature of his history is unchallengeable. But for Livy verse was out of the question. By the standards of his day, historical epic stood discredited, not merely on artistic grounds (because it was a way of writing that had worn out), but because it could not, as a form, cope with the stricter standards which were emerging for what constituted historical truth. Cicero had claimed (in a discussion at the beginning of his *De Legibus*) a special kind of poetic licence for his epic on the life and times of Marius: he hoped, he said, he would not be regarded as a liar for taking liberties with fact; it was the job of the historian (by which he meant the prose chronicler) to concern himself with truth; the poet's task was to give his readers pleasure (*in illa omnia ad veritatem referantur, in hoc ad delectationem*). In the Augustan Age new habits of critical, rational thought were taking hold. They were at once an incentive to, and the product of, disciplined thinking in prose. If you wanted to tackle a subject rationally, you found yourself using prose, not verse; once you began expressing your thoughts in prose, you found that the different etiquette of prose imposed a different attitude of mind, a habit of analysis which the etiquette of verse excluded. A turning point had been reached. A case can be made for Lucan's use of verse: verse both permitted and gave legitimate scope for the emotional incitement of his epic on the Civil War; Silius Italicus' epic poem on the Punic Wars, written a century after Livy, is a perverse denial of the inevitability of change.

The work Livy planned and executed was breathtaking in its scale. Ennius' *Annals* comprised eighteen books. Livy's history ran into 142 books; it covered seven and a half centuries (735–9 BC) and took forty years to write; he had reached Book 45 before he came to the point where Ennius broke off. It was the longest single work in Latin, longer than the whole of Cicero. Only a quarter survives: the first ten books (from the beginning to 293 BC) and a solid chunk out of the middle (Books 21–45, from the start of the Second Punic War to 167 BC); altogether, four largish volumes in a modern printed text; in addition, short summaries have come down to us of all the books except Books 136–7. As is to be expected, the emphasis is on military history. But Livy's concern is always to bring his story to life and this leads him from time to time into detailed reconstructions of events of especial importance. There is, for example, the charming story of the honest whore (*scortum nobile*, Livy calls her) who by denouncing a plot against her lover brought the Bacchanalian scandal of 186 BC out into the open (Book 39. 9–19).

We move back from the personal stance of Sallust into the public mode. This is prose epic and often, especially in the earlier books, prose epic in the grand manner. Take Livy's account of how Rome fell to the Gauls in 390 BC. The invaders enter a city from which all except the Senators had fled (Livy 5. 41, in the wonderful Elizabethan prose of Philemon Holland):

> All things being now set at Rome (as in such a time could be)
> in order sufficiently, for the defence of the castle, the aged
> persons abovesaid being returned to their houses, waited for the
> comming of the enemie, with hearts prepared and resolved to
> die. Such of them as had borne offices of the chaire, to the
> intent, that they might end their daies in the ornaments and
> robes of their former estate and honour, and according to their
> vertue and deserts, in their most stately garments and habili-
> ments, which they ware when they caried their sacred chariots
> upon festivall daies, or wherein they rode in triumph, now sate
> upon their yvorie chaires in the very mids and entrie of their
> houses. There be that write, how they willingly devowed and
> bequeathed themselves to die for their countrie and cittizens
> of Rome, and that *M. Fabius* the high priest read and pro-

nounced unto them a certaine hymne and prescript forme of praier, to that purpose. The Gaules, both for that now they had rested from fight a whole night, and so their choler was somewhat cooled, and also because they had not in any place fought a bloudie and dangerous battell with them, nor even at that time wan the cittie by any assault or force, entred the morrow after into the citie, without anger and heat of furious rage, by the gate Collina, standing wide open, and so passed forward to the common place of assemblies, casting their eies about them towards the temples of the gods, and to the castle, which onely presented some shew of warre. And there leaving a sufficient guard, least happily from the castle and Capitoll they should be violently assaulted, after they were once as under parted, they fell to ransacke and rifle: and meeting none at all in the void streets, some rush by heapes into the houses next hand, others goe to those that were furthest off, supposing them at leastwise to be untouched, full of riches, and fit for to fill their hands. From thence again (as frighted by reason of such desolation, and fearing least haply any fraud of the enemie might entrap them as they wandered one from another) they returned round in a ring together, into the market-sted, and the places neere thereto. Where, when they saw the Commoners houses fast shut & locked, & contrariwise the stately palaces of the Noblemen and cheefe Senators standing wide open, they were at a stand and doubted more to enter upon the open places, than the shut. And they beheld as it were with capping and crouching after a reverend manner, certaine ancient personages sitting in the porches and entries of their houses, who besides their ornaments and apparrell, above the ordinarie estate of men, for a certaine majestie which they carried in their countenance and gravitie of visage, resembled the gods. And when as they turned to them, and stood looking upon them, as if they had been Idols and sacred Images, *M. Papyrius*, one of them, when a Gaule began to stroke his beard (which then they used all to weare long) with his yvorie staff (as they say) gave him a rap on the pate, and mooved his patience. Where-upon hee was the first that was murdered, and so the rest were all killed as they sate in their chaires of estate. After this massaker of these honourable personages of the Nobilitie, they fell upon all the rest and spared no creature: they ransaked their houses, and when they were emptie set fire on them.

[Translation: Holland]

229

As the result of a century and a half of social change Livy is writing for a different public from Ennius, one that has a more assured sense of national pride. Not Rome between the Second and Third Punic Wars, a city only just becoming conscious of the direct impact of Greek culture, but the capital of a country that was now united, with a vigorous culture of its own. It mattered little whether Livy's readers agreed with the official Augustan claim that the new regime represented a reaffirmation of past achievements, or whether their sentimentality (like that of Livy himself) was tinged with republicanism and wistful regret for old Roman virtues now gone for ever.

By comparison with Sallust's mordant cynicism, an atmosphere of bland optimism in the future greatness of Rome is suffused into these early books. Livy sets out to present, as something which emerges from the facts he has gathered together, what in Virgil's *Aeneid* is a matter of prophecy: the grandeur of the role Rome was to play in the world. But the rational, critical tone is always present. The difference in approach is clear if we put Virgil's treatment of legend alongside Livy's. Here is Virgil's version of the old story of how Hercules, on his way back to Greece from Spain, paused by the River Tiber and had his cattle stolen by Cacus. In Virgil the tale, as told to Aeneas by Evander, is a miniature epic in itself, occupying 140 lines. Let us take a passage near the beginning (*Aeneid* 8. 193–212):

> There was a cave here once, vast, remote—
> in it Cacus, a dread, half-human figure dwelt—
> a place cut off from the sun's rays, its floor ever
> splashed with fresh blood; at the entrance, in defiance
> hung, the heads of men, blanched, decaying, a cruel sight.
> Of this monster Vulcan was the father, his the murky
> fire the great creature spat forth as it moved about.
> Time passed, and then one day in answer to our prayers,
> a god arrived and help, our most powerful avenger,
> Hercules: he'd chanced to pass our way, proudly leading
> the cattle he had despoiled Geryon of, and he'd set
> the great beasts to graze where the land slopes to the river.
> Like the crazy thief he was, Cacus couldn't leave alone
> the chance to try one of his impudent, knavish tricks.
> He drives off from their stalls four steers—powerful animals
> they were—rounds up four beautiful heifers too,
> and, so their hoofprints wouldn't point the way they'd gone,
> he drags them tail-first into his cave, leaving the prints
> reversed, and makes to keep them there, hidden behind a rock.
> If anyone was looking for them, nothing pointed to the cave.

Livy's version is more succinct (Livy 1. 7. 3–7):

> For the fame goeth, that *Hercules* vpon a time, after hee had
> slaine *Geryon*, drave that way exceeding faire Oxen, and neere
> the riuer Tybris, where hee had swum ouer with his drove afore
> him, laid him downe in a faire greene meddow, as well to refresh
> himselfe, being wearie of his way, as also to rest and bait his
> cattell in so plentifull grasse and forage. There, falleth he into
> a sound sleepe, as having well charged himselfe with wine and
> viands, and one *Cacus* a sheepherd dwelling thereby, a man
> right fierce, and bearing him prowdly of his strength, being
> greatly in love with the fairnesse of the beasts, had a good will,
> and minded to fetch away that bootie: but for that if he had
> driven the beasts into his owne cave, the verie trackes would
> have led the owner of them thither, he drew the goodliest and
> biggest of them backeward by their tailes into his hole. *Hercules*
> earely in the morning when he awoke, and beheld his droue, and
> missed some of his count, went on toward the next cave, if
> haply their footing would traine him thither: But seeing all
> traces fromwards, and leading no other way, as one troubled
> in spirit, and doubtfull what to doe, he began to drive farther
> out of that theevish and dangerous corner. But as some of the
> Oxen in driving, missed their fellowes behind, and honing
> after them, bellowed as their nature is, *Hercules* chanced to
> heare them loow again, and answere from out of the cave
> wherein they had been bestowed: whereat he turned backe,
> and made in hast thither. But as *Cacus* forciblie made head
> against him, and would have kept him from entrance, *Hercules*
> smote him with his club: and for all his calling upon other
> heardmen for helpe, slew him outright.
>
> [Translation: Holland]

In Virgil the lines quoted are only a preliminary to the spectacular
battle which follows: the fire-breathing monster is bearded in his lair, and
lair and monster are destroyed by a spectacular feat of strength. Where
Virgil mythologizes, Livy rationalizes. He coolly scrutinizes the core of
the story, the theft and its detection, and then presents a straightforward
account of what took place. The care he takes to impress rational, critical
form upon legendary material is evident. His Cacus is a wild, powerful
fellow (*ferox viribus*), but no more than that; a shepherd who happens to
live in these parts; an ordinary thief with a streak of low cunning who is
disposed of by Hercules without trouble. Questions are anticipated with
which Virgil makes no attempt to deal: how did Hercules get his cattle

across the Tiber? (he swam across); why did he decide to stop where he did? (it was an attractive spot, Hercules was tired and wanted to rest after his heavy meal); why was Cacus able to steal the cattle unobserved? (Hercules had had too much to eat and drink, and he fell asleep); what was Cacus' motive? (he just couldn't resist an attractive ox or cow). Livy realizes that when Hercules wakes up he is bound to notice that some of the cattle are missing: why does he not do something about it? The answer is that Hercules simply feels the place is uncanny and decides to move on without searching further; it is a natural-sounding explanation in the ancient world where ordinary people believed themselves surrounded by unseen, malevolent forces one was wiser not to meddle with. But at the same time it is an explanation that cuts Hercules down to human dimensions.

Livy's audience was also the audience Virgil wrote for, but he catches that audience in a more reflective frame of mind, prepared for a different kind of literary experience. The etiquette of prose demands clarity about the kind of detail a poet can safely leave to the aroused imagination of his audience, but frowns upon abuse of the picturesque. Graphic detail, the vivid image for its own sake, are things Livy wastes no time over: where Virgil has 'four steers—powerful animals they were . . . four beautiful heifers too', he has simply 'the goodliest and biggest'. Emotional incitement has to be held in reserve for the truly moving scenes, the great moments in history, such as the entry of the Gauls into a deserted Rome: these are the real stuff of history, and imaginative reconstruction is legitimate. About the old legends scepticism is permissible.

Livy writes for readers who, while willing to indulge sentimentality, prefer their history on the dry side. They are prepared to allow Virgil to make his Hercules a demi-god of supernatural powers; but they are able to respond equally to the challenge Livy extends when he makes the cult-hero a wandering adventurer armed with a club, able to look after himself in the ordinary rough-and-tumble of life, but not anxious to get mixed up in things he doesn't understand. It is the note Livy strikes in his Preface:

> As for such things as are reported, either before, or at the
> foundation of the citie, more beautified and set out with Poets
> fables, than grounded vpon pure and faithfull records, I meane
> neither to averre nor disprove. This leave and priviledge hath
> antiquitie, by interlacing the acts of gods and men together, to
> make the first rising of cities more sacred and venerable. And
> if it may be lawful for anie people under heaven to consecrate
> and ascribe vnto the gods their Original, certes, such is the

renowmed martiall prowes of the Romans, that all nations of the
world may as well abide them to report Mars above the rest,
to be the stockefather both of themselves and of their first
founder, as they can bee content to liue in subiection vnder them.
But these and such like matters, howsoeuer they shall hereafter
be censured or esteemed, I will not greatly weigh and regard.
This would I haue everie man rather to thinke upon in good
earnest, and consider with me, what their life, and what their
carriage was: by what men and meanes both in war and peace,
their dominion was atcheeved and enlarged: afterward, as
their discipline began by little and little to shrinke, let him
marke how at the very first their behaviour and manners sunke
withall: and how still they fell more and more to decay and
ruine, yea and began soone after to tumble downe right even
untill these our daies, wherein wee can neither endure our owne
sores, nor salves for the cure. For this is it that is so good and
profitable in an historie, when a man may see and behold as in
a conspicuous monument and lightsome memoriall, the lively
examples of all sorts, set up in open view.

[Translation: Holland]

By comparison with Livy's sombre pessimism, Sallust's moralizing
platitudes seem shallow. At the same time Livy can show, when the
occasion calls for it, a genuinely creative historical imagination. Take
these lines from his introduction to the Second Punic War (21.1 1–3):

The same may I well say, in the Preface and entrance of this one
part of my worke, which most writers of histories have promised
and made profession of, in the beginning of the whole, to
wit, That I will write the most famous and memorable warre that
ever was, even that, which the Carthaginians under the conduct
of *Anniball* fought with the people and State of Rome. For
neither any other citties or nations are knowne to have warred
together, more wealthie and puissant than they; nor at any time
ever, were they themselves so great, so strong in forces, and so
mightie in meanes, as nowe they were. Moreover, they came not
newly now, to wage war, without knowledge of the prowesse and
martiall skill, one of another; for triall they had made thereof
sufficient alreadie, in the first punicke warre. Besides, so
variable was the fortune of the field, so doubtfully were their
battailes fought, that neerer losse and daunger were they, who
in the end wan the better, and atchieved the victorie. And to

conclude, if a man observe the whole course and proceeding
of these their warres, their malice and hatred was greater in a
manner than their forces: whiles the Romans tooke foule
skorn and disdaine, that they, whose hap before was to be
vanquished, should unprovoked, begin warre afresh with the
Conquerors; and the Carthaginians again were as mal-content,
and thoroughly offended, as taking themselves (notwithstanding
they were overcome) to bee abused too much at their hands,
by their prowd, insolent, and covetous rule over them.

[Translation: Holland]

Livy's history, in the magnitude of its concept, is rivalled in modern times only by such enterprises as Gibbon's *Decline and Fall* and perhaps the histories of Spengler, Michelet and Toynbee. Only in the context of a society like that of Rome in the Augustan Age is such a work even possible. The historian depends on access to the researches of others. He depends also on an intellectual climate where some understanding of history exists, which lives in awareness of the past and can be made to think of the past as something more than facts or a glamorous pageant of events.

Where the assimilation of his material is concerned, Livy hardly ranks, by modern standards, as a competent historian. About the details of military history he is ingenuous; the critical analysis to which he submits his sources seems amateurish to the modern professional. His strength lies in his ability to submit his material to a controlling understanding of the underlying significance of what is taking place. He lacks Gibbon's cynicism. But his work reflects a gentle, critical irony tinged with pessimism that must have put Livy in the front rank of intellectuals of his day: a sceptical conservative, respected for his learning, possessed of genuine imaginative insight and able to communicate that insight in a style which met exactly the needs of the occasion. Livy's style is complex but relaxed; the syntax is distinctive, but not showy, avoiding equally the commonplaces of rhetoric and the posturing aphorisms of Sallust. Its distinctive quality is mellowness, but the mellowness of a reflecting, not complacent, mind.

VIII   TACITUS' *Annals*

On the Roman historians of the first century AD one can quote Tacitus himself (*Annals* 1.1):

The fortunes and the disasters of the Roman people in former
times have been recorded by distinguished writers. Nor has the

history of the age of Augustus suffered from a lack of talent
until the rising tide of flattery began to have a deterrent effect.
Fear made liars of those who wrote of the reigns of Tiberius,
Caligula, Claudius and Nero in their lifetimes; the accounts
written after their death were composed while hatred was still
fresh.

In order to make his point, Tacitus is a little generous to the historians of
the Republic and the Augustan Age. What survives and what we hear
about does nothing to threaten the lonely eminence of Sallust and Livy.
His comments on the historians of the next half-century are undoubtedly
just. We should remember that men went on writing history. If our
interest is in Roman history we cannot avoid consulting the histories that
survive. If our interest is in literature a quick look is still justified, if only
to see the rubbish they wrote. We have to wait till the beginning of the
second century to make up our trio of Roman historians worth worrying
about as literature.

The third member of the trio is a remarkable figure. He is not, like
Livy, a professional historian who devoted his life to the diligent
reconstruction of the past. In range and in output as in attitude he is closer
to Sallust. Like Sallust, he began with a study of his own times, the
Histories: the twelve books covered the twenty-eight years AD 69–96
(Tacitus was born about AD 56 and was appointed *consul suffectus* in AD
97). Only the first four books and part of the fifth survive; these deal with
the events of two years, the year of the three Emperors Galba, Otho and
Vitellius, and the first year of the reign of Vespasian. Like Sallust again,
Tacitus then moved back a couple of generations: the *Annals* cover the
period from the death of Augustus to the death of Nero (AD 14–68). This
work too has reached us in incomplete form: there seem to have been 18
books in all. We have Books 1–6 (devoted to the reign of Tiberius) and
Books 11–16, which cover the years AD 47–66 (the second half of the
reign of Claudius and most of the reign of Nero); Books 5, 6, 11 and 16 are
incomplete. The two works thus comprised 30 books, of which not much
more than half survive, and covered in all the space of something more
than eighty years. In addition we have a short biography of Tacitus'
distinguished father-in-law Agricola, a monograph on the land and
peoples of Germany and a study in the decline of Roman oratory (the
Dialogus).

It is a respectable achievement, though hardly to be compared with the
142 books of Livy. And yet one is almost tempted to deny Tacitus the title
of historian. He does not approach his task in the frame of mind one
expects of an historian. With facts as facts he is impatient and careless. On

his own admission he is less concerned with reconstruction of the past than with denunciation of tyranny, castigation of those whose spineless servility allowed tyranny to prosper, exposure of villains and recognition of those acts of personal courage which give hope for the future of the human race (*Annals* 3. 65, in the Victorian version of Church and Brodribb);

> This I regard as history's highest function, to let no worthy
> action be uncommemorated, and to hold out the reprobation of
> posterity as a terror to evil words and deeds.

The victims of tyranny are not an eloquent class. Mostly, they do not live to tell their tale. When they do, they tend to arouse our pity more than our indignation. Above all, they are too involved to keep experience in its proper perspective; personal tragedy blurs their understanding of its causes. Tacitus claims a detachment not available to those who survived the tyranny, or to those who had collaborated with tyranny and must now defend themselves (*Annals* 1.1):

> My intention is to give a summary of the end of the reign of
> Augustus, and then describe the reign of Tiberius and what
> followed without anger or concern to justify what occurred,
> as one remote enough to feel no reason to surrender to these
> emotions.

As always, he chooses his words with care. He claims only to write from a sufficient distance to be innocent of the emotions which distort the accounts of those who were personally involved: anger, the desire to get one's own back; the desire to justify one's actions at the time or one's failure to act. He does not pose as an impartial observer, nor is he; his passion, however, is intellectual, not personal; the tone of voice he adopts is marked by a dry, withering contempt.

It is also the voice of a consummate artist in words. The structural problems of historical narrative do not interest him: he accepts as his framework the year-by-year record of events usual among Greek and Roman historians. Like any other convention it has its uses: it permits a slackening of tension in passing from detailed description of the madness and degradation of the Imperial court to brief reviews of events on one or other of the frontiers of Empire where the disciplined might of Rome is engaged in bringing (or has failed to bring) the benefits of civilization to the savage races of the distant north and east.

Tacitus uses words to construct an impressionistic picture of a complex event, or to bring a character to life. Sallust had tried to do that, and so in a sense had Livy, though in Livy the individuals have to take their place in the pageant. But where Sallust and Livy are explicit in their delineation of character, Tacitus prefers suggestion. Sallust employs antithesis to build up a portrait in contrasting tones of black and white; Livy prefers the patiently worked at, finished portrait. Tacitus sketches his characters with the savage economy of the political cartoonist. When motives are ascribed, they are not presented as explanations based on an analysis of what occurred, but slipped in surreptitiously: Tacitus nudges us at the appropriate moment, to draw our attention to further proof of what we are tricked into believing we already know. Put like that, it sounds a technique which would deceive nobody. The technique is backed up, however, by a wonderfully compact, exciting style in which words always seem to mean more than they say. The result is a very distinctive kind of poetry in prose, a complex literary experience to which the reader has to subject himself in an effort of total concentration.

Let us take as an example the trial in AD 16 (some two years after the accession of Tiberius) of a young and rather fatuous Roman of good family. In itself the trial was an event of minor importance. The significance Tacitus attaches to it is that it was the first of a long series of trials in which Tiberius disposed of political opponents or personal enemies, or men he had decided to destroy on the whim of the moment, by trumped-up charges of treasonable conduct. A modern historian might present the facts of the case first, then add the sort of comment I have just given. If he were a responsible historian he would feel obliged to add that the so-called treason trials extended over a period of many years and that the circumstances differed a great deal. Tacitus' method is to introduce the trial of Libo as the first of the treason trials, and then, by a careful selection of detail, to use it as proof of the mad malevolence of Tiberius. Thus we are invited to regard as a clear, fully formed pattern of conduct what can only have become such over a long period of time (*Annals* 2. 27–29):

> About the same time Libo Drusus, of the family of Scribonii, was accused of revolutionary schemes. I will explain, somewhat minutely, the beginning, progress, and end of this affair, since then first were originated those practices which for so many years have eaten into the heart of the State. Firmius Catus, a senator, an intimate friend of Libo's, prompted the young man, who was thoughtless and an easy prey to delusions, to resort to astrologers' promises, magical rites, and interpreters of dreams, dwelling ostentatiously on his great-grandfather Pompeius, his aunt Scribonia, who had formerly been wife of Augustus, his imperial cousins, his house crowded with ancestral busts, and

urging him to extravagance and debt, himself the companion of his profligacy and desperate embarrassments, thereby to entangle him in all the more proofs of guilt.

As soon as he found enough witnesses, with some slaves who knew the facts, he begged an audience of the emperor, after first indicating the crime and the criminal through Flaccus Vescularius, a Roman knight, who was more intimate with Tiberius than himself. Caesar, without disregarding the information, declined an interview, for the communication, he said, might be conveyed to him through the same messenger, Flaccus. Meanwhile he conferred the praetorship on Libo and often invited him to his table, showing no unfriendliness in his looks or anger in his words (so thoroughly had he concealed his resentment); and he wished to know all his saying and doings, though it was in his power to stop them, till one Junius, who had been tampered with by Libo for the purpose of evoking by incantations spirits of the dead, gave information to Fulcinius Trio. Trio's ability was conspicuous among informers, as well as his eagerness for an evil notoriety. He at once pounced on the accused, went to the consuls, and demanded an inquiry before the Senate. The Senators were summoned with a special notice that they must consult on a momentous and terrible matter.

Libo meanwhile, in mourning apparel and accompanied by ladies of the highest rank, went to house after house, entreating his relatives, and imploring some eloquent voice to ward off his perils; which all refused, on different pretexts, but from the same apprehension. On the day the Senate met, jaded with fear and mental anguish, or, as some have related, feigning illness, he was carried in a litter to the doors of the Senate House, and leaning on his brother he raised his hands and voice in supplication to Tiberius, who received him with unmoved countenance. The emperor then read out the charges and the accusers' names, with such calmness as not to seem to soften or aggravate the accusations.

[Translation: Church and Brodribb]

The first day of the trial goes badly. After the adjournment, Libo goes home to stage a macabre farewell party for his friends. If we may believe Tacitus, that too was to become a regular feature of social life under the Julio-Claudian emperors. Here is Tacitus' narrative of Libo's final hours (*Annals* 2.31):

Meanwhile his house was surrounded with soldiers; they
crowded noisily even about the entrance, so that they could be
heard and seen, when Libo, whose anguish drove him from the
very banquet he had prepared as his last gratification, called for
a minister of death, grasped the hands of his slaves, and thrust
a sword into them. In their confusion, as they shrank back, they
overturned the lamp on the table at his side, and in the darkness,
now to him the gloom of death, he aimed two blows at a vital
part. At the groans of the falling man his freedmen hurried up,
and the soldiers, seeing the bloody deed, stood aloof. Yet the
prosecution was continued in the Senate with the same persis-
tency, and Tiberius declared on oath that he would have
interceded for his life, guilty though he was, but for his
hasty suicide.   [Translation: Church and Brodribb]

The most remarkable feature of Tacitus' narrative of the Libo trial is the
contrast between Tiberius' conduct as described by Tacitus himself and
the motives he reads into that conduct. On the surface, Tiberius' conduct
is exemplary. He does nothing to encourage Firmius' denunciation of
Libo; on the contrary, he redoubles his demonstrations of goodwill
towards Libo; throughout the trial he remains detached, impartial; when
the trial is over, he swears it was his intention to pardon Libo, 'however
guilty'. Considered out of context, each individual action of Tiberius is
beyond reproach. Tacitus presents Tiberius, however, as a pastmaster of
dissimulation. The individual actions need only be pointed to; everything
Tiberius does reveals the monster behind the mask. The climax of this
technique of exposing the villain by noting his most innocent-seeming
actions comes when Libo appeals to Tiberius' mercy as he enters the
senate-house for his trial, and the spotlight falls on the expressionless
features of Tiberius (*et manus et supplices voces ad Tiberium tendens
immoto eius vultu excipitur*). Tacitus has learnt from Virgil the art of
picking out the significant detail for graphic description and the art of
making words appear to speak for themselves. When he tells us that
Tiberius proceeded to read out the charges in a completely neutral voice,
it is almost as though he had unmasked this monster of dissimulation
before our eyes.

Libo calls for nothing like the same delicacy and tact in denigration; he
can be treated as the fool his conduct demonstrates him to be. The stroke
of genius here is the detailed reconstruction of the final dinner party and
the apparently detached description it permits of the histrionic behaviour
of this poor, silly victim of the sadistic cruelty of Tiberius.

Such reconstructions are a recognized feature of ancient historical writing once history crosses the border into literature. It is the tradition which permits Livy's imaginative reconstruction of the Gauls wandering through the streets of Rome. In Livy scenes of this kind are used as atmosphere, to bring the past to life. In Tacitus they are part of a ruthless technique: the past is not only made more vivid; it is reconstructed in such a way that our judgment is adroitly manipulated. The skill with which it is done in scene after scene is extraordinary. Tacitus succeeds because, after all, he does write, as he claims, without anger. The *Annals* is not a partisan attack upon Tiberius, or Claudius, or Nero: it is a whole mad epoch that stands condemned in his pages.

Tacitus has learnt too from Virgil the effect to be gained from a judiciously placed death-scene. Three of the twelve books of the *Aeneid* end with the death of a major character: Dido at the end of Book 4, Mezentius at the end of Book 10, Turnus at the end of Book 12. Each time there is a true tragic catharsis. In Tacitus the death-scene becomes a special exercise in the tragicomedy of the absurd. Tiberius is pronounced dead, unexpectedly revives and has to be smothered with a heap of bedclothes. Claudius, poisoned by his wife Agrippina, shows signs of lingering; on instructions from Agrippina, the imperial physician, under pretext of getting Claudius to vomit, passes a feather tipped with a deadlier poison down his throat. Comparison with the corresponding accounts in Suetonius is instructive. Suetonius mentions an attenuated version of the suffocation story as one of several rumours about the manner of Tiberius' death; he confirms that Claudius was poisoned with a dish of mushrooms, for which, he tells us, Claudius had a passion; about the poison-tipped feather Suetonius says nothing; instead we have a summary of different accounts of Claudius' last moments. In Tacitus there is no hint of uncertainty about the facts: of the death of Claudius he says simply, 'later the whole story became known' (*cuncta mox pernotuere*). In short, Suetonius reports gossip. Tacitus reconstructs the death-scene with a sure dramatic instinct: each time the picture is clear and damning.

The Emperors' victims get more sympathetic treatment. When Agrippina's turn comes, she is brutally murdered by the henchmen of her own son Nero, but dies with a kind of theatrical dignity (*Annals* 14. 5–8). (Here Tacitus takes up the version presented as part of a tragic chorus by the author of the *Octavia* [310–76] and beats the tragedian at his own game.) Or take the death-scene of a character more respectfully treated than Libo, but still a minor character, a certain Gaius Petronius, generally assumed to be the author of the *Satyricon*, whom we shall meet again in Section X. Tacitus' obituary tells us all we know of him (*Annals* 16. 18–19):

With regard to Caius Petronius, I ought to dwell a little on his antecedents. His days he passed in sleep, his nights in the business and pleasures of life. Indolence had raised him to fame, as energy raises others, and he was reckoned not a debauchee and spendthrift, like most of those who squander their substance, but a man of refined luxury. And indeed his talk and his doings, the freer they were and the more show of carelessness they exhibited, were the better liked, for their look of a natural simplicity. Yet as proconsul of Bithynia and soon afterwards as consul, he showed himself a man of vigour and equal to business. Then falling back into vice or affecting vice, he was chosen by Nero to be one of his few intimate associates, as a critic in matters of taste, while the emperor thought nothing charming or elegant in luxury unless Petronius had expressed to him his approval of it. Hence jealousy on the part of Tigellinus, who looked on him as a rival and even his superior in the science of pleasure. And so he worked on the prince's cruelty, which dominated every other passion, charging Petronius with having been the friend of Scaevinus, bribing a slave to become informer, robbing him of the means of defence, and hurrying into prison the greater part of his domestics.

It happened at the time that the emperor was on his way to Campania and that Petronius, after going as far as Cumae, was there detained. He bore no longer the suspense of fear or of hope. Yet he did not fling away life with precipitate haste, but having made an incision in his veins and then, according to his humour, bound them up, he again opened them, while he conversed with his friends, not in a serious strain or on topics that might win for him the glory of courage. And he listened to them as they repeated, not thoughts on the immortality of the soul or on the theories of philosophers, but light poetry and playful verses. To some of his slaves he gave liberal presents, a flogging to others. He dined, indulged himself in sleep, that death, though forced on him, might have a natural appearance. Even in his will he did not, as did many in their last moments, flatter Nero or Tigellinus or any other of the men in power. On the contrary, he described fully the prince's shameful excesses, with the names of his male and female companions and their novelties in debauchery, and sent the account under seal to Nero. Then he broke his signet-ring, that it might not be subsequently available for imperilling others.

[Translation: Church and Brodribb]

IX   THE YOUNGER PLINY: OBITUARY OF A MINOR POET

The letters of the younger Pliny are the third of three very different collections of letters which have come down to us from the Roman world. First in time and in historical importance there is the correspondence of Cicero; it is by far the largest collection (some 930 letters in all) and it consists of real letters, the majority to personal friends, some to public figures, a largish handful to his brother Quintus, over 400 to his friend Atticus. Since they have been preserved it is reasonable to suppose that Cicero had the thought at the back of his mind that what he was writing to Atticus, to Julius Caesar, to his brother or his wife might one day be read by others. To us the letters are precious documents for the intellectual and social life of the time and often a delight to read and a welcome corrective to the public persona of Cicero; but they cannot be reckoned as literature.

By the time we come to our second collection a hundred years later the situation has changed: prose has become the normal medium for the expression of a writer's thoughts at the literary level as well as in the practical situations of everyday life: Seneca's *Letters to Lucilius*, though superficially the formal model might seem the letters of Cicero to Atticus, are written for publication. They are intended to be read by others; in them Seneca undertakes a careful, if deliberately unsystematic, discussion of the fundamental problems of human existence as seen by a convinced practising Stoic.

Our third collection, the *Letters* of Pliny, belongs to the first decade, roughly, of the second century AD, the years during which Tacitus was writing the *Annals*. There are nearly 250 letters addressed to something like a hundred friends and acquaintances. Though undoubtedly real letters, in the sense that they were actually sent to their recipients, there is little reason to doubt that they were written with publication in mind, and no reason at all to doubt that they were carefully selected and worked up for publication by their author. To the nine books into which Pliny divided his collection a tenth has been added as a kind of appendix: it contains a further 121 letters, mostly very short, exchanged between Pliny and the Emperor Trajan during Pliny's terms of office as the Emperor's special legate in the province of Bithynia-Pontus (Catullus' old province); Pliny seems to have died in office there about AD 112.

If the *Letters to Lucilius* are to be compared with the *Epistles* of Horace (open letters written primarily for publication), Pliny's *Letters* are better compared to those short poems of Catullus which are addressed to his mistress or to a friend: each letter, like each of these poems of Catullus, has its genesis in an actual set of circumstances. The thought that the letters were worth publishing may have only emerged gradually; but once publication had been decided upon, Pliny clearly did not simply take the letters out of his files and publish them as they stood. What we have is a selection, artistically rather than chronologically arranged, which has been revised for publication of permanent value. Like the poems of Catullus, the letters reflect, rather than document, a personality and a way of life: that of a respectable and successful lawyer with literary interests.

The nineteenth century and the first part of the twentieth century tended to see the role of the educated man of assured means almost in old Roman terms as a leader in action, the active participant in the crises of public life, willing and competent to give the lead to others. So long as a mood of confidence prevailed in the fundamental reasonableness and stability of the social contract, Seneca seemed to be a cowardly intellectual and Pliny an ineffectual trifler. It was easier to admire Cicero: though his attempts to save Rome failed and were often foolish, he had at least tried. One of the insights we have been granted by the events of more recent history is that there are times when the civilized, clear-sighted, conscientious man is reduced to a level of ineffectuality by the progressive erosion of his position in a world over which he has no control. We now read Seneca and Pliny with a new sympathy. Something like a more just appreciation of them as men and as writers has become possible. Certainly, we can learn far more about the workings of a highly sensitive Roman mind from reading Seneca's letters, and more about Rome at the time of its greatest material prosperity from reading Pliny than from most things written in verse in the second half of the first century AD. Pliny supplements Martial and Juvenal; he is a useful corrective to Tacitus.

As was the case with Seneca (and Cicero at the end of his career), Pliny's literary studies are a refuge from and a consolation for life (*Letters* 8. 19. 1; the version is that of William Melmoth, 1746):

> I find my joy and my solace in literature: and as there is no
> pleasure I prefer to it, so there is no sadness it does not alleviate.
> In this time of trouble, then, caused by the ill-health of my wife,
> the dangerous sickness of some of my servants, and the death of
> others, I fly to my books as the sovereign alleviation of my
> sorrows. They do me this service—they make me understand my
> troubles better, and bear them more patiently.
>
> [Translation: Melmoth]

Pliny is the almost over-civilized product of a highly refined but utterly demoralized culture. The members of that class of society which under the old Republic took a prominent part in public life have survived the traumatic experience of a period in which tyrannical cruelty was rendered even harder to endure by the arbitrary malevolence with which the power of life and death was exercised over all imprudent enough to draw attention to themselves by the display of talents that had traditionally brought honour and distinction. Pliny's contemporaries are uncomfortably and helplessly aware that the present lull in barbarity may be no more than temporary. There is none of the revival of confidence at the end of the first century AD which followed the end of the Civil War a century and a quarter before. Men with the courage of a Tacitus to strike back in the hope that by attacking the mad horror of tyranny they can do something to ward off a further descent into tyranny are few. Pliny is content to do his duty as a public official and as a human being.

The *Letters* are a chronicle of his times, consciously composed as literature but stopping short of any formal claim to rank as social history. We can apply to them the words Pliny used of C. Fannius' chronicle of the crimes of Nero: they are 'half-way between conversation and history' (*libros inter sermonem historiamque medios*). One quality they possess which puts them ahead of everything written in verse at this period is their sincerity.

It may seem an odd word to use of Pliny because Pliny's sincerity is not that of a simple-minded or naturally modest man. To our ears his love of antithesis and the nicely turned phrase makes the expression of his thoughts sound artificial. Pliny is after all no profound thinker. He is apt to sound like watered-down Seneca. Where Seneca is sharp and to the point, Pliny's short, neatly balanced sentences seem precious; his besetting sin in fussiness. An obvious, and to us patently insincere, flattery was obligatory in his day in all personal relationships. But we can learn to penetrate the flattery: it is never fawning; there is never any real attempt to deceive; it is more a social ritual. By the standards of the circle in which Pliny moved, it would have been as uncouth to fail to observe that ritual as it would have been simple-minded to take what was said at its face value. Once we have learnt to allow for the flattery (and the urbane, posturing vanity which is its counterpart when Pliny speaks of himself) we can establish contact with a man who really was trying to say what was in his mind, to paint a picture of the times through which he had lived, and to express his understanding of the people he had known.

Cicero's letters abound in frank portraits of his associates and adversaries in political life. In a letter intended for publication one has to be more circumspect. If one is not to give offence wantonly, it is better to wait. Pliny excels at obituary. Death is the moment for taking stock. There are obituaries of leading public figures such as Verginius Rufus (2.1: it was years since Rome had seen such a funeral); writers such as C.

Fannius (5. 5: he had a dream just before his death that Nero came and read what Fannius had written about him); and Martial (3. 21: Pliny remarks to his correspondent, 'You may object that his verses will not be immortal; perhaps not, but he wrote them with that intention'); the philosopher Corellius Rufus (1. 12: he starved himself to death to put an end to a life of pain); and a society lady of sybaritic tastes, Ummidia Quadratilla, who died in her seventy-ninth year (7. 24: 'She kept a troupe of mimic actors whom she treated with an indulgence that was out of place in a lady of her high position').

The death of a friend or a public figure permits reflection, moreover, on wider issues than the character of the deceased. Here is Pliny on the death of the epic poet Silius Italicus, author of the longest Latin poem, who died about AD 101 at the age of seventy-five (*Letters* 3. 7):

> I am just now informed that Silius Italicus has starved himself
> to death, at his villa near Naples. Having been afflicted with an
> imposthume, which was deemed incurable, he grew weary of life
> under such uneasy circumstances, and therefore put an end to it
> with the most determined courage. He had been extremely
> fortunate through the whole course of his days, excepting only
> the loss of his younger son; however, that was made up to him
> in the satisfaction of seeing his elder, who is of a more amiable
> character, attain the consular dignity, and of leaving him in a
> very flourishing situation. He suffered a little in his reputation
> in the time of Nero, having been suspected of forwardly joining
> in some of the informations which were carried on in the reign of
> that prince; but he made use of his intimacy with Vitellius,
> with great discretion and humanity. He acquired much honour
> by his administration of the government of Asia; and by his
> approved behaviour after his retirement from business,
> cleared his character from that stain which his former intrigues
> had thrown upon it.
>
> He lived among the nobility of Rome without power, and con-
> sequently without envy. He was highly respected and much
> sought after, and though he was bedridden, his chamber was
> always thronged with visitors, who came not merely out of regard
> to his rank. He spent his time in philosophical discussion, when
> not engaged in writing verses; these he sometimes recited, in
> order to try the sentiments of the public, but he discovered in
> them more industry than genius. Lately, owing to declining
> years, he entirely quitted Rome, and lived altogether in
> Campania, from whence even the accession of the new Emperor

did not draw him. A circumstance which I mention as well to the honour of the prince, who permitted such a liberty, as of Italicus, who was not afraid to take it.

He carried his taste for objects of *virtù* so far as to incur reprehension for greedy buying. He had several villas in the same districts, and the last purchase was always the chief favourite, to the neglect of the rest. They were all furnished with large collections of books, statues and portraits, which he more than enjoyed, he even adored; above all the portrait of Virgil, whose birthday he celebrated with more solemnity than his own, especially at Naples, where he used to approach his tomb with as much reverence as if it had been a temple.

In this tranquillity he lived to the seventy-sixth year of his age, with a delicate, rather than a sickly, constitution. It is remarkable, that as he was the last person upon whom Nero conferred the consular office, so he was the last to die of all those who had been raised by him to that dignity; and again, that the last survivor of Nero's consuls was the one in whose year of office that prince was killed. When I consider this, I cannot forbear lamenting the transitory condition of mankind. Is there anything in nature so short and limited as human life, even in its most extended period? Does it not seem to you, my friend, but yesterday that Nero was upon the throne? and yet not one of all those who were consuls in his reign now remains! But why should I wonder at a circumstance so common? Lucius Piso (the father of that Piso who was infamously assassinated by Valerius Festus in Africa) used to say he did not see one person in the Senate whom he had called upon to speak on the motion before the house when he was consul.

[Translation: Melmoth]

X   THE BEGINNINGS OF IMAGINATIVE PROSE: PETRONIUS' *Satyricon*

Throughout the Preclassical period and for most of the Classical period a writer who had a story to tell wrote in verse: hexameter verse if the storyteller proposed to tell his story in the impersonal persona of the epic poet; iambic verse, most often (the metre which came closest to reproducing the rhythms of actual speech), if the story was allowed to unfold of its own accord, so to speak, upon the stage. It did not matter whether the story told was one reshaped for the occasion from the old legends of the Greeks and their gods, or one based on the comparatively recent events of Roman history; in either case verse was the obvious choice.

Storytelling started in that way because, as we saw, verse was the only appropriate form available. By the middle of the Classical period this had ceased to be true: prose had reached a level of sophistication and flexibility that made it more than adequate for most uses a writer cared to put it to. If writers chose instead to go on telling their stories in verse, it was because of that deep-seated conservatism involving the relationship between the writer and his audience of which I have had occasion to speak more than once.

The breakthrough came, as we have seen, with history. On the whole the decision to use prose seems to have been made on grounds of efficiency: it was simply easier to write history systematically, logically, analytically in prose than in verse. There was an old tradition of paraliterary historical writing in prose and a rather more sophisticated tradition of didactic writing to build upon: Livy's prose epic of the history of the Roman people could thus appear less shamelessly unconventional.

Long after Livy conservatism continued to induce writers to do the old thing in the old way out of unthinking respect for the past. But from Livy onwards it was generally understood by those who talked about literature that, if you chose to treat an historical theme in verse, you weren't interested in writing history. You might still have a serious purpose in writing, as Lucan had, though even Lucan is derided by Petronius for working in a worn-out form; he seems at any rate the obvious victim of the parody of epic style with which the elderly homosexual pseudo-poet and critic Eumolpus proudly regales the travellers on the way to Croton in Petronius' *Satyricon*.

By way of justifying his high-flown style Eumolpus introduces his recitation with some preliminary remarks on just the point we are discussing, arguing that, even when dealing with the facts of history, poetry must be poetry and avoid all appearance of dealing with reality. Eumolpus speaks in character, but his impromptu lecture amounts to a tongue-in-cheek travesty of current views on the subject (*Satyricon* 118):

> Eumolpus broke in on this duet. 'My young friends,' said he,
> 'many a young fellow is tripped up when he takes to poetry.
> As soon as he has constructed a line that scans and has wrapped
> up a sentimental idea in a cloud of words, he imagines that he
> has climbed straight into Mount Helicon. So when they are
> weary of their forensic duties they regularly slip away into the
> serener atmosphere of literature as though to a harbour of
> refuge, under the impression that a poem can be put together

more easily than an address to the court tricked out with sparkling, thrilling epigrams. The truly noble soul, however, is above such vanity: he does not attempt to create or give his thoughts to the world until he has been baptized in the mighty river of the Muses. We must shun all, may I say, cheapness of phrasing, and adopt language that is caviare to the general, that our standard be

"I loathe the vulgar herd, and keep clear of it."

Above all, beware that our fancies be not exaggerated so as to overdo the subject-matter, but shine with the colour that is woven in the texture. Witness Homer and the lyric bards, our Roman Virgil, and Horace with his subtle grace. For the rest, either they did not see the road that led to poetry, or when they saw it they dared not tread it. Behold, a "Civil War" is a mighty theme, and whoso essays it, if he be not ripe of scholarship, will faint under the burden. For not in a poem can we describe the deeds of men—the historians do this far better; nay, through dark ways and the service of the gods, through the tossing maelstrom of the imagination, must the free spirit be hurled, so that it may seem rather the prophecy of a soul inspired than the prosaic record of authenticated facts?'

[Translation: Mitchell]

In fiction, unlike history, efficiency is not a relevant consideration. It is not self-evident that the task of a writer of fiction is to tell his story as fully and as clearly as he can. There were two factors, moreover, which militated against change. One was that the greatest writers of the past (Homer, the Athenian tragedians) had used verse; the other was that they had confined themselves to a particular kind of story. In two ways conventions based on impressive precedents restricted the initiative of the writer of fiction. A double breakthrough was necessary before literature could free itself from the restraining inspiration of the past and move closer to the characteristic literary form of modern times: the work of fiction that deals creatively in prose with the real world around us.

Coming as he does at the end of the chapter on 'The Uses of Prose', Petronius is apt to sound like the writer everybody had been waiting for: the author of the single, startlingly original work which achieved this double breakthrough and changed the course of Roman literature. It would be nice to be able to say 'the novel was discovered by Petronius and lived happily ever after'. But that is not what happened. The reason is, once again, a matter of social circumstances and a matter of the nature and extent of the impact of the individual work.

The *Satyricon* is the product of the highly unusual circumstances which surrounded the production of literature at the court of Nero. Like the tragedies of Seneca, like Lucan's *On the Civil War*, the *Satyricon* is a hothouse plant displaying all the qualities of overstimulated growth. It was apparently an immense work. We possess only fragments, some long and more or less consecutive, others no more than broken potsherds of the original fiction. There seem to have been something like twenty books, of which we have perhaps a substantial part of no more than three. The story is pretty much a transposition into the real contemporary world (but against a backdrop of fantasy and magic) of the typical epic plot from Homer's *Odyssey* to Virgil's *Aeneid*. The hero Encolpius has incurred the unforgetting anger of a god (Encolpius' offence, it seems, was against Priapus, the god of lust), is driven from place to place along with a faithful companion (Ascyltus)—to say nothing of a more intimate companion, the boy Giton— and undergoes a series of adventures in expiation of the curse of impotence imposed on him by Priapus. As in the *Odyssey* and the *Aeneid* a dinner party occupies a major part of the story. The role of the host is played, not by a king or a queen, but by the *nouveau riche* Trimalchio, a caricature of the man of the people who has made good and lives a life of cheerful, mindless extravagance. One quickly realizes, in short, that, although Petronius is a natural storyteller able to cover the rough skeleton of his plot with the rich, shining flesh of his fertile imagination, his story is more a boisterously executed exercise in parody, a superb extravaganza symptomatic of its time, than the single startlingly original work that had in it the power to change the course of literature.

For nearly a hundred years the *Satyricon* fell, if not upon deaf ears, upon ears too refined to heed. The literary extravagances of the age of Nero (a movement largely inspired by Nero himself, whose patronage of the arts was as capricious as it was unconventional) did not survive the age which produced them. Indeed, not one of the major writers at Nero's court survived his imperial patron, for to have one's talent recognized by Nero was to receive the kiss of death. The suicides of Seneca, Lucan and Petronius were all at the Emperor's orders, and as superbly staged, if we may believe Tacitus, as if Nero himself had not only commanded the performance but directed it as well. If, like the Romantics they were, they had been imprudent enough, in one way or another, to get involved in an underground movement which was ruthlessly stamped out, that is more a symptom of the writer's relationship with his imperial patron and of his image of himself than grounds for seeing in any of these three a hero of the resistance.

Under Nero's philistine successors respectability became the keynote. It was attained and preserved by the cautious, dilettante practice of the established genres. In the earlier part of the reign of Domitian, there was even something of an Indian summer for literature, before the re-descent into those years of mad, cruel tyranny which cast a grim shadow upon literary production at the turn of the century. Epic enjoyed a brief period of artificial resuscitation, if those who assumed charge of the patient were careful not to allow him to excite himself unduly. There was a more assiduous revival of occasional verse, allegedly in the tradition of Catullus: to be witty, or to be indecent, was to be safe; only ideas were dangerous.

Under such circumstances, the creativity which verse had lost did not easily pass to prose, even when a measure of freedom returned following the assassination of Domitian. Pliny's *Letters*, though they deserve their place in these pages, are little more than an agreeable vehicle for a minor talent. With history, of course, the battle had been won. But even Tacitus' *Annals*, the greatest single work of the Postclassical period, though it transforms historical writing into something closer to poetic prose, is the work of a conservative of genius: his models are Sallust and Virgil. It is not until right at the end of the Postclassical period that we come to a major work, a genuinely creative piece of writing in prose, the *Golden Ass* of Apuleius. The *Golden Ass* is an obvious descendant of the *Satyricon*, but it is a remote descendant: Apuleius, the African, the master of a strange exotic prose style, is one of the most interesting writers in Latin, but he hardly belongs to the history of Roman literature.

If we can call the *Satyricon* a parody of epic, however, it is not a parody in the usual sense of a work which is a *reductio ad absurdum* of an established form or of an individual work. Whether the object of such a parody is to demolish the reputation of the original, or simply to entertain the reader, close imitation is essential. The *Satyricon* is not a close imitation of anything; it is a superbly nonchalant work the plot of which just happens, as it were, to resemble the plot of some of the best-known epic poems. We may be sure Petronius was aware of the resemblance and found it amusing, and hoped his readers would also. But the function of the plot is to give a kind of form to a large-scale work which sets out to realize hitherto unsuspected possibilities of that traditionally formless medium, Roman satire.

Because of Horace and Juvenal, the modern world associates satire with verse. But originally it was all part of the formlessness which was the essential feature of satire to mix prose with verse. That was the formula followed by Varro in his *Menippean Satires* (named after the Hellenistic writer Menippus, a Cynic philosopher, who seems to have originated the form). For reasons of his own—because he was more scrupulous about form, because he wished to emphasize his relationship with Lucilius—

Horace stuck to verse. Persius and Juvenal followed Horace. Petronius, sensing no doubt the possibilities of prose, went back to the older, looser mixture of prose and verse. The *Satyricon* has a basic narrative structure in which the action stops from time to time while one of the characters breaks into verse, most often a short lyric which serves as an ironically elaborate expression of the character's feelings at a high point in the action. Petronius' originality is that characteristically Roman originality which consists in combining two traditions nobody had thought of combining before. The *Satyricon* is the sort of off-the-cuff story Varro might have related in passing, told on an epic scale.

Where the *Satyricon* is genuinely creative is in its style. Petronius goes far beyond relaxed casualness. His style is racy, vivid, full of colourful expressions and brilliant flashes of fantasy. Where Plautus' dialogue creates no more than the illusion of real speech (it is after all in verse), Petronius' dialogue comes close to the way we may suppose ordinary Romans of the first century AD actually spoke, or would have spoken if they had possessed the eloquence of Petronius' characters and found themselves in circumstances so conducive to conversational exuberance. Here is one of the speakers at Trimalchio's dinner party waxing eloquent on that familiar theme: the sort of people who find their way into politics nowadays (*Satyricon* 44):

With this Phileros gave way and Ganymede chimed in: 'You fellows are talking of things which don't matter a scrap in heaven or earth, and no one seems to care about the ruinous rise in corn. I take my oath I couldn't find a bite of bread to-day. And look how the drought continues! We've been on short commons for a whole year now. Devil take the commissioners; they're hand in glove with the bakers. "You help me, and I'll help you"; the unhappy public is between the upper and the nether millstone, while your lordly gluttons have one long beanfeast. Ah, for a week of those sturdy warriors whom I found here when I first arrived from Asia! That was real life! Those money-grubbing magistrates used to get a gruelling as bad as if Jupiter himself had been annoyed with them. I recollect Safinius. He lived by the old arch, when I was a boy, and a peppery fellow he was. The very pavement smoked when he walked. But he was as straight as a die, and never went back on a pal. You could play "Up Jenkins!" with him in the dark without a qualm. In the House he laid out opponents right and left: there was no finesse about him—he hit straight from the shoulder. When he argued a case in the Courts his voice resounded like a trumpet. He

251

never mopped his brow, or hemmed and hawed. I think he had
Asiatic blood in his veins. How genially he returned a greeting!
He knew us all by name, and addressed us like comrades. And
so in those days corn was dirt cheap: for a penny you could buy
a loaf bigger than you and a pal could eat; now they run smaller
than bulls' eyes. Alas, alas! It gets worse every day; this
place is growing downwards like a calf's tail. But why do we put
up with a third-rate minister who thinks more of a penny in
his own pocket than our very existence? So he chuckles gleefully
at home, and nets more in a single day than his neighbour has
in his whole fortune. I could tell you here and now of a single
deal in which he made 1,000 guineas. If we had the courage of a
mouse, he would soon cease to feather his nest. Now-a-days
the public is a lion indoors, but a fox in the open.'

[Translation: Mitchell]

It is refreshing to read Latin so simple and direct. The narrative of the
Satyricon is all first-person narrative, and therefore all in a sense
conversational. But the narrator Encolpius when speaking in his own
person has a remarkable talent for vivid, imaginative description. Here is
a specimen: it comes at the point in the tale where Encolpius is travelling
under the pseudonym Polyaenus, 'full of wise speech', one of the stock
epithets of Ulysses (*Satyricon* 126):

Her complimentary remarks filled me with pleasure. 'Tell
me,' I said, 'I suppose you aren't the lady who has fallen in love
with me?'

The maid laughed heartily in mockery of my cool impertinence.
'No,' she cried, 'don't flatter yourself. I never yet allowed a slave
to kiss me. Heaven forbid that I should waste my sweetness on a
gallowsbird. Such a thing may suit grand ladies, who stroke the
weals where the whip fell; I may be only a servant, but I never sit
in the pit.'

My breath was taken away by love's perversity: it seemed to
me a strange anomaly that the maid should have the fastidious-
ness of a matron, a matron the simple taste of a maid.

This merry banter went on some time, and at last I asked
the maid to produce her mistress in a neighbouring grove of
planes. The girl agreed: she drew her skirts about her ankles,
and darted into a bank of laurels which bordered on the path.
After a few moments' delay she escorted her mistress from the
shadow of the trees and led her to my side. She was a lady of
surpassing charms, beyond all dreams. No words can set forth

252

her beauty; whatever I say will limp behind the truth. Her
glorious hair fell like a cloud over her shoulders in natural
curls; her brow was low, and above it the hair waved smoothly
back upon her head; her eyebrows curved even to the contour
of her cheeks, and almost met again between the eyes; the eyes
gleamed brighter than stars when the moon has set; her nose
slightly retroussé; her lips such as Praxiteles gave to Diana. Now
her chin, now her neck, now her hands, now the whiteness of
her feet set in a tiny ring of gold, threw into the shade the gleam
of Parian marble. Then for the first time I forgot my Doris, the
dream of my earliest love.

[Translation: Mitchell]

One can only regret that so much of Petronius' eccentric masterpiece
has been lost and that he had no successors.

Bibliography

The works of Roman authors which have survived have come down to us in *manuscripts,* some as early as the fourth and fifth centuries AD, but most dating from the ninth and tenth centuries or later (the oldest manuscripts of Catullus, for example, belong to the fourteenth century). These are available to the modern reader in printed texts, or *editions.* The best known belong to the various collections of texts which have been built up, mainly in the present century. The most comprehensive are the Teubner texts (*Bibliotheca Scriptorum Graecorum et Romanorum Teubneriana,* originally published in Leipzig, now issued also in Stuttgart). Others include the *Oxford Classical Texts,* the *Loeb Classical Library* (published in London by Heinemann and in Boston by Harvard University Press) and the *Collection Guillaume Budé* (Paris, Société d'Edition 'Les Belles Lettres').

In all these editions, readings of different manuscripts have been compared and systematic efforts made to present a text free from the errors of transmission in manuscript over a period of many centuries; the texts are printed in accordance with modern printing conventions, punctuation, division into paragraphs, use of capital letters and, to some extent, spelling being decided by the editor. In twentieth-century texts the older practice (originating in mediaeval times) of printing consonantal *i* as *j* is abandoned; the use of *v* to distinguish consonantal *u* remains fairly general. Usually a short list of *variant readings* (divergences between manuscripts) and *conjectures* (emendations proposed by scholars attempting to correct passages believed to be corrupt) is given at the foot of each page. The Loeb collection includes an English translation on alternate pages and the Budé collection a similar translation into French. The quality of both texts and translations varies a good deal.

Verse authors are usually referred to by work, book and line (e.g., *Aeneid* 1. 234), prose authors by work, book (where the work comprises more than one book), chapter or paragraph (or both), the practice varying from author to author.

INTERPRETATION

The Teubner texts and the Oxford Classical texts contain no discussion of the work in question (the Latin introduction being confined to textual matters); the Loeb and Budé series usually contain a brief general introduction. Detailed interpretation of the works of all major authors is to be found in *commentaries* (some of which include a text of the work discussed). These vary greatly in scope: some are scholarly works in which problems of interpretation (*cruces*) are debated at length, others are intended primarily for students. A few include critical evaluation of the work discussed, but many of the best commentaries are strictly exegetical, critical comment being incidental or rigorously excluded. For most authors modern critical studies are available (see below under individual authors).

LITERARY HISTORY

Most histories of Roman literature interpret the term 'literature' in its broadest sense and attempt discussion of all that has survived. The following will be found most useful:

ROSE, H. J.: *A Handbook of Latin Literature* (first published, 1936). A strictly factual survey in the German positivist tradition.

DUFF, J. WIGHT: *A Literary History of Rome in the Golden Age* (first published, 1909); *A Literary History of Rome in the Silver Age* (first published, 1927). The critical evaluations reflect the subjectivist approach typical of English criticism prior to the First World War; the judgments are arbitrary rather than analytical, discussion of texts is limited to brief quotations. Both volumes are now available in revised form, but revision has not altered the character of the work.

BIELER, LUDWIG: *History of Roman Literature* (1966). A brief, sensible introduction along conventional lines.

COPLEY, FRANK: *Latin Literature* (1969). Similar in scope to Bieler, but longer and with somewhat fuller critical comment.

Most university libraries will contain the much longer histories of SCHANZ and HOSIUS (in German, essentially factual with minimal critical comment, along lines similar to Rose), the standard reference tool for scholars; and ROSTAGNI (in Italian, an excellent critical survey).

The following more specialized introductions are also worth consulting:

SULLIVAN, J. P. (editor): *Critical Essays on Roman Literature* (vol. 1, 1962; vol. 2, 1963). Short critical surveys by different scholars of individual authors.

DUDLEY, D. R. and DOREY, T. A. (editors): *Studies in Latin Literature and its Influence.* More recent volumes have appeared under the title *Greek and Latin Studies, Classical Literature and its Influence* (editors C. D. N. Costa and J. W. Binns). This series began in 1965 with a volume on Cicero; subsequent volumes have dealt either with particular authors (Lucretius, Virgil, Horace, etc.) or with individual genres (Roman drama, the Latin historians, etc.). Each volume contains chapters by various hands. The quality of the critical comment varies considerably.

The *Oxford Classical Dictionary* contains articles on individual authors as well as useful background information. The much shorter *Oxford Companion to Classical Literature* by Sir Paul Harvey is an excellent vade-mecum.

TRANSLATIONS

The translations included in the Loeb series of texts (see above) are intended as an aid to understanding the Latin and make little attempt to represent the literary quality of the original. Most of the major works of Roman literature have been translated in the Penguin Classics series; a few are excellent, the general quality good. Older translations (some of them represented in this book) often capture the spirit or the style of the original more successfully.

The most difficult case is naturally personal poetry. Here useful guidance to available translations is given by R. J. Tarrant, *Greek and Latin Lyric Poetry in Translation* (1972).

INDIVIDUAL AUTHORS

The following is a short list of useful books on the principal authors discussed in this book and a guide to translations. The dates given are those of first publication. Only works in English are considered.

Bibliography

Catullus

QUINN, KENNETH: *The Catullan Revolution* (1959); *Catullus, an Interpretation* (1972).

The best translations are those by Horace Gregory (1956), Frank Copley (1957) and Peter Whigham (1966). Gregory is probably the closest in style and spirit, Copley's version in the style of e. e. cummings is a *tour de force* popular with students, the Penguin translation by Whigham is very readable but arbitrarily misrepresents the original. There are numerous other modern versions.

Cicero

D. R. Shackleton Bailey's *Cicero* (1971) is a useful modern biography by the editor (and translator) of Cicero's correspondence. No comprehensive study of Cicero's literary achievement exists in English. A. E. Douglas's *Cicero* (1968) in the Greece and Rome *New Surveys in the Classics* series is an excellent introduction to all aspects of Cicero's life and works. The volume on Cicero edited by T. A. Dorey in the *Studies in Latin Literature and its Influence* series (1965) deals chiefly with the orator and politician. Penguin translations are available in some cases. The Loeb translations of the philosophical works are in general good.

Horace

L. P. Wilkinson's *Horace and his Lyric Poetry* (1945) is a useful introduction. Eduard Fraenkel's *Horace* (1957), a personal evaluation by a distinguished scholar, is always interesting and sensible, often warmly appreciative and illuminating; it ranges over the whole of Horace's poetry but is concentrated on those poems which most interested Fraenkel (there is virtually no treatment of Horace's love poetry). Steele Commager's *The Odes of Horace* (1962) is the work of a scholar trained in critical theory and procedures; stimulating rather than penetrating. David West's *Reading Horace* (1967), like R. G. M. Nisbet's chapter on Horace in J. P. Sullivan's *Critical Essays on Roman Literature,* is an attempt to clear the air which has been somewhat overpraised for its forthrightness. Niall Rudd's *The Satires of Horace* (1966) is readable and sound. The *Arion* special number on Horace (vol. 9, numbers 2–3, Summer and Autumn 1970) and the volume on Horace edited by C. D. N. Costa in the *Greek and Latin Studies* series (1973) contain interesting material of varying quality.

The best translations of the *Odes* and *Epodes* are those by Joseph P.

Clancy (1960) and the Penguin version by James Michie; the version by Smith Palmer Bovie of the *Satires* and *Epistles* (University of Chicago Press, 1959) is excellent. There is a very readable version of the *Art of Poetry* by Roy Campbell (1960).

Juvenal

Modern works on Roman satire may be consulted. H. A. Mason's 'Is Juvenal a classic?' in Sullivan's *Critical Essays on Roman Literature*, vol. 2, is stimulating but eccentric. The Penguin translation by Peter Green and that by Jerome Mazzaro (1965) are lively and readable, but older, more formal translations, such as Hodgson's version of 1807 (quoted in this book), give a better idea of the spirit and rhetorical manner of the original.

Livy

P. W. Walsh's *Livy, his Historical Aims and Methods* (1967) is a useful introduction. The Elizabethan translation of the whole of Livy by Philemon Holland (1600) remains one of the greatest of all classical translations; there is a good, readable version by A. de Selincourt of Books 1–5 and Books 21–30 in the Penguin series (1960, 1965 respectively).

Lucan

No comprehensive study exists in English of Lucan's literary achievement. The translation by Nicholas Rowe (1718) can be recommended; there is a version of Book 1 by Christopher Marlowe (*Poems*, 1598, edited by Millar Maclure, 1968); J. Wight Duff's version in the Loeb series (1928) is intended mainly as a crib.

Lucretius

The volume edited by D. R. Dudley in the *Studies in Latin Literature and its Influence* series (1965) is a useful starting point. Most studies of Lucretius deal with the philosopher rather than the poet. An exception is David West's brief, stimulating (and somewhat eccentric) *The Imagery and Poetry of Lucretius* (1969). There are numerous modern translations; of those in verse, that by R. C. Trevelyan (1937) can be recommended; the prose version by R. E. Latham in the Penguin series (1951) is clear and readable.

Bibliography

Ovid

The best introduction is L. P. Wilkinson's *Ovid Recalled* (1955; reissued in abbreviated form as a paperback under the title *Ovid Surveyed,* 1962). H. Fränkel's *Ovid, a Poet between two Worlds* and Brooks Otis's *Ovid as an Epic Poet* (to be consulted in the second edition of 1972, in which the author modifies his views) are standard works.

The best translation of the *Metamorphoses* is that by Arthur Golding (1567; reissued as *Shakespeare's Ovid* by W. H. D. Rouse, 1904; reprinted in the Centaur Classics series, 1961). There is a brilliant translation in heroic couplets by A. E. Watts (1954); either is to be preferred to the versions currently available in paperback. The *Amores* is best read in the Elizabethan version by Christopher Marlowe (*Poems,* 1598, edited by Millar Maclure, 1968) and the modern version by Guy Lee (Murray, 1968). The best version of the *Art of Love* is that by Rolfe Humphries (Indiana University Press, 1971) in an English adaptation of the original metre.

Petronius

P. G. Walsh's *The Roman Novel* (1971) is a useful introduction. The translation of the *Satyricon* by William Arrowsmith (1959) and the Penguin translation by J. P. Sullivan can be recommended. The version used here is that by J. M. Mitchell (1922).

Plautus

W. Beare's *The Roman State* (1950) is the standard introduction. Erich Segal's *Roman Laughter* (1968) is a stimulating introduction to Plautus. There is a volume on *Roman Drama* in the *Studies in Latin Literature and its Influence* series (edited by D. R. Dudley and T. A. Dorey, 1965). The Penguin translation by E. F. Watling (two volumes, nine plays in all) is the most useful.

Pliny the Younger

Betty Radice's excellent Penguin translation (*The Letters of the Younger Pliny,* 1963), which contains an introduction and a bibliography, provides a useful starting point.

Propertius

The recent brief studies by Margaret Hubbard (*Propertius,* 1974) and

J. P. Sullivan (*Propertius, a Critical Introduction*, 1976) may be consulted, but Propertius continues to defy critical appraisal. The Penguin translation by A. E. Watts is serviceable.

Sallust

Ronald Syme's *Sallust* (1964) deals chiefly with the historian. D. C. Earl's *The Political Thought of Sallust* (1961) is worth consulting. The Penguin translation by S. A. Handford is good.

Seneca

A satisfactory modern introduction to Seneca as a literary figure, other than T. S. Eliot's famous essay, is conspicuously lacking. The Penguin translation of selected letters (*Seneca, Letters from a Stoic*, 1969) by Robin Campbell contains an introduction and a brief bibliography. The Elizabethan translations of the tragedies (*Seneca, his Tenne Tragedies*, edited by Thomas Newton, 1581; reissued, with Eliot's introductory essay, 1927, still in print) remain the best.

Tacitus

Ronald Syme's *Tacitus* (1958) is monumental and comprehensive, C. W. Mendell's *Tacitus, the Man and his Work* (1957) conventional in its judgments, B. Walker's *The Annals of Tacitus* (1952) more interesting to the literary student. The Penguin version of the *Annals* by Michael Grant offers a clear paraphrase rather than a translation; the older version by Church and Brodribb (1882, still available in paperback) is a less inadequate representation of Tacitus' style. There are Penguin translations of the *Histories* by Kenneth Wellesley, and the *Agricola* and *Germania* (in one volume) by H. Mattingley and S. A. Handford respectively.

Terence

For books on Roman drama see under Plautus. The Penguin translation by Betty Radice (two volumes) is excellent.

Tibullus

G. Luck's *The Latin Love Elegy* (second, revised edition, 1969) and J. P. Elder's chapter in Sullivan's *Critical Essays on Roman Literature*, vol. 1, do something to meet the lack of a modern critical evaluation. The Penguin translation by Philip Dunlop is adequate, that by Guy Lee (1975) much superior.

Virgil

The best comprehensive modern study is Brooks Otis's *Virgil, a Study in Civilized Poetry* (1963). W. F. Jackson Knight's *Roman Vergil* (1944) is stimulating. On individual poems the following may be mentioned. *Eclogues*: M. C. J. Putnam, *Virgil's Pastoral Art* (1970); E. W. Leach, *Vergil's Eclogues* (1974). *Georgics*: L. P. Wilkinson, *The Georgics of Virgil* (1969). *Aeneid*: Kenneth Quinn, *Virgil's Aeneid* (1968).

The best modern translation of the *Eclogues* is probably that of C. Day Lewis (1963, available in an Oxford paperback translation of the whole of Virgil); of the *Georgics*, that by Smith Palmer Bovie (1956); of the *Aeneid*, that by Allen Mandelbaum (1971). All the above are verse translations; Dryden's version (1697), though rather too free with the sense, comes closer to the original in its more formal metre and diction, as well as its general elegance. The Penguin translation of the *Aeneid* by W. F. Jackson Knight is a prose crib, often interesting as an interpretation of the original, but less readable than the versions of Day Lewis and Mandelbaum; the sober, economical version by Frank Copley (1965) is a useful corrective to the more advanced version by Mandelbaum.

General Index

Helvius Cinna, 158, 163
Hendecasyllable, 157
Hesiod, 122
Hipponax, 157, 173–4
Holroyd, M., 124–5
Homer, 41–2, 43–4
Horace, 1, 2, 14–15, 19, 20–1, 23–4,
    39, 46, 51–2, 104, 207, 250–1; *Ars
    Poetica,* 197–8, 208; *Epodes,* 173–5;
    Odes, 175–81; *Satires* and *Epistles,*
    194–8; and preciousness, 191; as
    moralist, 121, 143, 179–81;
    compared with Catullus, 165, 176,
    178–9, 181; compared with Juvenal,
    199–200; compared with Ovid, 144;
    compared with Propertius, 186;
    compared with Terence, 105–6;
    compared with Virgil, 141–2; his
    attitude to love, 174–5; his
    pessimism, 141–2

Johnson, Samuel, 49, 218
Jugurtha, 225–7
Juvenal, 57, 143, 153, 198–201, 207
    250–1

Laevius, 158, 162
Leavis, Q. D., 34
Licinius Calvus, 163–4
Literacy, 33–4
litterae, 2–3
Littérature engagée, 131
Livius Andronicus, 15, 55, 82
Livy, 20, 22, 82, 120, 219; as historian,
    227–34, 247; compared with Virgil,
    230–2
Lucan, 47, 56–7, 59, 81, 247; compared
    with Virgil, 88
Lucilius, 173, 195, 207
Lucretius, 30, 154; compared with
    Catullus, 149; compared with
    Cicero, 132, 206–7; compared with
    Virgil, 134, 139–41
Lutatius Catulus, 156–7
Lygdamus, 189

Macabre, in tragedy, 114–15, 116
Maecenas, 166, 172, 174, 195, 196
Manilius, 121, 127, 143
Marius, 225

Martial, 26, 153, 167
Marxist interpretation of literature, 45
Memmius, 130
meretrix, 97
Messalla, 190
Metre, 53–4
Milton, 218
Mime, 92
mimesis, 1
Molière, 30, 93, 209
Mommsen, 210–11
Mozart, 43

Naevius, 82, 219
Nero, 84, 249
nugae, 158

Ovid, 6, 30–1, 47, 55–6, 59, 115, 170;
    Amores, 190–4; *Art of Love,* 122,
    142–8; *Metamorphoses,* 68–81;
    compared with Catullus, 81;
    compared with Horace, 144;
    compared with Lucretius, 71–3;
    compared with Seneca, 118–19;
    compared with Virgil, 61–4, 68–70,
    77–8, 80, 82–3; his *Fasti,* 122; his
    letters from Pontus, 194; his *Medea,*
    112–13; his *Metamorphoses* as a
    didactic poem, 121–2; his *Tristia,*
    194

Paraliterature, 157, 166, 167
parasitus, 109–10
Persius, 143, 198, 207
Personal poetry, 149–53
Petronius, 32, 166, 208, 240; compared
    with Homer, 249; compared with
    Lucan, 249; compared with Plautus,
    251; his *Satyricon,* 246–53
Pharsalus, 85
Plato, 121
Plautus, 5, 44–5
Pliny, the Elder, 31, 209
Pliny, the Younger, 58, 92, 166, 191,
    250; compared with Catullus, 242–3;
    compared with Cicero, 243, 244;
    compared with Seneca, 244; his
    correspondence, 242–6
Pompey, 85–91, 112
Pound, Ezra, 162, 187

263

Index of Poems
and Passages Discussed

266